The Anatomy of Art

The Anatomy of Art

Unlocking the Creative Process for Theater and Dance

Alexandra Beller

BLOOMSBURY ACADEMIC
LONDON • NEW YORK • OXFORD • NEW DELHI • SYDNEY

BLOOMSBURY ACADEMIC
Bloomsbury Publishing Plc, 50 Bedford Square, London, WC1B 3DP, UK
Bloomsbury Publishing Inc, 1359 Broadway, New York, NY 10018, USA
Bloomsbury Publishing Ireland, 29 Earlsfort Terrace, Dublin 2, D02 AY28, Ireland

First published in Great Britain 2026

Online resources to accompany this book are available at https://www.bloomsburyonline
resources.com/the-anatomy-of-art. If you experience any problems, please contact
Bloomsbury at: onlineresources@bloomsbury.com.

A catalogue record for this book is available from the British Library.

A catalog record for this book is available from the Library of Congress.

ISBN:	HB:	978-1-350-56418-3
	PB:	978-1-350-56417-6
	ePDF:	978-1-350-56419-0
	eBook:	978-1-350-56420-6

Typeset by Integra Software Services Pvt. Ltd.
Printed and bound in Great Britain

For product safety related questions contact productsafety@bloomsbury.com.

To find out more about our authors and books visit www.bloomsbury.com
and sign up for our newsletters.

For the artists who stay awake to the making,
who keep faith when the air grows thin
or the world says no.
We have held each other through the quiet work of continuing.
May these pages be your companion in risk and renewal.

Contents

Figures

Contributors

The following artists and thinkers generously contributed reflections that appear in this book.

Anne Bogart is a director, writer, and teacher whose influential work in contemporary theater and the cofounding of SITI Company have shaped ensemble-based performance and actor training worldwide.

Emanuel Gat is a choreographer and dancer whose work explores compositional structures, musicality, and collaborative processes in contemporary dance.

Liz Lerman is a choreographer, performer, writer, and educator known for integrating civic engagement, critical dialogue, and interdisciplinary collaboration.

Katherine Profeta is a dramaturg, translator, and scholar whose research focuses on rehearsal processes, movement dramaturgy, and interdisciplinary collaboration.

Kelly Bartnik is a performer, choreographer, and educator working across dance, theater, and immersive performance contexts.

Janet Wong was the associate artistic director of the Bill T. Jones/Arnie Zane Company, whose work bridges performance creation, mentorship, and education.

Deborah Hay is a choreographer and writer whose pioneering approaches to movement and perception have shaped generations of experimental artists.

Okwui Okpokwasili is a performer, choreographer, and writer whose interdisciplinary practice centers embodied histories and Black feminist thought.

David Dorfman is a choreographer, educator, and performer known for physically charged, community-oriented contemporary dance that explores vulnerability, risk, and connection.

Bebe Miller is a choreographer, performer, and writer exploring the interplay between movement, language, and evolving creative process.

Brenda Dixon Gottschild is a dance scholar, writer, and cultural historian whose research articulates the Africanist presence and its foundational influence in American performance.

Kate Hamill is a playwright and actor recognized for her bold feminist adaptations of classic literature for contemporary theater.

Barbara Adrian is a voice teacher, author, and actor specializing in creative process, vocal performance, and actor training.

About the Author

Alexandra Beller is a choreographer, performer, director, and educator based in Brooklyn, New York. She was a member of the Bill T. Jones/Arnie Zane Dance Company from 1995 to 2001 and is the artistic director of Alexandra Beller/Dances. Her work bridges dance and theater, integrating somatic practice, creative process, and embodiment. Beller has choreographed and directed more than sixty works for concert dance, regional and Off-Broadway theater, and university programs nationwide.

Beller is core faculty at the Laban/Bartenieff Institute of Movement Studies and teaches internationally in the fields of choreography, movement for actors, and somatic education. Her creative and pedagogical work has been presented at institutions such as Lincoln Center, La MaMa, Goodman Theater, and Folger Shakespeare Library.

The Anatomy of Art: Unlocking the Creative Process for Theater and Dance reflects over thirty years of Beller's research in performance, teaching, and the creative process. She is also the coauthor, with Dr. David Vickerman, of the book *The Embodied Conductor: A Somatic Approach with Laban and Bartenieff*. She lives in Brooklyn with her family.

Acknowledgments

Much of my early training consisted of being told to quit dancing. I am grateful to the exceptional teachers who advised me otherwise: Ryanne DeGoode, Shane O'Hara, Joe Lanteri, Richard Pierlon, Natasha Baron, Gina Buntz, Jackie Villamil, Judy Rice, Janet Lilly, and Barbara Grubel.

As my path widened, I met artists who changed me. Bill T. Jones taught me about fire, conflict, power, ferocity, exposure, and proclamation. Martha Clarke taught me delicacy, patience, and the resonance of a single image. Irving Penn taught me about the risk inherent in stillness. Anne Bogart taught me that there is always another way in and that storytelling is sacred. My teachers at LIMS (John Chanik, Ellen Goldman, and Cheryl Clark) empowered me to change the aperture of my lens.

I'm indebted to the dancers who graced my work for years—Andrew Avery, Carly Berrett-Plagianakos, Eric Jackson Bradley, Megan Brunsvold, Sarah Carlson, Andi Clegg, Tim Cusack, Justin Donham, Lea Fulton, Charlotte Gibbons, Jocelyn Greene, Mira Kingsley, Doug LeCours, Jill Locke, Meg Madorin, Brendan McCall, Toni Melaas, Milvia Pacheco-Salvatierra, Greta Parsons, Jennifer Phelps, Kendra Portier, Brian Reid, Jenna Riegel, Tamara Riewe, Edward Rice, Christina Robson, Emily Skillings, LiYana Silver, Lillian Stillwell, Simon Thomas-Train, Rebecca Wender, and Ryoji Yamaguchi—for their relentless faith and talent.

I *wish* I could name and thank *each* of my students and clients for their bodily and intellectual offerings, patience as I grew, adaptability when I failed, and the honor they bestowed by trusting me with their bodies and art. You are patrons of this work.

Thanks to designers Jessica Ames, Anton Martynov, Carl Skutsch, Emma Hoette, Ian Douglas, Judith Stuart, Karen Graham, Kato Hideki, Katherine Profeta, Kristin Marting, Mandy Ringger, Martijn Hart, Robert Poss, Steven Schreiber, and Brian Ireland for their questions, answers, and material. Thanks to theater collaborators, including Rebecca Taichman, Eric Tucker, Mark Clements, Jose Zayas, Stephen Brackett, Christopher Edwards, Victor Malana Maog, and GT Upchurch, for inviting me into their world of theater, where I've found my forever home. Thanks to Stephen Cook at Brockport University for manually retrieving the rough draft of this book from the depths of Google Docs purgatory when I thought it was lost forever.

Thanks to my chosen family—Anna Azrieli, Laura Baranik, Joanne Barrett, Rose Pasquarella Beauchamp, Nicco Beretta, John Blesso, Donna Bouthillier, Joe Bowie, Joan Bradford, Shaina Branfman, Kelsey Burns, Catherine Cabeen, Christian Canciana, Gerald Casel, Janessa Clark, Donna Costello, Todd Coulter, Matthew Cumbie, Crystal Davis, Alberto Denis, Kate Digby, Justin Donham, David Dorfman, Meredith Fages, Lea Fulton, Renee Gerardo, Daniel Giel, Kelsey Greenway, Kayla Hamilton, Jenna Hanlon, Kristen Hollinsworth, Tumi Johnson, Soomi Kim, Meredith Koloski, Mirah Love, Scott Lyons, Bea Martino, Toni Melaas, Brendan McCall, Krista Miranda, Luisa Muir, Stevie Oakes, Laura Peterson, Jenny Pommiss, Sarah Pope, Robin Pringle, Katherine Profeta, Jenna Riegel, Allegra Romita, Ethan Ruby, Alexx Schilling, Myah Shein, LiYana Silver, Angie Simmons, Benny Simon, Emily Skillings, Nicole Smith, Rebecca Stenn, Dawn Stern, Jeremy Steward, Antonio Suarez, Ivan Talijancic, Pamela Terry, Marisa Tomei, Amy Upton, Jason Van Orden, Angelica Vessella, Rebecca Wender, Sarah White-Ayon, Matthew Williams, Nicole Wolcott, Stephan Wolfert, Jeramy Zimmerman, and so many more friends—for their grace, love, humor, intelligence, tough love, humanity, activism, integrity, and support over a lot of years.

Four assistants—Melanie Holm, Kelsey Greenway, Lane Dupuy, and Kyle Masson—helped me immeasurably to gather evidence and organize my scattered ideas. Thank you!

A book cannot arrive without feedback, and I am awed and so grateful for the feedback of Anna Brewer, Katherine Profeta, Daniel Schatzman, LiYana Silver, Martin Beller, Kelsey Greenway, Jill Randall, and Jason Van Orden. I have deep gratitude to the nearly eighty artists who peer-reviewed this in its Beta phase. Your feedback was transformative.

Thanks to my kids for their patience with mommy at the computer, mommy at the theater, mommy teaching, mommy staring off into space.... Lucas and Ivo Hart are the best kids I could ever hope for, and their questions are the most magical. Thanks to Martijn for years of artistic cheerleading.

Thanks to Jason for having my back in every possible way, holding faith in me even when mine lapsed, and always having another question for me.

Preface

by Marisa Tomei

This book trusts you.

It trusts your body, your rhythms, your not-knowing. That's where it begins, and that's where I'll begin, too. When my friend Alexandra invited me to write this, I said **yes**, not from certainty, but from the flutter in my chest, that physical recognition that arrives before thought: an embodied yes, not yet shaped into language.

And then I got queasy, as my mind caught up with my instinct. You see, I'm in a period of my life where I'm inside a pocket of not-knowing. But… my heartbeat continues, steady and insistent, and with it the practice I've always returned to:

I begin again. I begin again. I begin again.

So, lately, I feel the need to rummage—to root around in what I haven't said, what I've silenced, what might be silly or wild or too fierce/too soft. I have a feeling to name what's been living in me for years—what has carried weight in my body without ever finding rest.

So I ask:

Can I trust my *body* even more?

Can I trust the *not-knowing* even more?

Can I trust the *begin-again* even more?

Beginning again is a kind of faith. A faith in **the Creatrix** inside me, the one who won't stop showing up.

(By the way, beginning again isn't always noble or poetic. Sometimes it's messy. Sometimes it's lonely. Sometimes it's the only thing left.)

Coaching myself: Trust the one who stirs before dawn, who arrives uninvited, who doesn't wait for approval. Soften into deep listening and follow it to carve—fiercely, precisely—a body-mind offering of what I suppose is the "innermost manifesto."

That carving doesn't come from nowhere. It comes from years of listening. From giving breath to other people's words—not as a vessel, **but as a body that listens back**, responding to what those words ask me to hold. From tracking the pulse of a scene (the weight of a silence, the meaning inside a gesture).

I've always loved interpreting—not just performing, but collaborating, attuning, responding. Feeling into where the heartbeat is. Into the tension and texture of what's unsaid—because that's where I find *myself*, again and again.

But in beginning again, I've felt the pressure not just to interpret, but to originate! To generate!

Why?

What used to hold shape doesn't hold in the same way anymore. The world has changed. We have to reshape, too. Not by discarding ourselves, but by finding new scaffolding to trust who we are and how we create.

That's where this book comes in.

This isn't a manual. It's not about mastery or answers. It's a companion.

It helps you build that scaffolding one question, one choice, one return to the body at a time.

My curiosity has never been about just the work. It's about the transformation it invites. The presence it requires. The attunement it demands.

That's why I'm in it: for the warm-up and the stretch, the late-night fries, and the dance party. I'm in it for the communion.

The happiest place for me has always been an empty rehearsal room—a sprung floor, a ballet bar, a curtain pulled across the mirror, a folding table, maybe a few bagels.

And the rest of it? *Dream time.* The liminal hours, the early morning when things begin to stir, when the dreams start speaking into the piece. When time moves differently and everything feels permeable. When the veil is thin and the piece reveals itself, not all at once, but just enough. That's the boon. That's the hallelujah moment.

Being an artist or an actor, to me, has never been about pretending. It's about revealing. Walking in someone else's shoes and living many lives. It's the greatest privilege, and the most humbling.

But, as you walk, know this: You are the **source**.

You are not raw material waiting to be shaped. You *are* the shape.

I wish someone had told me that at *my* beginning. Especially as a woman. Your body, your wisdom, your longings, your questions: **They are the art, not the obstacle.**

"Listen to that inner voice, even when it whispers, even when it contradicts what you've been taught. Make it manifest in movement, in sound, in language, in space. Make something. Make what you want to express, specifically."

No one ever explained this to me in words, but I understand it now in my bones.

Art, at its most alive, is not performance; it's transmission.

When I follow what wants to move, it's not what I've planned or practiced, but what pulses up through breath and feeling, something ancient emerges. Something that knows. And it teaches me—not through explanation, but through *sensation*. Through the shape of a truth my mind hadn't caught up to yet.

And that kind of knowing? It starts in the body.

Not the *idea* of the body, but the body you wake up with.

The one that senses before it speaks.

The one that tightens or tingles or turns away before your mind can name why.

No method, no director, no system knows that body better than you do.

Learning to trust it—to listen and stay close, even when it contradicts what's expected—is not easy. Especially now. But it's essential.

That's the work.

I didn't always have a guide for it. But I've learned how much it helps to walk with one.

This book doesn't tell you where to go. But it maps the terrain. It helps you see the contours of the work—what questions it asks of you, what choices it offers, what patterns it might trace. It doesn't hand you a path. It shows you what the land looks like, so you can walk it with your eyes open.

Trusting yourself doesn't mean doing whatever you want. But it also doesn't mean following the rules. It's about listening closely—to what's true, not just what's loud. To what's alive, not just what's easy.

It means knowing the difference between instinct and fear.

Between what's yours and what's borrowed.

Between liberation and collapse.

That knowing isn't static.

It takes concentration, dedication, imagination, meaning.[1]

---

[1]Susan Polgar, Hungarian American chess grandmaster and former Women's World Chess champion, described the values behind her success—"It takes concentration, dedication, imagination, meaning"—in a *New York Times* interview at age fifteen. This quote has served as my guiding mantra since I was eighteen. See Howard W. French, "Top-Rated at 15, Girl Challenges Chess World," *New York Times*, March 30, 1985.

It takes unlearning.

It takes faith.

That's what this book supports.

That's why I'm here.

People sometimes ask what kept me in it, or what brought me back, when it would be easier to quit. But stopping has never felt like the easier choice. If anything, it's been harder to stop! I've wanted to!

But I've also been snakebit.

Bit by art, by transformation, by curiosity, by luminosity.

The thing that keeps me here is the wildness of it—the wilds of the psyche, the wilds of the spirit, the moments when I fly, when I am being breathed, when the muses carry me.

That's not sentiment.

That's what **happens**.

That's why I stay.

Not because it's easy.

Not because it's **clear**.

But because I still believe.

What keeps me here? The same thing that brought me here: a body that says **yes**, even now.

So if you're standing there starting, or uncertain, or unfinished, or unsure if you can keep going—just listen.

Not to the noise, not to the rules.

To your own body.

To that flicker of *yes*.

You don't have to know.

You just have to begin.

And begin again.

How to Use This Book: Navigating Your Creative Process

This book is designed as a **choose-your-own-adventure** experience. You can read it cover to cover or dip into sections as inspiration strikes. Each chapter enters art through different windows, doors, and thresholds. These topics will not be new to you. They are the scaffolding not only of art but of a conscious life. Because they are so fundamental, we often overlook their power.

The sections in each chapter invite different modes of intelligence to drive. Some are for **thinking**, some for **making**, some for **questioning**. All are in service of your artistic autonomy. I won't tell you what to do. I'll offer frameworks, provocations, and reflections to help *you* define what matters. I'll ask you to try things that don't feel like *you*. That's the point. Not to remake you, but to climb to a different vantage to see yourself anew.

Where to Begin?

You can read the book as I wrote it. There is logic to the order, but I could have reordered it fifteen *other* ways. Consider whether you prefer analytical or intuitive systems.

If you want to begin **intuitively**, ask yourself:

- What am I most curious about right now?
- Where am I stuck?

Let your response guide you to a **title**, **exercise**, or **question**.

If you want a more **reflective** approach: The *x* and *y* axes in this book are the **What** (chapter) and the **How** (section). The chapter title gives you the **topic**: Time, Space, Relationship… These are the deep currents of creative life. You might choose a chapter because it names what you're grappling with right now, and move through it, beginning to end.

The sections within each chapter serve different **functions** in your process: **generating**, **reflecting**, **embodying**, and **problem-solving**. Each offers a particular engagement. Do three embodiment exercises across different chapters to shift your state, or go through all the writing prompts during a weeklong retreat.

Or flip to a random page, like pulling a tarot card, letting your instinct and chance lead.

There's no right way. The structures exist to support you in making meaning and momentum.

Chapter Descriptions

Time investigates how duration, rhythm, tempo, and sequence shape meaning, attention, and experience in creative work.

Space invites you to reimagine your surroundings as an active collaborator in your art-making.

Relationship addresses the complex and shifting dynamics between people, things, and ideas in your work.

Meaning delves into how content, structure, and resonance are built and dismantled in process and performance.

Environment explores how surroundings shape your sensory state, compositional decisions, and social context.

Process offers ways to track, trust, disrupt, and deepen your creative unfolding.

Facts considers how research, documentation, and specificity serve imaginative rigor.

Faith examines the emotional and existential resilience required to navigate doubt, risk, and revelation.

Communication plays with how intention, action, and reaction intersect to create meaning between *you* and *not you*.

Material looks at the building blocks of art as both substances and collaborators.

Context and Culture encourages you to interrogate the histories, identities, and conditions that shape how work is made, seen, and understood.

Priorities helps you clarify your values, ensuring that every decision aligns with your larger artistic inquiry.

Conclusion reflects on change, growth, and continuity in a creative life—and invites you to articulate your own evolving ethos.

Appendix A: Laban offers a grounding in the Laban/Bartenieff framework to articulate movement, perception, and presence with greater clarity.

Appendix B: The Art of Feedback reimagines critique as a generative, relational practice that supports rigor, clarity, and mutual respect.

Section Descriptions

1. **Before You Begin:** Somatic and Poetic Threshold
   Six personal questions—a felt, rhythmic gateway into the theme. These are for sensing, noticing, entering.
   Use It: when you want to enter through intuition.

2. **Groundwork:** Conceptual and Philosophical Grounding
   The intellectual foundation. Helps reframe assumptions, question structures, and broaden perspective.
   Use It: when you need artistic or intellectual stimulation.

3. **In Practice:** A Cheat Sheet for Quick Reference
   Bite-sized takeaways. A mental Post-it note—a touchstone for clarity in the midst of making.
   Use It: when you want a simple idea to carry with you into rehearsal.

4. **Frameworks:** Rewiring Through Structure
   Schematics, diagrams, prompts, or processes that offer structured ways to rethink, reframe, or repattern. These are architectures for generating insight, disrupting defaults, and organizing action.
   Use It: when you're ready to interrupt a habit, clarify thinking, or apply a structure, and don't feel like reading.

5. **From the Field:** A Lived Example of the Concept
   A brief memoir of one work in which I made a discovery about the chapter's theme.
   Use It: when you're looking for artistic companionship or camaraderie.

6. **Guidance:** Practical Tools from Experience
   Concrete strategies for being an artist. Real-world creative decision-making from the trenches.
   Use It: when you're facing a practical challenge and need advice.

7. **Tuning In:** Physical Exploration of the Concept
   A somatic investigation to center the body's wisdom.
   Use It: when you need to reconnect with your physical intelligence.

8. **Studio Lab:** Process Without a Fixed Product

Open-ended invitations help you test, explore, and improvise with a theme, without trying to produce an end result.
Use It: when you want to field-test a method without expecting an outcome.

9. **Pagework:** Excavating Personal Insight
To dig into your patterns, instincts, resistances, and priorities so you can name what matters and why.
Use It: when you want to use writing as a way to unearth your unsaid truths.

10. **Movements + Maps:** A Score for Generating Material
Recipes that help you generate material for eventual performance, staging, or refinement.
Use It: when you're composing, choreographing, or devising and want a new way in.

11. **Contributor's Note:** Intergenerational Advice from Working Artists
Small gems of wisdom from luminaries in dance and theater to offer another perspective on the chapter's theme.
Use It: when you crave a different voice, or want to hear from one of your art idols.

12. **Studio Provocations:** Catalytic Questions in Real Time
Questions. A mentor's voice in your studio, asking you to sharpen your focus or knock you off autopilot.
Use It: when something isn't working.

13. **Viewing (Online):** Examples to Watch and Learn From
Art by other artists curated to illuminate the chapter's theme. Watching as research, absorption, and orientation.
Use It: when you want to learn by witnessing.

14. **Book Recommendation (Online):** Cross-Disciplinary Deepening
Links to recommended books that extend the chapter's theme into other minds, bodies, or fields.
Use It: when you want to dive deeper into the topic.

Tuning In: Setting Yourself up for Pleasure

Many of the exercises, especially the embodiment explorations, are best done with your eyes closed, or while moving. You'll find audio recordings on the companion website. You can also record the instructions yourself; centering your rhythm and voice can be transformative.

These are best done in your safest space, whether that means alone or in good company. They do not require a studio, a large space, or any equipment. Plan for aftercare: a ritual, moment, or activity that nurtures you after a vulnerable experience.

Studio Provocations: Finding the Right Question

The studio provocations are lists of questions that served as the seed for this book. They began in rooms—labs, rehearsals, post-show circles—where I would ask an artist a question and the atmosphere would shift. Postures lengthened. Eyes brightened. Someone would whisper, "Yes… that's it." I started writing them down. But translating them into a book meant writing not for one, *particular* artist but for *every possible* artist, an impossible task. I released the need for each question to apply to everyone and worked to ensure that every reader would find *one* that offered that electric moment of recognition.

Find the one that catches your breath, that names something true. One that lights you up or unsettles you. Cross two together. Read one out loud. Tape one to your wall. Anchor it in a specific section of your work. Add "today" to bring it into the now. These questions are not a syllabus. They are a thrift store: a mix of gems, oddities, and just-right surprises, each waiting for the right person to find them the perfect fit. Ignore the ones that don't suit your needs.

In time, I plan to create card decks to accompany the book. Until then, you might handwrite or print your favorites on cards and draw from them when you need orientation or disruption. Or paint yourself a fancy artistic tarot deck!

A Final Note

As a mentor, I prioritize consent, specificity, and safety in the vulnerable work of self-expression. Translating that ethos into a book—where I can't read the room, listen to your questions, or repair in real time—was a challenge. I chose to speak clearly and trust you to take what serves, question what doesn't, and revise freely. Disagreement can be its own form of clarity. Let this book be a resource, not a rule. You are the final authority on what matters in your work. Some ideas will be uncomfortable. The distance of a book can't tell me whether that discomfort means you need to "deepen" or "divert." **I trust you to know.** I urge you to discern when friction is simply irritation and when it is molting—shedding your skin and revealing who you are.

Start where you are. Return when you need. Let the book change with you.

Introduction

I was lost.

The plan for my new work wasn't yielding what I'd imagined. I knew where I wanted it to start and end, but the middle wouldn't come together. My rehearsals felt sluggish, my confidence shaky. Sitting across from my friend and dramaturg Katherine Profeta, I voiced my frustration.

"I've been alternating working the beginning and the end of the piece, moving forward and backward," I explained. "I feel I know where I want it to start and end, and I am trying to connect them now. But I'm worried I can't make them meet."

Katherine tilted her head and said, "Is it possible they're two pieces?"

That simple question changed everything. Suddenly, I saw it. One piece was complete; the other belonged to something else entirely. With that realization, a new work, *milkdreams*,[1] emerged.

This is the power of a question. It is a scalpel that opens the art, revealing its fascia, muscle, and bone. A question doesn't impose meaning; it **unlocks** what we already know.

My art has always been an act of asking: asking to be seen, asking if we know one another, asking for permission, forgiveness, or love. Asking for change. The deeper I've leaned into questions, the more I've come to understand others and, paradoxically, myself.

But letting go of the need for answers is an ongoing process that is not without discomfort. Sitting in the unknowable space of questions can feel unsettling, even dangerous. But a room without questions is far more destructive; it is steeped in assumptions about ourselves, our audience, and our work.

---

[1]Alexandra Beller/Dances, *milkdreams*, world premiere, Ellen Stewart Theatre, La MaMa, New York City, June 11–21, 2015.

> The enemy of art is assumption: the assumption that you know what you are doing, the assumption that you know how to walk and how to talk, the assumption that what you "mean" will mean the same thing to those who receive it. The instant you assume who the audience is, or what the moment is, that moment will be asleep. Assumptions can prevent you from entering new and embarrassing territory.[2]

This book began as "Things I Would Ask You If I Were There: 1000 Questions for the Studio." As I wrote down these questions, I realized they needed context: statements, scores, prompts, anecdotes, and recommendations that revealed *me*. Each chapter in this book turns toward one facet of practice—Time, Space, Relationship, Meaning, Environment, Process, Facts, Faith, Communication, Material, Context and Culture, and Priorities. These are not abstract concepts but the forces already shaping your work.

Time holds the tension of lived experience; **Space** invites orientation, disorientation, and new ways of seeing; **Relationship** maps how we meet, resist, and transform one another. **Meaning** slips between intention, interpretation, and perception, while **Environment** holds atmosphere, setting, and the living world's imprint. **Process** reveals patterns inside chaos and openings inside failure. **Facts** anchor us in what is undeniable and present; **Faith** sustains trust before proof appears. **Communication** holds the tension between intention and interpretation. **Material** is the tactile weight of *idea* becoming *form*. **Context and Culture** are the ground from which meaning arises. **Priorities** clarify what matters most. To notice these elements is to expand the field of choice. This book also insists that art making is never neutral: inherited frameworks, genres, and hierarchies shape what becomes possible. Later chapters, especially **Context and Culture**, return to this challenge in depth.

The Anatomy of Art is not an instruction manual. Instead, it is a map of the tangled, luminous terrain of the artistic process. It is a mentor, a conversation, and a provocation for those ready to lean into **discomfort** and embrace the **unknown**.

While many artists resist setting goals for fear of diminishing the process, this book invites you to consider goals as **compasses**. Your goal might be clarity, disruption, visibility, or healing. Your process will shape the goal, and your goal will shape the process. To become your own mentor, you'll need to notice how you experience and respond to your ideas—with curiosity, with judgment, or with assumptions. Let's start there.

---

[2] Anne Bogart, *A Director Prepares: Seven Essays on Art and Theatre* (Routledge, 2001).

Beyond the Binary

We must challenge our inherited assumptions, particularly binary thinking, to provide rigorous and empathetic feedback, both to ourselves and others. Many of our systems operate within the rigidity of yes/no, good/bad, light/dark, positive/negative, and so on, rather than on a continuum and within an ecosystem where friction, disruption, and contradiction are essential to growth. We are beginning to deconstruct long-held binary beliefs about gender, race, religion, culture, capitalism, and sexuality. We must incorporate art and education if we want to inspire a genuine revolution. Stripping the binaries from art frees us to live and create with our full range of nuance, choice, contradiction, and complexity.

Just as the body isn't a simple set of levers but a tensegrity system of interconnection, our art is a web of tensions. Replace the idea of *opposites* with a *continuum*—an infinite field between two poles. A spectrum leaves space for us to disagree, change our minds, hold two truths, and find balance. Increasing from two options to an infinite number of shading options gives us more tension points, an indispensable tool in art making.

The tension of contradiction and multiplicity is fecund and ripe with potential. A binary limits us to two options, inhibiting our imagination. It is hot or cold, humor or pathos. A continuum makes space for both to exist, even in their maddening complexities, a more truthful representation of our lives. Rejecting the binary opens our imagination to cultural and contextual information, which diminishes prejudice. It is challenging to see an artist's work clearly without questioning our social, political, racial, geographic, and religious "givens."

Art Is Not Life

If art were a replica of life, mirroring its mundane stretches and scattered focus, it would fail to captivate. Art's magnetism lies in its ability to distill and intensify the lived experience, clarifying, deconstructing, and poeticizing reality. To achieve this, art condenses life into its essence, distilling images and relationships to their most profound, even primal, sources. By clearly using time, space, relationship, meaning, communication, process, facts, faith, context, material, and priorities, we can elevate our lived experience to meet the audience in theirs.

In *You Are Here*,[3] my evening-length work based on Sartre's *No Exit*, a character awaits life-altering news. The moment vibrates with uncertainty. I wanted the audience to feel it viscerally. I searched my body's memory and remembered from my own high-stakes moments the way my heart fluttered,

[3]Alexandra Beller/Dances, *You Are Here*, world premiere, Dance Theatre Workshop, New York City, ca. 2006.

stomach churned, and breath became ragged. The challenge was to create a stage moment that could captivate the audience, so they, too, would feel gripped by the physical tension of anticipation.

On stage, the scene is deceptively simple, driven by the tension of time. A phone, isolated on a pedestal, rings incessantly. A woman stares at it, her body rigid, gaze fixed. God is on the phone with an answer about her future: heaven or hell. The ringing continues; we feel the strain between the phone's magnetism and the woman's hesitation. Her frozen stance mirrors our anxiety; we are desperate to stop the ringing and find resolution. Finally, she steps forward, her hand reaching for the receiver. It flies upward suddenly, dangling out of reach. **Blackout.**

Tension is the foundational structure of this beat. It holds the scene together, condensing time and space into an emotional crucible. It distills the audience's focus, creating a shared physical experience of suspense and release. Tension transforms the mundane into the extraordinary, not by replicating life but by coalescing and heightening it, offering a poetic intensity that resonates long after the lights fade.

On Value

Our artistic home is much like our actual home: a collection of materials gathered over a lifetime, shaped by priorities, habits, and desires. Like any home, it can become cluttered with outdated choices or unquestioned routines. This book asks you to open the closets you've forgotten, notice the hidden rooms, and reconsider what you keep.

Resisting the urge to rank and evaluate can feel counterintuitive—we are conditioned to label one thing as *better* than another. Yet that reflex often traps us in habit, reinforcing inherited beliefs rather than chosen ones. What if, instead of asking whether something is "good" or "better," we asked: What attracts, repels, delights, or disturbs us?

By diminishing hierarchies of attention, our entire creative palette becomes available. Every dynamic, technique, frame, and duration becomes an option. From this state of openness, we can assign value intentionally without being limited by habit, bias, or assumption. Letting go of our proclivities and cultural norms opens up a world of choice.

The Anatomy of Choice

I've noticed this acutely in parenting. Society tells me I must be nurturing because I'm a mom. That may sound logical, but it's still an assumption. If we adhere to the expectation that I "should" be nurturing, even that I *must* be, I end up with no choices.

What if I said that until I have a *goal* for my parenting, there's no good or bad method—just choices? If my goal is to help my children feel safe and loved, then nurturing becomes a *decision*, not a *default*. The distinction matters. The act of choosing, rather than defaulting, imbues the same behavior with authenticity and intention.

Similarly, releasing value judgments in art allows us to recalibrate our goals. By setting aside assumptions, we gain a clearer perspective on the work and make choices that are grounded in our unique visions and desires.

Once we have removed "value" from our work, we can decide what we genuinely care about. What do we want now, when the expectations, habits, and pressures have been removed? What do we *need* to share with the audience? What are our goals for this *particular* work and our practice overall?

The concept of "goals" is fraught in creative practice. Goals are often associated with capitalism's emphasis on productivity and exceptionalism, reducing them to *end products*. Many artists resist this framing, preferring to focus on "the process." But process and goals are not oppositional; they are interdependent. Every process has a *purpose*, whether experiential, material, or conceptual.

What if we reframe the idea of a goal? Instead of seeing it as a fixed endpoint, we might think of it as a compass: a way to orient ourselves without constraining the journey. In this sense, a goal is fluid, evolving in response to the process. It becomes a shared energy between the maker and the work, not an objectifiable product, but a *relational practice*.

In this way, a goal is not unlike love: a journey, not a destination. I recall a conversation with Lea Fulton, about our work *milkdreams*. She was surprised when I told her there had been a goal to my process. "What was it?" she asked. "Searching for a form of god inside our bodies," I replied, "going on an internal pilgrimage to find some answer to the question 'Why am I here?'" This goal wasn't about aesthetics or a specific outcome. It shaped every decision we made and permeated the process, which, in turn, created the final product. The goal wasn't a destination we reached but a guiding star that focused the work.

This is not to say we should erase our ancestral or communal histories. These containers—our personal, familial, and cultural frameworks—are critical for identity and celebration. But opening these containers and examining what they share is a powerful tool of communion. As Audre Lorde reminds us, "It is not our differences that divide us. It is our inability to recognize, accept, and celebrate those differences."[4]

---

[4]Audre Lorde, *Sister Outsider: Essays and Speeches* (Crossing Press, 1984).

Of course, part of decolonizing the body and mind is to *question everything*, assume nothing, and rigorously interrogate our strategies, products, intentions, passions, materials, and choices. This makes the practice of questions, especially questions devoid of inherited assumptions, so powerful in providing feedback. A question is an act of both survival and subversion. It is both the keyhole and the key. Questions name *both* the obstacle and the way in.

This book aims to be the type of mentor who does not tell you what to do, but asks you the right question at the right time. It is here to disrupt, challenge, and reveal—to help you discover what you already know but might not yet see. So let's begin. Let's step into the unknown—bravely, together.

Start Here: A Wayfinding Guide

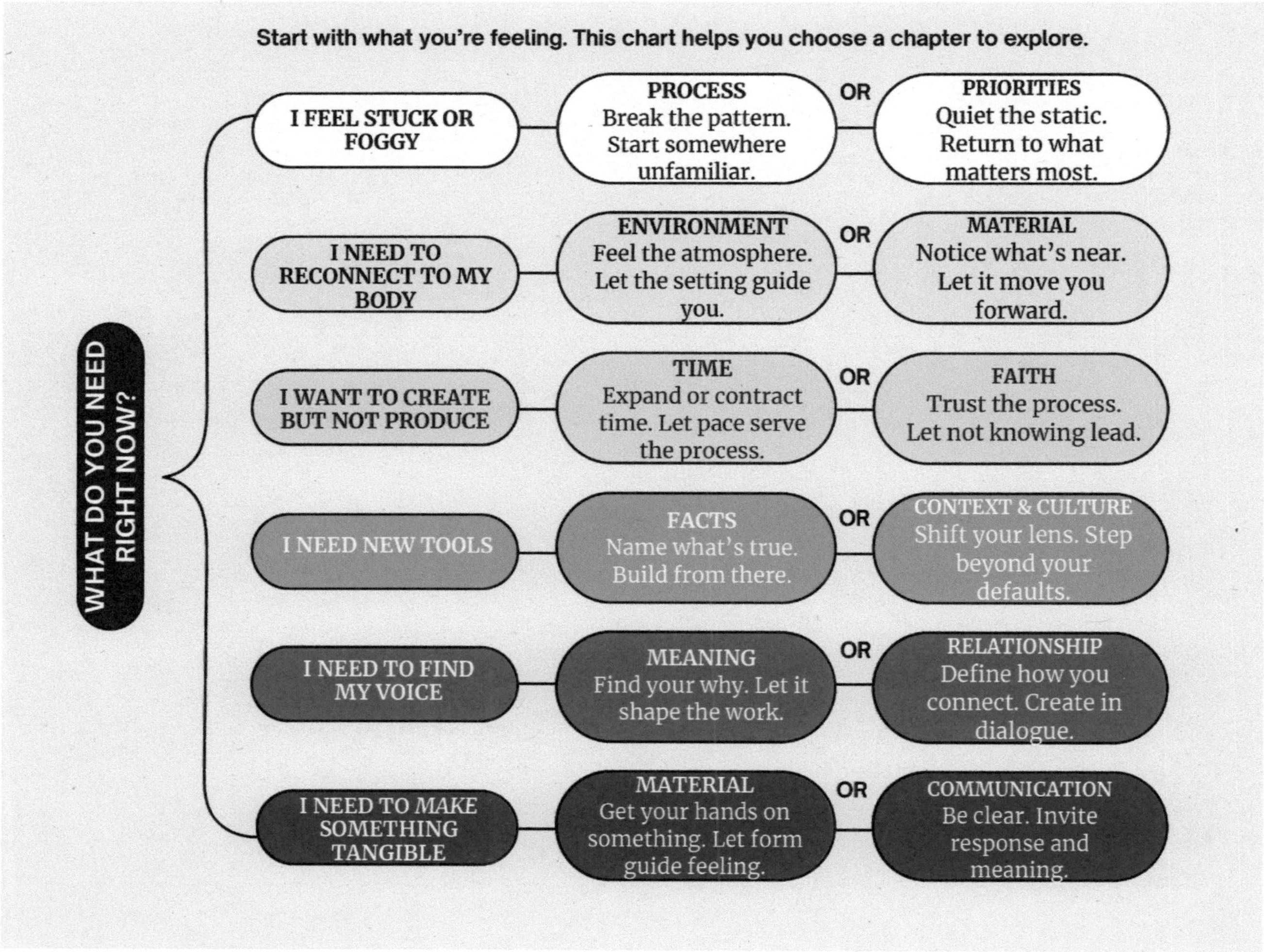

Figure 0.1 *Chapter Flow Chart.*

1

Time

Before You Begin: Priming Curiosity About Time

Take a breath. Consider these questions. Let them settle in your body before moving forward. They are not for solving, but for sensing.

Who am I when I am not rushed?

What rhythms guide me right now?

When do I trust that time is *enough*?

Where in my life feels too fast or too slow?

How did I come to understand time the way I do?

Why do I fear wasting time—and what would it mean to waste it *beautifully*?

Groundwork: The Sense of Time

"How did it get so late so soon?"
(Dr. Seuss, *Dr. Seuss's Book of Poems*)[1]

The Tempo of Creative Tension

In 2009, when my son Lucas was two and a half years old, I brought him on an eight-week tour with my dance company to Amsterdam, Norway, Poland, and Russia. One day, with the dancers and crew out at a party, I found myself in a Russian apartment with a sick and hungry kid. There was a watchperson inside our apartment, so I left him happily ensconced in bed watching *Cars* and ran outside to grab him dinner. Time slowed in my body; each minute stretched as the urgency to return elevated my anxiety.

I ran back to the complex, where I realized with horror that I could not differentiate one building from another, and there were no numbers. I was trapped outside, with no cell phone and no idea how to get back to Lucas. Every second felt like a day, yet my inner body was racing, with a heartbeat to match.

I rang buzzer after buzzer, waiting to find the right one. Each pause, listening for that click, was eternal. I finally rang the correct buzzer, heard the salvational sound, and sprinted up the stairs. My son glanced up at me before returning to his movie, unaffected, happy for pizza. I hugged him for ten minutes as my system slowly regulated. In those minutes outside, I was reminded how time can stretch, compress, and command our attention when our actual or imagined survival is at stake. This tension between urgency and control mirrors how we experience time in both art and life.

Time as a Bodily Experience

Time is a visceral experience. We are mortal bodies living in the tension between what we know—the inevitability that life will end—and what we don't: how much time we have left. If time is a metronome, beating out our life's duration, we can syncopate our rhythm to create tension and flow. This propels us forward, shaping our choices and creativity. In art, time is a tool to create stakes and meaning through rhythm. We've all experienced three relationships with time. Suddenness rushes in with impulse, velocity, and surprise, sometimes bringing shock. The elastic elongation of time tautens our attention, sometimes painfully. The even meter of monotony can be, in turns, meditative or numbing. All three can be useful in art, but we must ask which serves *this* moment.

---

[1]Theodor Seuss Geisel, "How Did It Get So Late So Soon?," *Dr. Seuss's Book of Poems* (Random House, 1980).

Time brings unanswerable questions: Why are we here, and what will happen? Consider the slow-motion agony of waiting for test results or the split-second reflex that saves a child from falling. Time's elasticity in these moments is embodied, generating our choices, emotions, and actions, and showing the world and our audience how life *feels to us.* Time shapes our daily lives and brushes up against our feelings about death.

The fact of our mortality is all we can be sure of. Everything else is a question. And, yet, death brings the biggest question… and *then* what? That question propels so much of our choice-making, emotional experience, and relationship to fear. For some, the "not knowing" is freeing, and for others, a terror. *Not knowing* has inspired religion, politics, psychology, philosophy, and art. **My question is:** How does *not knowing* affect you in life and your creative process?

Time and Mortality

Time stretches like a bowstring between birth and death. Our nervous system lives inside that tension: fight, flight, and freeze are temporal reflexes. Death often hinges on a fraction of a second: looking up from your phone as a car barrels past, pausing long enough to see that it's a rattlesnake not a rock, reacting to the sudden fall of an object before it smashes. These calibrations of time are survival itself. We read them in animals, and in human bodies alike, though we are rarely taught to notice what the body knows.

The most charged moments in art emerge from the same pulse. A dancer caught midfall, a pause that stretches before a confession, a line like "Can we talk?"—each bends time until it nearly snaps. These moments show how mortality and attention to time hold each other in the breath, the heartbeat, the silence before the break.

The Storytelling of Time

Time works in layers: Seconds that decide survival become years that arc across a life. The past and future are powerful stories, but the present is our only active space, constantly shedding itself into memory and jettisoning itself into the future. But admonishments to "be present" lack context. To be truly present, we must consider *how* the past and future are affecting us *now*.

The present contracts beneath the weight of past stories. The failed premiere, the insensitive feedback, or the rules we were conditioned to follow limit the choices, even the view, of *this* moment if we let them.

The same contraction occurs when we fix our attention too sharply on a single outcome. What the piece must look like, what success means, and even what genre we use to describe our work will close off the experiments that lead to the unimaginable.

The practice is to loosen that grip: to uncouple from what has already happened, to release our fantasies about the outcome, and to meet the present with enough openness that new paths can emerge.

Time in Performance

In Butoh, performers stretch time to create a trance-like state, while in Elizabeth Streb's athletic and high-octane choreography, time is measured through explosive action. Both reveal how time shapes meaning at the opposite ends of tempo. The felt sense of meaning often surfaces through *changes* in time, rather than the difference between *fast* and *slow*. We might assume fast will keep us on the edge of our seats, while slow will calm us, but both can lull and hypnotize us. It is usually a *change in time* that activates our nervous system, enlivening our attention.

Butoh rejects time and Streb catalyzes it. Both engage the audience bodily. It is when we take time for granted that our art suffers. When we take the audience's time for granted or let our assumptions about time dictate our dynamics, we slacken the tension and risk losing them.

Constructed and Subjective Time

Time can be understood as both **constructed** and **subjective**. **Constructed time** is the system we have made to regulate and coordinate society: clocks, calendars, milestones, and schedules that unify human activity. **Subjective time** is how we feel its passing: sometimes as a rush, others as a trickle, sometimes seeming to vanish.

In performance, constructed time creates rules, rhythm, and a shared reality. This includes the following:

- **Chronology:** Events unfold in a specific order, shaping plot and progression.
- **Duration:** Moments occupy a defined span, giving weight to scenes and beats.
- **Tempo and rhythm:** Speed determines velocity, and rhythm organizes flow.

The *sensation* of time—its subjectivity—offers us a view into a character or performer's inner world. This can be shaped through the following:

- **Flashbacks and flash-forwards:** Memory and expectation bend narrative and meaning.
- **Temporal layering:** Multiple timelines interweave, complicating memory and identity.
- **Varied durations and repetition:** Lengthening or shortening time shifts perception and builds tension. Repetition accumulates meaning and reshapes what each return carries.
- **Pacing:** Pauses build tension; acceleration or surprise generates urgency or disorientation.

The tension between constructed and subjective time is often where meaning resides in art. Here, we glimpse what the world expects of a character *and* how they experience that expectation. Playing with this tension reveals the inner experience and unsettles the audience's assumptions. Three common approaches are **dissonance, resonance**, and **subversion**:

- **Dissonance:** When constructed time and subjective time move in friction. A character's panic might be shown through slow motion, heightening tension and stakes. Or perhaps everyone freezes and the character remains in motion.
- **Resonance:** When constructed time and subjective time align and reinforce one another. The final note of a symphony landing exactly on time, or the drop of a rollercoaster, brings deep satisfaction through resolution.
- **Subversion:** When the expectations of constructed time are deliberately disrupted. A pause held beyond comfort, or a work extended beyond convention (a twenty-four-hour song cycle, a forty-five-minute "evening-length" piece), asks the audience to recalibrate their sense of time.

Cultural Constructions of Time

Every culture builds expectations that bind us to time. Rites of passage, schooling, professional milestones, marriage, procreation, retirement—all are steeped in unspoken timelines. Even those who resist the mainstream carry these timelines in their bodies. Fourteen years of school, the annual reset of New Year, the shifting expectations of your twenties, thirties, forties, sixties: each embeds a clock inside us, whether or not we respond to its alarms. The details vary across cultures, but time sits at the center of most social systems.

Most of these expectations have little to do with biology; they are pressures of productivity, creativity, sexuality, and belonging. These hegemonies are invisible, ubiquitous, and difficult to reject.

I once had a client who asked for two-hour sessions. He knew his own tempo well enough to insist on the space he needed to expand into thought and sensation. I worried I'd "run out" of things to say and do, but working at his pace changed me: my ideas slowed and opened, my communication shifted, and my body released the pressure to make his time "worth it" by producing quick answers. Moving slowly through the veil of *not knowing*, I found myself generating ideas I doubt would have surfaced in a one-hour session.

It was not only the extra time that mattered, but the way he had already chosen to release the social construct of what a "normal" session should be. His refusal of the clock altered my own sense of what was possible. In that space, time itself became part of the wisdom.

In the studio, the same questions apply. What habits and assumptions about time shape your process? If you released all artistic expectations, might you commit to one idea for a lifetime, or generate something new every day for a month? Would you stretch a performance to eight hours, or compress it to fifteen minutes? What are your defaults around tempo, duration, repetition, meter, rhythm, pulse, and flow—and what happens if you turn them upside down?

Time is mathematics, poetry, and instinct. It is both measure and pulse, calculation and breath. It is the rhythm of survival and the current of creation. When we attend to it consciously—embracing its tension, resisting its pull, or shaping its flow—we open ourselves to infinite possibilities in life and art. At its core, time governs the thresholds we live by: survival, mortality, fear, love, connection, desire.

Takeaway: Time is about survival. Treat it with intention and care.

In Practice: Tips About Time

1. **Create tension.**
    - **Countdowns:** Use visible or implied countdowns to escalate urgency (visible clocks, repeated cues, or rhythmic buildups).
    - **Prolonged pauses:** Hold a beat just past comfort. The space where nothing happens becomes charged with *everything*.
2. **Elicit empathy through time.**
    - **Temporal perspective:** Show the same moment through two bodies at different speeds or densities—one racing, one suspended, allowing us to *feel* what each character is experiencing.
    - **Friction with the world:** Let a character's inner tempo clash with their environment (suspension inside frenzy, rushing inside stillness).
3. **Challenge assumptions.**
    - **Break chronology:** Refuse narrative time, like Butoh's timelessness or "dream logic."
    - **Nonlinear structures:** Interrupt the expected order. Begin at the end. Loop midmovement. Scramble chronology entirely (think Christopher Nolan).
    - **Invert expectations:** Place silence at the climax. Slow everything down when we expect speed.
    - **Expose the bias:** Western time prizes speed, productivity, and linearity ("time is money," "you're late," "wasted time"). Show what it feels like to live under the weight of the clock.
    - **Offer alternatives:** Draw from cyclical, relational, or ritualized time. Structure a piece around sunrise and sunset, lunar phases, seasons, or communal rhythms rather than the clock.
    - **Disrupt the metric:** Stretch or compress duration. Defy social and artistic rules about length.
4. **Craft the audience's attention.**
    - **Tempo shifts:** Accelerate and decelerate. Invent new rules for how time passes. Invite time to surprise, even betray.
    - **Stillness and silence:** These are events. Stillness reframes what just happened and charges what comes next. Silence holds the last sound and seeks the next. They can also be used in contradiction (noisy stillness, frenetic action in silence).

5. **Heighten the stakes.**
   - **Compressed time:** Use montage or acceleration to collapse chronology.
   - **Extended time:** Linger. Hold. Let the audience want the next beat—and *deny* them a moment longer.
6. **Let the body measure time.**
   - **Performer's time:** Let duration emerge from sensation. Stay in action until you fail, falter, or complete. The body decides when it ends.
   - **Creator's time:** Watch your work with your body. When do you hold your breath, flinch, drift, or brace? Let those responses guide what stays or shifts.
7. **Manipulate time structures.**
   - **Layered timelines:** Give each performer a different era—childhood, present, future. Repeat gestures, cycle memories, and interrupt each other's time. Overlap the past, present, and future.
   - **Temporal rupture:** Build a slow crescendo, then cut it. Insert a sudden burst, freeze, or silence.
8. **Personify time.**
   - **Time as antagonist:** Make time the enemy: a ticking deadline, aging body, or approaching loss.
   - **Time as witness:** Use silence, echo, or repetition to show how the past affects the present.
9. **Deconstruct cultural clocks.**
   - **Reject dominant time:** Break from "beginning-middle-end." Spiral, pulse, double back—refuse conclusion.
   - **Invent your own clocks:** Invent rules like "each breath starts the next gesture" or "no event can last more than two seconds" or "repeat every new idea three times."
10. **Negotiate shared time.**
    - **Shared tempo:** Rehearse a phrase with a partner without presetting timing. Let tempo emerge between you. Notice who accelerates, who yields, and how rhythm becomes relational rather than individual.
    - **Collective duration:** Let a scene end only when everyone senses it has completed. No one exits alone. Completion becomes communal rather than dictated.

- **Asynchronous time:** Allow different performers to inhabit distinct temporalities at once. One sustains and stretches. Another moves in sharp bursts. A third loops a short phrase while the others evolve. Do not resolve these into a single rhythm. Let the friction, harmony, or disorientation create meaning.

Frameworks: The Time Map: Letting Tempo Tell the Story

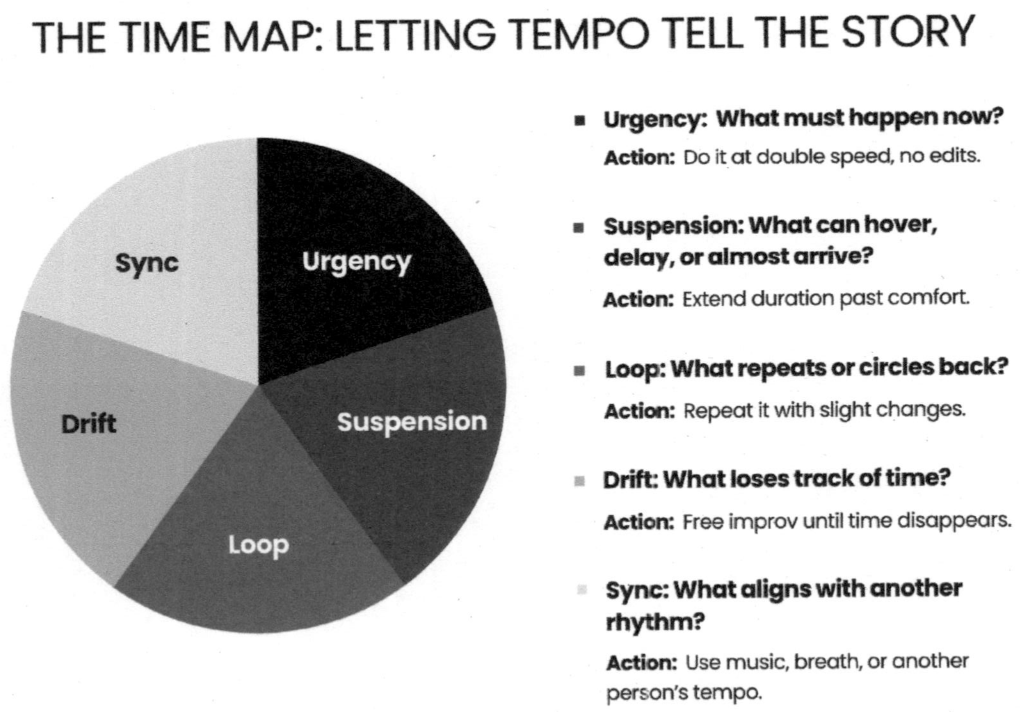

Figure 1.1 *The Time Map: Letting Tempo Tell the Story.* Diagram linking five temporal modes (Urgency, Suspension, Loop, Drift, Sync) with corresponding movement actions.

From the Field: *milkdreams*

For years, my process followed a formula: nine months creating half the work, a thirty- or forty-minute repertory piece. I'd spend six to nine months expanding it. The final work was ninety minutes long. I rehearsed four hours, two to three times weekly. Without knowing it, my process defined my work. My assumptions about "how to create" were *givens* I'd inherited.

Figure 1.2 Lea Fulton and Edward Rice in *milkdreams*. Reproduced with permission of Judith Stuart.

In my last evening-length work, *milkdreams*, I let go of them. I spent two and a half years making it. I worried my dancers would leave the process because of the balance between rehearsing and performing (and one did). I rehearsed once weekly for six hours. I worried we'd have no momentum. The work was forty-five minutes long. I feared the audience would feel I'd "cheated" them.

The dancers expressed that slowing down had been transformative, allowing them to find subtlety and release long-held habits. The space between rehearsals allowed my subconscious to marinate, synthesize, and stay open to wonder. The audience seemed grateful for the short show and stayed for the postperformance gathering, a transition from the trancelike *milkdreams* back to the "real world."

The slow burn of two and a half years, at first unfathomable to me, allowed the work to emerge with a quiet complexity I hadn't accessed before; it changed my work forever. The intensity of a single weekly rehearsal made it a sacred, high-stakes event. The outcome, to me, was magical.

Guidance: Ecosystems

I looked out the window recently, and there was a nest on my fire escape—a tiny, perfect nest housing one egg and a mama bird. I was rapt to watch the story of a new life unfold. Each day, I eagerly turned to "Mama Bird and Her Little Egg," like a show I was binge-watching.

One day, torrential sheets of rain came down. The nest had no coverage, and after an hour or two of being battered by the weather, Mama Bird flew off. The rain lasted two days, and she never came back. The egg never hatched. I was terribly sad.

At first, I ruminated on Mama Bird's "choices." *Where had she gone? Why didn't she return?* I almost judged her. But nature doesn't work like that. Neither does creativity. She was responding to an ecosystem, not failing at her role.

We blame ourselves for not creating, but it's rarely a flaw of character. More often, something in the ecosystem is misaligned.

Artistic ecosystems are tied to time. Time governs how inspiration emerges, motivation is sustained, and processes unfold. We judge ourselves for how long it takes us to make a decision, finish a sentence, or create a product. When time feels imbalanced—either slipping too quickly through our fingers or stretching into endless inertia—the strain ripples through the entire system. In an artistic ecosystem, time determines which ideas flourish, which go dormant, and when things bloom.

We can consider the phrasing of five things: **inspiration**, **motivation**, **action**, **feedback**, and **community**. How these work, individually and in conversation with each other, defines how, what, when, and where we create.

Inspiration often sparks in a fleeting moment. But without the **motivation** to act, the creative impulse withers. We may have motivation, but lack the infrastructure or process to take **action**. When we don't have a supportive **community** or thoughtful **feedback**, the time spent in creative isolation can feel stagnant rather than fertile. Each piece contributes to an environment in which creativity may manifest into art.

When we think about time as part of a creative ecosystem, we can begin to ask: Where is the imbalance? Is time moving too fast or too slow for our imaginations to achieve flow? Are we allowing ourselves the time to recover, dream, and work deeply? Just as Mama Bird responded to the pressures of her environment, our creative lives are shaped by how time and external forces interact.

A healthy ecosystem has three essential aspects:

- **Productivity:** In art, *productive* doesn't always mean *producing a product.* A conversation that clears tension or a research rabbit hole can be productive. Redefine what counts.
- **Resilience:** External pressures—deadlines, rejection, distraction—distort time. How do we adapt, compensate, or even celebrate our nervous system's unique rhythms?
- **Organization (Biodiversity):** Balance time for inspiration, work, feedback, and rest. Which element dominates, and what is underfed?

A disruption in any of these areas is like a storm hitting a fragile nest—it threatens the system's balance. Understanding time as part of our ecosystem allows us to locate the strain and take action to protect and support ourselves.

Our relationship with time requires elasticity. Time can feel oppressive when overly rigid—like in rehearsal, when we refuse to sit with *not knowing* and force decisions before they're ready. Sometimes the better move is to clean a section, or invite inspiration through table work or improvisation. Yet, without applying structure to time, it drifts, unmoored and purposeless—like wanting to create but never booking rehearsal space. Without *crafting* our time, the process dissolves into nothing more than ideas.

The Mama Bird's absence wasn't a failure but an adaptation to circumstances beyond her control. Stepping away—resting, rethinking, responding to life—is not abandonment. Sometimes the ecosystem requires us to yield control and trust that balance will return. When letting go becomes necessary, grief may rise. Allowing that grief is part of the balance too: a sign of care.

Tuning In: Attuning to Time

This practice invites you to attune to time, feeling its elasticity, urgency, ease, and memory.

1. **Find stillness or motion.**
   Find a comfortable position: sitting, standing, or lying down. Close or soften your gaze.

2. **Listen to your inner clock.**
   When you believe a minute has passed, gently open your eyes or mark the moment. Was your sense of time faster or slower than the clock?

3. **Slow time, speed time.**
   Begin moving, finding your organic pace. Gradually slow to half speed. Notice the effort required and the details that emerge. Gradually accelerate, to double your original speed. Alternate between tempos, noticing how time reshapes perception and sensation.

4. **Find your tempo.**
   Return to your own organic tempo (it may be a different tempo now). Release how fast or slow is "acceptable."
   - What tempo arrived?
   - What happened when you lived in it?
   - How different is this from your usual pace?

5. **Expand and contract perception.**
   Return to stillness and focus on breath.
   - Inhale slowly, imagine time expanding—more space, possibility, and patience.
   - Exhale quickly, imagine time contracting—urgent, concise, immediate.
   - Do the opposite: inhale quickly, as if a great idea had suddenly occurred.
   - Exhale slowly, releasing fixed ideas and assumptions.
   - Notice how your body responds to all four breath patterns. Did one feel healing? Did one challenge you?

6. **Reflect.**
   Write or vocalize any sensations, thoughts, or realizations.
   - What is one action in your daily life that would support a more authentic tempo? (For example, walking slower from work to home.)
   - How might you bring this awareness into your creative process?

Studio Lab: Time Mapping

This is not about making a phrase but about practicing ways to shape, break, or ride time.

1. **Feel time in your body.**
   Stand, sit, or lie down for one minute. Ask: *How is time moving through me right now?* Let one gesture, sound, or breath pattern arise. Repeat it ten times, letting it evolve.

2. **Recall a charged experience.**
   Choose a short, specific memory that *moved through different speeds*. Pick something charged but not a trauma:

   - Waiting for, then getting, a call.
   - Waiting in the wing, then entering the stage.

   Improvise the memory physically or vocally. Express how time felt.

3. **Build a time phrase.**
   Name **three to five distinct time feelings** from that moment. Examples: urgency, impatience, anxiety, relief.

   Create a **simple gesture or movement** for each one. Let the tempo and rhythm shape it. Make a clear time choice for each without overthinking ("This one is sustained and fluid," "This one is sudden and jagged").

   Combine into a **phrase** (10–30 seconds total).

4. **Disrupt with intuition.**
   Run your phrase **listening for friction**:

   - When do you lose interest?
   - When do you want to stay longer?
   - When do you feel something catch or shift in your body?

   When you feel an urge for difference, **DJ the phrase**:

   - **Repeat** a gesture until it changes quality.
   - **Reverse** the direction, rhythm, or emotion.
   - **Hold** still.
   - **Replace** one section with another.

   Let your body tell you when to disrupt, not your conscious mind.

5. **Improvise with time.**

   Use your new phrase as vocabulary. Follow or abandon the structure as you go. Use **tempo,** **breath,** or **pressure** as your score.

6. **Reflect.**

   - When was I most engaged?
   - What surprised me?

Pagework: Writing into Time

Freewrite on one or more of these questions. Don't overthink; just drop in.

1. **What part of your creative life lags behind? What part do you rush? What would happen if you reversed them?**
2. **Where do you wait "too long"? Where do you move "too fast"? Where do you hesitate? Where do you leap?**
3. **What does "too long" mean to you, and where did you learn that? Where did you learn the "right" amount of time for:**
    - Dreaming/Imagining
    - Planning
    - Rehearsing
    - Performing
    - Celebrating
    - Grieving
4. **When was the last time you took the time you truly needed—for a piece, a conversation, a recovery, a meal? How did you know when it was done?**
5. **If your art had its own clock, what kind of time would it keep? Would it tick, pulse, spiral, lurch, or loop? What kind of work would that rhythm create?**

Movements + Maps: Disrupting the Clock

This score makes time your primary tool for meaning. Let form emerge from time, not content; let rhythm lead structure.

1. **Create a base phrase through accumulation.**
   - Begin with one clear action or gesture; make it feel as tangible as an object.
   - Repeat it until your body *insists* on the next.
   - Keep adding only when a new gesture demands to emerge.
   - Allow one action to repeat twenty or more times if needed. Stay in the tempo that feels right.
   - Keep building until you have a one- to two-minute phrase. Let it emerge *through* time, not against a stopwatch.
2. **Strip it down and clarify time.**
   - Once you've built the whole sequence, **remove all repetition.**
   - If something appears twice—even on the other side of the body—cut it.
   - Define the time quality for each event. One is lightning fast. Another is lingering. The next is thoughtful but direct. Don't be arbitrary for the sake of novelty. Ask each movement what dynamic it requires to be its fullest self.
3. **Choose to repeat one thing.**
   - Reintroduce **only one repetition**—but only where it feels essential. Make repetition a crack in the logic.
   - Be brave when deciding on the duration of that repetition. Does it want to repeat three times or for a minute?
4. **Distort time.**
   - **Improvise** from your set material, playing with tempo, duration, and repetition.
   - Let tempo drive the relationships, inviting tension, indifference, dominance, reverence. What does time communicate that movement alone does not?
   - Rebuild the choreography using discoveries from your improvisation.

5. **Edit your phrase by breaking time rules.**
   - **Name three unspoken beliefs** about time in performance ("Start with a bang," "Going slow will bore the audience").
   - **Break two** (add a durational pause, speak too fast).
   - **Invest in one rule** ("You cannot pause too long or you'll lose the audience" becomes "Never pause longer than five seconds").
6. **Make time disappear.**
   - Insert a moment where time slips: sustained motion, extreme repetition, suspended stillness, unpredictable shifts.
   - **Ask:** What dissolves the clock? Let that moment anchor the piece.

Contributor's Note: And Then, You Act

by Anne Bogart

Time is a vital ingredient in the recipe for making art, a partner rather than an enemy in the process of making the music more intense. The treatment of context, articulation, intention, attention, magnetism, attitude, and content are all contingent on your relationship to time—the time of a project, the time span of a relationship, your time on earth, and so on. The art of time is intuitive. Sense when to wait and when to plunge, and be brave enough to articulate in the face of transient experience. If you hesitate, you will miss the boat. You cannot force things to happen at a particular time, but you can prepare and pave the way for the eventuality of expression in the same way that you pave the way for visits of inspiration in your daily life: you create the proper conditions and circumstances. And then, you act.

Studio Provocations: Questioning Time

Bigger questions, questions with more than one answer, and questions without an answer are the hardest to cope with in silence. Once asked, they do not evaporate and leave the mind to its serener musings. Once asked, they gain dimension and texture, trip you on the stairs, wake you at night time. A black hole sucks up its surroundings, and even light never escapes. Better then to ask no questions? Better then to be a contented pig than an unhappy Socrates? Since factory farming is tougher on pigs than it is on philosophers, I'll take a chance.

(Jeanette Winterson, *Gut Symmetries*)[2]

Existential

What role does time (felt, chronological, linear) play in this work?

How do urgency or survival factor in?

- Is time a pressure or a release?
- Are you stretching time or trying to dissolve it?

Are biological or natural rhythms forces at play (breaths, seasons, tides, cycles)?

- What happens if you highlight, distort, or break these rhythms?

Neurological

How much are you trusting your instinct?

- Are there places where you could invite more intuition?
- Are you craving more structure, logic, or objectivity?
- What happens if you switch dominant modes—lead with analysis where you've been intuitive, or vice versa?

How important is analysis for you?

- Do you feel overly cerebral, or not rigorous enough?

---

[2]Jeanette Winterson, *Written on the Body* (Vintage, 1993).

- Could more ambiguity or contradiction expand your options?
- What kind of thinking (mapping, list making, improvising, wandering) helps you reenter your work when you're lost?

What sensation do you want your audience to have around time? When should they be

- Breathless or rushed?
- Suspended or slowed?
- Held in stasis?

Is your personal rhythm visible?

- Do you have ingrained rhythmic habits or preferences?
- Is it useful to resist or subvert any?

How does physics operate here?

- Can you amplify or distort physics with props, surfaces, costumes, or illusion?
- What changes when you make weight visible, invisible, natural, or exaggerated?

Are you working with or against the body's internal clocks?

- Do your breath, heartbeat, or fatigue shape how time flows?
- Does the performer have agency over tempo and duration?

How does your audience's tempo influence you?

- How do you account for different nervous systems, thresholds, and attentional rhythms?
- Are you making room for neurodiversity in your performers, audience, and yourself?

What is your relationship with impatience?

- Does the audience's impatience activate, derail, or provoke you?

Cultural

How will different audiences experience your use of time?

- What might change for a theatergoer vs. a gamer versus a TikTok scroller?
- How will cultural background, age, or ability shape attention?

Narrative

What moment sparked this work?

- Can you trace back to a specific image, memory, or event?
- Is that moment are visible in the work?

What rules about time have you set?

- Is there a tempo, rhythm, or pacing the audience is meant to follow?
- Where do you break that expectation, and what effect does that have?
- Do you expect patience, restlessness, focus, or surrender—and how are those expectations seeded?

What clues are you giving about the past or future?

- Are you creating any history, memory, or backstory?
- Are you planting hints or tensions about what's coming next?

How does the emotional arc of your work map to rhythm or timing?

- When emotion intensifies, does tempo accelerate, stretch, or stay steady?

How are you using repetition?

- What patterns have emerged?
- Are they intentional or instinctive?
- What meanings or emotions arise from these repetitions?

How does your performance space affect the audience's perception of time (proscenium theater vs. open field)?

How quickly do you want the audience to start assembling ideas?

Process

What time-based assumptions are shaping your process?

- Do you assume "This section will take a week to make" or "It has to be at least *x* minutes long"?

How much *creative time* does this piece want?

- What's your ideal duration for this process?
- Does this actually want to be made more quickly or slowly?

What agreements are you making with your audience about their attention?

- Do they have control or flexibility (e.g., can they leave, stay, reenter)?

Is chronology essential during creation?

- Do you start where you left off, or work nonlinearly?
- Can you try working the other way?

How visible do you want your process to be in the final piece?

- Do you want the audience to see evidence of strategy or structure? Why?

Dramaturgical

What rules have you created about time?

- Have you seeded ideas about pacing, duration, or flow?
- Do you rupture the rules?

What duration is this asking for?

- If you dropped all expectations ("evening length"), how long would this be?
- What would a twelve-minute, a seventy-five-second, or a twenty-four-hour version look like?

What is the "EKG" of durations within the piece?

Try: Time each event/section. Do you see a pattern? Do you want to break it?

What is the "EKG" of tempos?

Try: Describe the time quality of each event/section (slow burn, sudden burst, even flow). How does this overlap with your duration EKG?

Do the performers have their own time signatures? How do they affect each other?

Try: Swap material and have another performer try a very different time tactic.

How much time do you leave between the question and the answer?

Try: Reverse your habit here, in rehearsal or in the work. (If you are quick to answer, pad more space; if you are methodical, be impulsive. This can be in relation to performers' questions or the audience's.)

What role does chance play in the timing of this work?

- What might shift if you introduced an element you couldn't control?

Flow

How much control are you exerting?

How fluid or seamless do you want this to be?

- Are you letting anything feel unresolved, broken, or jagged?

Where do interruptions happen?

- Are they deliberate?
- Could interruption become a driver?

Does this want more ongoingness or unpredictability?

What drives the progression (music, accumulation, story, character development)?

Application

Is the piece ruled more by constructed (clocks/cues) or felt (sensed/perceived) time?

What narrative time structures are you using?

- Is it linear, cyclical, chaotic, ritualized, or chance-based?
- What values or beliefs are embedded in these choices?

What expectations about time could you challenge for the performers *or* the audience?

How do silence, stillness, or repetition affect the audience's sense of time?

2

Space

Before You Begin: Priming Curiosity About Space

Take a breath. Consider these questions. Let them settle in your body before moving forward. They are not for solving, but for sensing.

Who am I when I am fully in my body?

When do I feel spacious—inside and out?

Where do I feel the most sense of belonging?

How did I learn how much space I'm allowed to take up?

What spaces, people, and actions do I shrink from without knowing?

Why do I trust or distrust the space around me, and how might I reimagine that trust?

Groundwork: The Shared Edge of Space

In a field
I am the absence
of field.
This is
always the case.
Wherever I am
I am what is missing.
When I walk
I part the air
and always
the air moves in
to fill the spaces
where my body's been.
We all have reasons
for moving.
I move
to keep things whole.
(Mark Strand, *Keeping Things Whole*)[1]

The Space Between: Reimagining Boundaries in Life and Art

When Martha Myers, in a feedback session, said, "I'm curious about the space above your head. What do you want from it?," her comment cracked open the entire piece for me. I'd never thought of the space above me as a place to consider. How would you enter it? Beyond a jump or a lift, that space seemed unreachable. Yet her question stuck with me: What if I choreographed into unreachable space? I began to hunger to enter the space above us.

The work, a backstory for Sartre's *No Exit*,[2] began with heated conversations between each character and god. I never explicitly named this for the audience, but Martha perhaps intuited that the characters were relating to something *beyond*. Grappling with the verticality, I suddenly imagined

[1]Mark Strand, "Keeping Things Whole," *Selected Poems* (Knopf, 1980).
[2]Jean-Paul Sartre, *No Exit* (French, Huis Clos), originally performed in 1944.

a single green balloon floating upward. One balloon became many: some drifting beyond our grasp, others sinking before we could save them. They were metaphors for the characters' relationship to their imminent deaths, rising and sinking into the unknown. This image ultimately drove the story for my evening-length work *You Are Here.*[3]

There is a mythology built by capitalism that we can *own* space.[4] The impulse to divide and claim space reaches back thousands of years. Anthropologists often locate a turning point in the agricultural revolution, when nomadic rhythms gave way to settlement, and the land became marked by boundaries, property, and inheritance. This framing of space as possession lingers in how we imagine our classrooms, studios, and stages.

How space is imagined depends on access, history, and circumstance. Some grow up moving freely through rooms without question; others are taught to shrink, defer, or disappear. Few of us are taught to confer with space itself—to notice it, to ask something of it, to offer it regard. We inherit boundaries that feel fixed, as if the room allows *exactly this much* presence and no more. Space itself instructs us. The way a classroom arranges its chairs, a studio its mirrors, a stage its sight lines—each carries unspoken lessons about power, visibility, and permission. To accept these constructions without question is to inherit a thousand invisible rules that govern how we move, create, and exist.

At one point, though, we made endless choices about space and had no limiting beliefs about what was available.

At birth, our vision is limited to the faces leaning over us. The rest of the world arrives through sensation. Safety, in those first months, is proximity—the nearness of a caregiver's body, the warmth of being held, the reassurance that someone will come when we cry. As we develop agency, curiosity pulls us outward. These twin forces—stability and desire—shape our earliest stories: *I want to go there... but you come with me.* In performance, doesn't this echo? The urge to explore the unknown, coupled with the desire for witnesses.

Watching a baby explore space reveals a fearless relationship with uncertainty. Reaching, crawling, grasping—each gesture is discovery, unburdened by ownership. Whatever is within reach becomes theirs momentarily; what lies beyond reach is opportunity waiting to be grabbed. Returning to this playful orientation lets space become collaborator, not backdrop.

At some point, that fearlessness shifts. We learn compartments, possessions, and boundaries. We are taught to separate *here* from *there*, *available* from *unavailable*, *safe* from *dangerous*. These categories

---

[3]Alexandra Beller, *You Are Here,*world premiere, Dance Theater Workshop, New York, 2005. 4.

[4]Samuel Bowles and Jung-Kyoo Choi, "The Origin of Private Property and the Neolithic Agricultural Revolution," *Journal of Political Economy* 127, no. S1 (2019): S1–S23.

begin to determine who enters, who stays out, and what movements feel permissible. How do such inheritances shape our art-making?

As we grow, proximity becomes a story. Intimacy, power, and fear show up in how close or far we place ourselves from others. Too close, too distant, too crowded, too empty. For artists, the question becomes: What assumptions about available or unavailable space am I carrying right now—and what might be possible if I set them down, even briefly?

The Story of Distance

Babies are curious, but they *do* have a maximum distance they'll travel from their caregiver before insecurity, fear, and eventually terror set in.[5] That early calibration of closeness doesn't disappear; it bleeds into culture. Every society teaches its own acceptable distances, and we carry them with us—into classrooms, studios, and stages.

In class, when I say, "Let's get in a circle," I give no parameters about space. Almost always, we form an equidistant ring, each person about eighteen inches from the next person. This spacing is *socialized.* Though it shifts across cultures, every society sets its own "safe" proximity. In the United States, that boundary is about eighteen inches—the threshold between "personal" and "intimate" space.[6] To illustrate, I'll edge closer and closer to the person beside me until I'm only two inches away. I ask them, "How do you feel about me right now?" Then I step back—four feet away. Instantly, the story changes.

All I shifted was distance. No expression, attitude, or gesture. Yet, in those sixteen inches forward, I become "intrusive," "seductive," even "threatening." Four feet back, I read as "remote," "rejecting," "diffident." The values we absorb about distance in daily life become the lens through which audiences perceive our work.

Interrupting Assumptions About Space

Our safe proximities may keep us protected in daily life, but when repeated in art, they tether us to habit and narrow imagination. Art is more vivid, intensified, saturated. Onstage, we want spatial relationships to be heightened, evocative, daring—to leverage space so our animal bodies recognize it as dramatic, surprising, charged with meaning. By challenging our spatial defaults, we

---

[5]This phenomenon has been widely described in attachment theory as the "secure base" behavior, where infants explore freely within a certain radius but return for reassurance when that distance feels too great. See Mary D. Salter Ainsworth et al., *Patterns of Attachment: A Psychological Study of the Strange Situation* (Erlbaum, 1978).

[6]Edward T. Hall, *The Hidden Dimension* (Anchor Books, 1966).

invite space to become metaphorical, allowing our stories to become more compelling, disruptive, even subversive.

Because humans read distance with remarkable consistency—as a signal of threat, desire, or intention—responses strike the nervous system before the mind can intervene. Researchers have traced this reflex to the amygdala, the part of the brain that governs our instinctive regulation of personal space.[7] Artists can harness this predictability to disarm, confront, or destabilize an audience with startling accuracy.

Space as a Storyteller

The arrangement of bodies is its own language, resonant before a word is spoken or a step is taken. Three dividing into two and one, a single figure set apart, a mass pressed into a corner, or one body drifting in vast emptiness—these compositions narrate before we clock vocabulary, dynamics, or content: stories of isolation, exclusion, fracture, or allegiance.

Yet the raw language of space is muffled by conventions: the givens of architecture, etiquette, and expectation.

What are our assumptions about space? Here are a few to consider:

- Space is a commodity to be fought for.
- Space can be controlled.
- Proximity means intimacy.
- Proximity is a threat.
- Endless space offers freedom.
- Endless space is terrifying.
- Space cannot be touched.
- Art requires a fixed amount of space.
- The front matters more than the back.
- The center holds more power than the edge.

A few questions to ask yourself:

- What remains if these assumptions are released, rejected, or reversed?

[7]Daniel P. Kennedy et al., "Personal Space Regulation by the Human Amygdala," *Nature Neuroscience* 12, no. 10 (2009): 1226–7.

- Can space be **invented**, **redefined**, or **reshaped** for a particular work?
- What does this work actually *need* from space?
- Do you partner with a rehearsal/performance space, or accept it wholesale?
- Can you listen to your art's request as you would to a partner, a child, or your own body's needs?
- What would emerge if you treated space as a consensual collaborator?

The Inner World Made Visible

Space is not only *around* us; it is *within* us. Our bodies breathe in space, shape it, compress it. Our sense of inner space tunes us to outer space. We are not a "missing piece" that completes the world, nor is the world simply a frame that holds us. Together, our body and the world coauthor a story. Through art, our inner experience becomes visible.

Space is our feeding ground, our playing field, our church, and our graveyard. It is where we risk, where we assert our existence, where we press against the edges of what we have been given. It is where we are seen, and also where we hide, the source of true safety and real danger. Space does not complete us, nor do we complete it. We move through each other, keeping things whole.

Takeaway: Space shapes both what we see and what we feel. Let it disrupt, provoke, and transform—not as a passive backdrop but as a dynamic, living collaborator in your work.

In Practice: Tips About Space

1. **Use proximity and distance as narrative tools.**
   Experiment with closeness and separation. A tight cluster can evoke intimacy or entrapment; a lone figure in a vast space can suggest loneliness or defiance. Create images where placement alone tells the story.

2. **Shift spatial relationships over time.**
   Create tension by altering arrangements. Let performers drift, converge, or collide. Use grids, diagonals, and pathways intentionally—then dismantle them.

3. **Interrogate spatial defaults.**
   Question why performers occupy certain areas. What if the center becomes the margin—or the margin the focus? Let something vital happen offstage. If characters are equidistant, why?

4. **Break the boundaries of the performance space.**
   Extend into unconventional areas: the audience, the lobby, the light grid. Project performers from elsewhere. Alter the stage itself—remove wings, open doors, reveal the scene shop.

5. **Use negative space with intention.**
   Emptiness is powerful. If it feels empty, try removing rather than adding. Test how much void the stage can hold and still feel alive.

6. **Explore all three spatial dimensions.**
   Work across vertical (up/down), horizontal (side/side), and sagittal (forward/back). Purposeful shifts across planes can radically alter a scene's psychology. The planes each hold meaning:

   - **Vertical:** sensing, intending, grounding
   - **Horizontal:** thinking, attending, connecting
   - **Sagittal:** deciding, intuiting, acting

7. **Activate the audience's spatial awareness**
   Invite them to move, change vantage, or enter a new proximity. Surprise them with where events occur.

8. **Tell emotional stories through micro-spatial shifts.**
   A few inches can change everything. Step closer to signal desire or threat, retreat to suggest rejection or withdrawal. Test how subtle distances transform dynamics.

9. **Express power through scale.**
   Expand or contract presence. Consider using contradictory signals. A puffed-up body may signal insecurity; a quiet, grounded one may hold authority.

10. **Create spatial hierarchies.**
    Position bodies unequally to expose status, intimacy, or need. Use isolation or grouping to tell a story before any action begins.

Frameworks: Three Approaches to Using Space

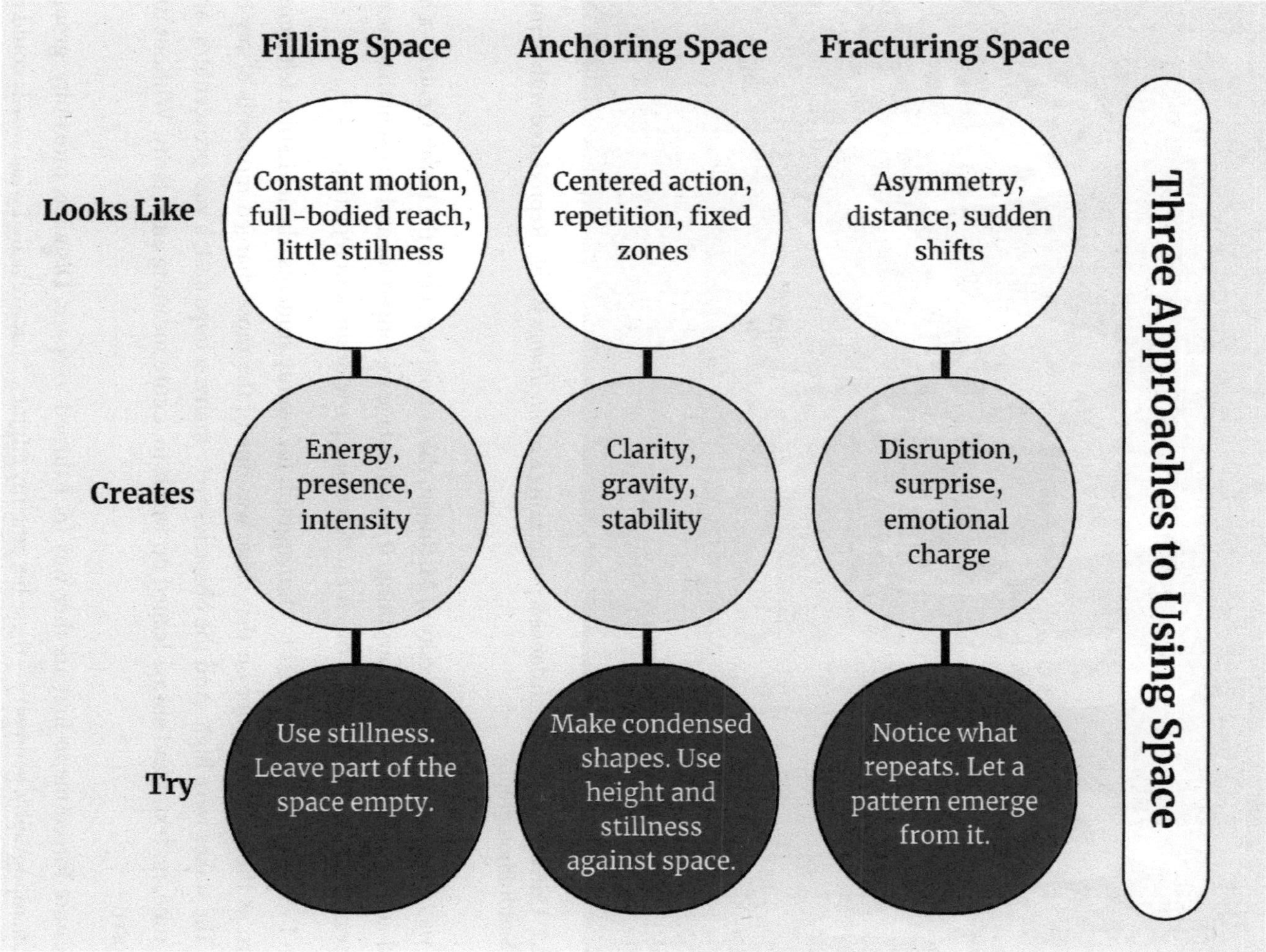

Figure 2.1 *Three Approaches to Using Space*. Chart outlining Filling, Anchoring, and Fracturing as spatial dynamics, each with characteristic actions and effects.

From the Field: *Keeping Things Whole*

Figure 2.2 University of Michigan dancers performing *Keeping Things Whole*. Reproduced with permission of Peter Smith Photography.

When I was a student at the University of Michigan, the annual concert at the Power Center—a fifteen hundred-seat opera house—was everything. It was the stage we longed for and an event that measured our success in the department. For me, it carried equal parts desire and rejection.

So when I was invited back in 2003 to choreograph for twenty students, the invitation felt immense. To return as the choreographer on that stage was one of the most charged moments of my career to date. The stakes were high. And the obstacles were many: a huge cast, a vast proscenium, and for the first time, no text. I had always leaned on words to secure meaning and clarity. Without them, I felt exposed.

That pressure forced me to find another way in. I turned to space. Distance, proximity, groupings, repetition, topography, geometry—these became my engines. Space revealed what words could not. A group leaving one body alone felt like grief. Two people, separated yet moving in unison, ached with longing. A mass moving wildly at an unbearably slow pace radiated power and dread.

Out of this inquiry, the theme surfaced: a meditation on climate change. The story didn't lead the spatial choices: space invented the story. The piece that emerged, *Keeping Things Whole*,[8] was piercing, unpredictable, and alive. The physical and thematic narratives birthed one another, shaping a work that told a piercing, haunting tale I could not have anticipated.

[8]Alexandra Beller/Dances, *Keeping Things Whole*, world premiere, Power Center for the Performing Arts, University of Michigan, Ann Arbor, 2004.

Guidance: Inspiration

> If the artist works only when he feels like it, he's not apt to build up much of a body of work. Inspiration far more often comes during work than before because the majority of the artist's job is to listen to the work and follow its prompts. Ultimately, when writing, you stop thinking and write what you hear.
>
> (Madeleine L'Engle, *Walking on Water: Reflections on Faith and Art*)[9]

Inspiration is often imagined as a rare, magical force—lightning that strikes without warning, something we must seize before it vanishes. But its very name tells a different story. Inspiration means *breath*.

Breath flows in cycles, often unnoticed, yet always sustaining. And breath is unusual among our vital functions: it runs automatically, and we can also choose to shape it.[10] Breath can be instinctive—a gasp of surprise—or intentional, like box breathing to calm the body. Inspiration works the same way: sometimes sudden and involuntary, sometimes summoned through choice and practice.

Breath is also the liaison between inner and outer worlds. Each inhale draws the world in even as it expands the body outward. Each exhale offers the inner world out even as the body retreats. Inspiration mirrors this reciprocity: it is both intake and offering, a constant negotiation between what is outside us and what rises within.

Inspiration, like space, waits within and beyond us. Outer inspiration enters through our senses—hearing, seeing, touching, tasting, and smelling the world, stimulating feeling. Inner inspiration rises through subtler awareness: interoception, equilibrium, the mapping of kinetic chains. Together, these pathways offer a two-way road for inspiration to flow.

If we approach inspiration the way we usually engage with breath—automatic, habitual, unexamined—we miss an opportunity. Our creative habits—same studio, same chair, same time of day—become tethers, attaching us to sameness. If we want freshness, an inhale, an initiation, we may need to alter conditions: a new space, an unfamiliar hour, even a different corner of the room. Change alerts the body into readiness. From readiness comes adjustment. And adjustment—the act of rerouting around what blocks us—is the body's earliest creative act.

---

[9]Madeleine L'Engle, *Walking on Water: Reflections on Faith and Art* (Wheaton Literary Series, 1972).

[10]Jack L. Feldman and Christopher A. Del Negro, "Looking for Inspiration: New Perspectives on Respiratory Rhythm," *Nature Reviews Neuroscience* 7, no. 3 (2006): 232–42, https://doi.org/10.1038/nrn1871.

Inspiration fuels your art's rhythm. It is personal, immediate, and ever-changing. And like breath, it is both a gift and a practice: automatic, yet something you can choose to affect.

Suggestions for Nurturing Your Inspiration

- **Work in a new location**, even a different corner of your room.
- **Change the time of day you create.**
- **Reset with breath.** Try a few rounds of box breathing (inhale 4, hold 4, exhale 4, hold 4) or coherent breathing (inhale 5, exhale 5) to regulate your nervous system. Then add a playful twist: an instinctive gasp, a sighing exhale, a slow, porous inhale, a sharp, cathartic exhale. Build a short breath composition, a score. Let each breath dynamic spark a movement, word, or image.
- **Cross-sensory translation.** Take one stimulus (a sound, a texture, a smell) and "translate" it into another form: movement, color, rhythm, words.
- **Interrupt the dominant channel.** If you always rely on sight, try closing your eyes. If you depend on music, work in silence. Let the absence awaken other senses.
- **Reverse a habit.** If you begin standing, start on the floor. If you start alone, invite someone in.
- **Speak your ideas aloud instead of writing them**; notice how they strike you through a new medium. Record yourself and listen as if to a podcast.
- **Draw, write, or gesture with your nondominant hand.** This activates underused neural pathways.[11]
- **Change your visual field.** Look at your work upside down, from the floor, or through a mirror. Create from a new orientation.
- **Alter your gait.** Take a short walk, moving slower or faster than feels natural, and let your thoughts catch up differently.
- **Engage a novel sense.** Hold an unfamiliar object, taste something sharp or sweet, or notice texture with your eyes closed.

Inspiration is also a *part* of us, with its own voice and needs. Just as breath bridges the unconscious and conscious minds, inspiration can move on its own or speak up when we listen closely. At times, what feels like a lack of inspiration may actually be *unmet needs*: your system may need more play, more quiet, more art watching, more collaboration. Approaching inspiration as a companion we can dialogue with offers another way to understand what it requires from us.

---

[11]Betty Edwards, Drawing on the Right Side of the Brain (New York: Tarcher, 1979).

Exercise: Interview Your Inspiration

Have a conversation with your inspiration as if it were a separate person. Speak aloud in a private space. **Ask it:**

- Where have you been lately?
- What do you need from me?
- When do you feel most alive?

Answer back aloud, without judgment. Listen for its requests. Make notes or agreements about how you will treat your inspiration moving forward.

Tuning In: Breath Reflection

This practice invites you to notice how breath reshapes the body and the world around it.

1. **Begin with breath.**
   Sit, lie down, stand, or move. Focus on breathing. Notice air entering and leaving. Notice how your body shifts shape, how volume adapts to the world, how the world presses back.

2. **Pause at the edges.**
   At the top of an inhale, **wait.** (Not *hold*—wait.) Let the exhale *occur*. At the bottom of the exhale, **wait again**. Let the next inhale come when the body truly *needs* it.

3. **Let your inhale lead the movement.**
   Let the inhale initiate a movement. Pause. Let the exhale settle your ending shape. Repeat until ready for a change.

4. **Let your exhale drive you.**
   Move on the exhale. Let the inhale nourish the shape before the next exhale moves you again.

5. **Allow choice.**
   Continue moving on either the inhale or exhale or both, organically. Let breath direct you—without planning or judging.

6. **Attend to space.**
   What changes in your awareness of space when movement begins with the inhale versus the exhale?

7. **Reflect.**
   What ideas, collaborations, or experiences feel like an expansive, nourishing inhale, feeding and sustaining you?

   What habits, pressures, or expectations could be released like an exhale?

Studio Lab: Shaping Space, Shaping Meaning

Compose with space as an active participant. Notice how it shapes your choices, and how your body inscribes meaning through distance, direction, level, and scale.

1. **Set up your space.**
   Choose a room, studio, or open area. **Notice** its size, boundaries, textures, and objects. **Sense** how it surrounds your body.

2. **Mark the invisible.**
   With tape, paper, string—or imagination—mark zones. Name them: **safe, forbidden, mysterious, charged, neutral.** Go with instinct, not logic. Improvise inside them. Notice how shifts in space affect your body and emotions.

3. **Challenge your defaults.**
   Identify three or four habits (prefer midlevel? avoid corners? stay small?). **Pick one and reverse it:** restrict yourself to a tiny area, pause often, use only the floor. Observe what changes.

4. **Create spatial interventions.**
   Introduce a barrier: an obstacle, real or imagined.
   - **Introduce a pathway:** a designated route, a line to cross, an invisible threshold.
   - **Introduce a focus shift:** move with constant peripheral vision or hold a single fixed gaze. Choose to use focus like a laser, a loose firehose, or an ocean.
   - **Change dimension:** explore *only* vertical, horizontal, or sagittal movement.

5. **Expand and contract.**
   Move as if you are *too large* for the space; extend, reach, and press against walls. **Shrink** as if the space is *too big*; hug the edges and find small nooks and pockets. **Notice** what these extremes reveal about presence and movement.

6. **Explore.**
   Choose a small creative event: Perform a phrase, create an object collage, or recite a monologue. **Perform it** in three different areas. **Track** how tone, meaning, and energy shift with location.

7. **Reflect.**
   - What spatial habits revealed themselves—where do you always return, what do you avoid?
   - How did space shift the tone of your story, presence, or relationships?
   - What surprised you—an impulse, an obstacle, an opening?

Pagework: Writing into Space

Freewrite on some or all of these questions.

1. **What spaces influence your inspiration positively or negatively?**
   Are you sparked by vastness, containment, nature, or crowds? Are you drained by fluorescent lights, noise, or monotone colors?
2. **What habitual spatial patterns do you see in your work?**
   Can you devise a plan to disrupt any?
3. **How do you nourish your inspiration? What conditions does it request?**
   If you ask your inspiration, as if it were a person, what it needs to feel alive, safe, playful, and curious, what would it say?
4. **When did you last notice the "space above your head?"**
   What opportunities, ideas, relationships, or dreams have you set aside as "out of reach"? What would happen if you allowed yourself to explore what feels beyond reach?
5. **What assumptions about space limit your imagination?**
   Do you feel confined by physical boundaries, creative rules, or inherited habits? How might you dismantle them?

Movements + Maps: Making the Space a Living Collaborator

This score invites you to break inherited habits, question your assumptions, and explore space as both physical and conceptual material.

1. **Make a rule about space, and break it once.**
   Define a spatial law ("I will always face one direction," "I will never cross center"), then disrupt it at a key moment.

2. **Use a tiny kinesphere.**
   Create a movement event that uses only a tiny amount of space (a finger dance, whispered monologue, series of nuanced focus shifts).

3. **Make a phrase that etches the space.**
   Create a phrase that inscribes geometry into the room—lines, arcs, spirals—so the space is marked.

4. **Draw your topographic pattern before moving.**
   Put a pen to paper and draw without lifting the pen. This is the map of your floor pattern.

5. **Use space as the *only* tool for meaning.**
   Set aside facial expression, language, and overt emotion. Use only spatial choices—distance, nearness, separation—to create shifts in meaning. In a solo, these distances can be to the audience, to an object, or to the room itself.

Contributor's Note: The Space/Time Paradigm Shift

by Emanuel Gat

Whenever I am asked what choreography is, I usually answer: It's the process of organizing movement, or action, through time and space. However, in recent years, I've begun to feel that this answer no longer accurately reflects what I observe.

The assumption is that time and space are fixed, objective fundamentals: preexisting frameworks, external to the action taking place. As a choreographer, I supposedly organize human movement and action within those two layers.

But the more I observe the relationships among time, space, and movement, the more I feel that time and space are not neutral or given but that they emerge from the internal logic of the choreography itself. In other words, something about the way choreography is structured and enacted actually *generates* specific spatial and temporal fields, or at the very least alters our experience of them. Choreography doesn't operate inside space; it reshapes it.

This means that each choreographic happening generates its own emergent time and space properties. Because choreography is only alive when and where it is happening, the same work performed in a different place, at a different time, in front of a different audience, produces a different spatial reality.

The choreographic process is a construction pathway, producing objects, structures, kinetic entities—assemblages of constraints and interactions that form complex systems. These systems accumulate information about their own making. Choreography is the embodiment of all the steps that led to its manifestation. And central to this process are constraints—rules or limits that require the dancer's receptivity. Acknowledging these constraints is what allows the choreographic reality to come into being. That acknowledgment is consciousness.

Through repetition and continued engagement with choreographic systems, dancers develop a form of autonomous choreographic intelligence—a collective intelligence distinct from that of any individual. Over time, this intelligence facilitates the emergence of a specific field of choreographic consciousness. That's why I've never felt that choreography is about reflecting reality. It's about building the conditions for a *parallel* one.

Back to space, then: if choreography is capable of generating its own consciousness field, it makes sense that a singular, external, fixed spatial reality doesn't bind it. It creates its own manifestations of space and time—each unique, each contingent on the living event of the work itself.

Maybe, just maybe, the purpose of choreography is to harness human energy in such a way that it opens a portal—a threshold—into an altered spatial and temporal field. If that's true, then the quality of a choreographic work is directly linked to the clarity, strength, and coherence of the spatial (and temporal) consciousness it manages to produce.

Studio Provocations: Questioning Space

> Have patience with everything that remains unsolved in your heart. Try to love the questions themselves, like locked rooms and like books written in a foreign language. Do not now look for the answers. They cannot now be given to you because you could not live them. It is a question of experiencing everything. At present you need to live the question. Perhaps you will gradually, without even noticing it, find yourself experiencing the answer, some distant day.
>
> (Rainer Maria Rilke, *Letters to a Young Poet*)[12]

Sensation

Are you aware of how space is framing this work?

- Do you more often track performers individually, or do you see them in spatial context?

Are you aware of your breath as you create? As you watch the work?

Try: Watch your work, allowing your breath to be incredibly sensitive to the dynamics. Inhale sharply when you are surprised. Let your exhale slowly drift as an event unfurls. Notice the score of your breath. Was it mostly even, jagged but at regular intervals? Let your breath score amplify your body's intuitive response to your work.

Does the rehearsal or performance space create pressure, safety, or resistance?

How are you attending to the ground?

- Could the "bottom" of space extend beyond the floor—into the earth below, or imagined depth above?

How are you attending to the space above?

- What is the "top" of the space?

Viewing and Proximity

How have you designed the audience's location and viewing?

- What separates the performers from the viewers?
- How does this architecture shape meaning, intimacy, power, or mystery?
- Could altering proximity change the work's emotional or narrative clarity?

---

[12]Rainer Maria Rilke, *Letters to a Young Poet*, trans. M. D. Herter Norton (W. W. Norton, 1934).

Are you crafting the audience's focus?

- Have you made decisions about angle, focus, facing, and directionality?
- Is there a "front"?
- What power dynamics arise from crafting the audience's attention or ignoring it?

How are the margins and unseen spaces functioning?

- Are there hidden or withheld areas of space that carry meaning?
- Are you using height, depth, and the sides of the space to tell the story?

Are the audience's other senses included?

- Can they touch, smell, or feel any part of the work?

Are you considering the audience's sensation of their space?

- How might different body types, neurodivergence, or cultural norms affect them?
- Have you provided agency in how they interact with the space?

Do you ever enter the "audience" space?

Distance and Connection Between Performers

How does proximity between performers tell a story or evoke emotion?

- Are those shifts choreographed, improvised, or intuitive?

Are any spatial rules or hierarchies established between performers?

- Who initiates, who follows, who yields?

Does your space use reflect or resist norms (personal space, intimacy, authority)?

Try: Make a radical spatial shift in a beat or section. Place two characters who were intimate across the stage from one another, or overlap two events that were far apart. You don't need to keep the spatial change, but did it offer any new information?

Architecture and Mathematics

How is architecture affecting the work? Consider:

- How far away are the viewers?
- Are you watching the work from every sight line?
- Are there obstacles for the audience?
- Where are the entrances and exits?
- Are there hiding spots?
- Are the workings (electricity, water, heat, lighting, etc.) visible?
- Where does the space feel bound, and where does it flow?
- Are there corners? Curves? Angles?

What is the vertical topography of your piece?

- Does it change?
- Have you considered rigging, platforms, dropping things, flying, floating, or levering?

Are you using spatial counterpoints?

Where are your spatial habits?

Try: Map your use of the grid (movement upstage/downstage/stage right/left), the diagonals, levels, and curvilinear pathways. How often are you close to or far from the audience?

Map your use of small, medium, large, and global kinespheres.

- What do you use most/least? Why?

Performance Space

Is there a difference between where you're *making* your work and where you're *showing* it?

- What excites you about your performance space that's unavailable in rehearsal?
- Will you miss anything about your rehearsal space? Can you re-create it?

How much do you want the work to "fill" the performance space?

- Have you considered intentionally leaving part of it untouched?

What feels most expressive or meaningful about the performance space?

- Is there any way to amplify it?

Can the performers see the audience?

- What decisions have you made around the fourth wall?

Is there space available (grid, lobby, dressing rooms) that you are not using?

Dramaturgical

What rules in the performance space are negotiable?

- Would working "outside the box" serve the work?
- Has the space been reimagined? ("The theater is an asylum.")

Does the audience enter your world, or do you enter theirs?

Does your work leave the space feeling changed?

Does the space have a known history (a church, factory, famous venue)?

- Are you leveraging that identity?

Does the performance space transform over the course of the work?

Narrative

Does your work imply or explicitly reference another space (a forest, a home)?

- Is it a real-life place?
- How are you indicating it (text, video, sound, scent, taste, imagery)?
- Are there ways to augment the audience's sense of it (a scent, taste, sound)?

Does the space have a character?

- How are you indicating it?

Are you using the space in a way that feels

- Sculptural?
- Enigmatic?

- Familiar?
- Architectural/geometric?
- Human/naturalistic?
- Charged/loaded?
- Irrational/absurdist?

Do performers share the same perception and rules of space?

- Do differences create any opportunities?

What is the difference between "space" and "environment"?

Is there a sense of outer *and* inner space? How do we see that?

Are some of your *spatial* choices actually *temporal* (could a pause replace a distance)?

What part of the space feels like

- A right?
- A privilege?
- A given?
- An unknown?
- Something familiar?

Is the space stable?

- Does it exist like this all the time, or does it get prepared for you?
- What goes into preparing it?
- Would you like to change anything about how it gets ready?
- Is it missing anything, including ritual?

Power, Politics, and Identity

Is there any violence in this space, historically or presently?

- Has this space been colonized?
- Did enslaved people build it?
- Has anyone been barred from this location?

- Is it ADA compliant? Can *every* body enter it?
- Does this affect how you want to present here?

What rules govern the space, and who polices them?

- Do they create tension for you? Are there any adjustments that would relieve it?

How much ownership do you feel in the rehearsal and performance space?

- Is it temporary, permanent, borrowed, or communal? How do you adjust for that?

Kinetics

If your movements left visible traces, what picture or pattern would remain?[13]

What space was the audience in before they entered the performance space?

- What did they need to do to arrive (climb stairs, pass through security, drink at a rooftop bar, take a hike)?
- What is the preshow experience, and how might it affect various bodies/systems?

Process

What is your ideal creative environment?

- How can you create it?

How much space do you crave in your process?

- Can you design the amount of space you need?
- If not, what opportunities does the adaptation offer?

In your fantasy, *with no limitations*, where does this piece want to be seen?

- On a cliff? In an abandoned factory? Through a peephole?
- What about that image feels most important?
- Are there any ways to bring part of it to life?

---

[13] *The Value of a Line* was a group exhibition featuring Heather Hansen's kinetic drawings created through her unique dance movements. Using charcoal and paper, Hansen translated physical motion into visual art, exploring the relationship between body, space, and mark making. Heather Hansen, *The Value of a Line*, group exhibition, Ochi Gallery, Ketchum, Idaho, 2014.

Have you made space for

- Dreaming?
- Failing?
- Organizing?
- Not knowing?
- Changing your mind?
- Waiting?
- Listening to others?
- Reading?
- Watching?
- Reviewing?
- Ignoring your work?
- Being uninterrupted?
- Having time alone?
- Asking for help?

3

Relationship

Before You Begin: Priming Curiosity About Relationship

Take a breath. Consider these questions. Let them settle in your body before moving forward. They are not for solving, but for sensing.

Who am I when no one is watching?

Where in my life do boundaries feel too porous or fixed?

How did I learn to show up—or disappear—in relationships?

When do I let connections deepen, without trying to control them?

What relationships shape me, even when I think I'm working alone?

Why do I walk away from some interactions fuller—and others emptier?

Groundwork: Moving Inside Relationship

> But once the realization is accepted that even between the closest people infinite distances exist, a marvelous living side-by-side can grow up for them, if they succeed in loving the expanse between them.
>
> (Rainer Maria Rilke, *Letters to a Young Poet*)[1]

Defining the Edge

We think of relationships as *connections*, but they are revealed through *boundaries*. Feeling the edge of oneself against the world—against the needs and stories of others—etches a picture of our sensed experience. Our skin, breath, and weight act as the first tools to craft relationships, measuring desire, action, and outcome. Sound, temperature, and touch arrive at the edges of our bodies passively at first. But relationships deepen when we send signals outward—crying, reaching, gesturing—and notice how the world answers back. This is the beginning of the echolocation of relating.

Echolocation works by emitting sound and receiving the feedback of its echo.[2] The time, direction, and quality of that echo reveal distance, shape, and even texture—whether what's out there is smooth, jagged, close, or far. It's not only proof that something is present; it traces the contours of how we stand *in relation* to it.

Relationships, both in life and art, are a form of echolocation. Every gesture is a signal, every response an echo, sketching not only who we are but who we are *to one another*. What returns carries the imprint of what it touched. In this moment, we glimpse two things—our **lived experience** and **the story the world is telling about us**.

Every return signal is both *about us* and *not about us*. What others receive is filtered through them; their response is theirs alone. Yet it still maps the distance and resonance between us, offering information about both ourselves and others. No one ever sees the whole picture. Each of us sketches a contour of the relationship—a reality that may align with theirs, or drift apart.

I explored this in my piece *other stories*.[3] A guest improviser, surrounded by my company dancers, began moving from their own lived story. When a gesture struck one of the dancers, they would raise a hand—"That one's mine"—and turn away to capture it. They set it and taught it back to the guest onstage over the course of the piece. By the time the guest reentered, they were performing a phrase of

---

[1]Rainer Maria Rilke, *Letters to a Young Poet*, trans. M. D. Herter Norton (W. W. Norton, 1934).
[2]"Echolocation is nature's built-in sonar. Here's how it works," National Geographic, February 3, 2021.
[3]Alexandra Beller/Dances, *other stories*, world premiere, Institute of Contemporary Art, Boston, 2011.

their "own" movement—now filtered through others' memories, interpretations, and bodies—which they shared in fragments with the others.

This is how relationships live in the world: we share gestures of attention, passion, body, and belief with different groups. I share certain things with women, others with artists, progressives, New Yorkers, or the neurodiverse. None *defines* me, but taken together, these mutualities shape my identity in both art and life. And because I never overlap entirely with anyone, every story *about* me will diverge from my own. No single overlap defines us, and no relationship completes us. Each encounter returns only a fragment—political, somatic, aesthetic, familial, spiritual. Together, these fragments form a shifting composite: never fixed, never whole. The edge between my lived truth and others' interpretation of me need not be a battlefield. It is difficult to sit with the discrepancies and contradictions between how we feel and how we are perceived, and it invites possibilities for harmony or collision, but hopefully negotiation.

Chemistry Versus Ecology

We often talk about relationships as having "chemistry," but in truth, they are far more complex. Chemistry may describe a spark, a bond, or a reaction—but there are only building blocks. Relationships behave more like *ecology*: webs of interdependence where countless forces shape one another over time. What we call "chemistry" is just a glimpse of this wider field, a shorthand for something far messier and more dynamic.

To glimpse that ecology in art, we can name some of the elements always at play:

- Our past work
- Our heritage/lineage/artistic genealogy
- Our collaborators
- The performers to one another
- The characters to one another
- The bodies to one another, to space
- The objects to one another, to us, to our performers
- Our work/performance/dreaming/thinking/creating space
- Time
- Money
- Our body
- The audience

- Our ego
- Our material
- Identity/culture
- Critics/press/media
- Community
- Technology

Each element exerts its pull. Some lie dormant, shaping quietly like roots beneath the soil. Others catalyze change when combined, reshaping what surrounds them. None of us acts alone. Every collaborator, choice, and response transforms the conditions for the rest.

Among them, the audience is the most catalytic. They arrive carrying their own composites—histories, identities, filters, curiosities—and when these meet our work, the ecology shifts instantly. A phrase, an image, a silence—each lands differently depending on who is there to receive it. The audience is the volatile element: impossible to predict, measure, or contain.

Relationship with the Audience

While we cannot control how others engage with our work, we can be intentional in meeting their gaze. The audience relates to our subjective art, ingesting it through their filters. Controlling their response isn't just impractical; it's impossible and antithetical to art's purpose. Relationships thrive on *consent*, not *force*.

We have all seen art that pushes, cajoles, or demands something of us that we are unwilling or unable to give. This alienates the audience, denying them the chance to meet the work on their own terms. Manipulative art *tells* the audience what to think or how to feel, often asking for admiration or validation. Just as the swelling orchestral score in a film urges the viewer toward sadness, a centering of virtuosity may be exposing a longing to be seen.

Then there is art that ignores the audience, sometimes with hostility. Some artists proudly proclaim, "I never think about the audience!" I believe this, too, limits us. Art can be so determined to be *itself* that it leaves the audience in the dark. I think of certain strands of postmodern dance where the performers were so absorbed in task or structure, they were indifferent to their legibility. Yvonne Rainer's *No Manifesto*[4] declared, "No to spectacle… no to involvement of performer or

[4]Yvonne Rainer, "Some Retrospective Notes on a Dance for 10 People and 12 Mattresses Called 'Parts of Some Sextets,' Performed at the Wadsworth Atheneum, Hartford, Connecticut, and Judson Memorial Church, New York, in March 1965," *The Drama Review* 10, no. 2 (Winter 1965): 178.

spectator," and some Judson-era works embodied that refusal to its endpoint. The dancers' attention was turned inward, their logic precise but often opaque, leaving the audience to hover outside the event.

Both extremes erode relationship; our task is to *hold attention* while *releasing control* over response. It is a fine line; walking it asks us to consider our need for acceptance, control, and visibility.

The Balance of Control and Surrender

Releasing control over the audience restores their agency. This shift can be uncomfortable, but it opens the possibility of a genuine encounter. Our task is not to engineer their response, nor to ignore it, but to make choices that are legible and purposeful, honoring the work's priorities without demanding admiration. This is the sweet spot of a relationship: *consent*.

I learned how volatile this balance can be in my one-woman show, *us*,[5] about my relationship with the United States. The audience stood in for the country. They surrounded me on four sides, like a boxing ring. I spoke, yelled, and sang to them, sat next to them, enlisted their help with props, taught them songs, and had them read aloud. The show depended entirely on their actions, responses, and engagement.

How the audience responded, and how I metabolized their response, determined whether the show flew or failed. On nights when they resisted or refused, I was sometimes flooded with rage: *You're ruining my show! You're not doing it right!* How I responded to that rage determined the tone of the show that night. On nights I could absorb their choices and let them change me, the piece transcended my control and became something larger than either of us. When I stayed too attached to "the way I wanted it to go," our relationship became adversarial.

So, if we let go of controlling or ignoring the audience, how *should* we relate to them? I believe the magic is in caring *about* them, but not *caretaking* them.

---

[5]Alexandra Beller/Dances, *us*, world premiere, HERE Arts Center, New York, 2007.

Do We Need an Audience?

Not every work calls for an audience. Some art lives privately—in a journal, in a rehearsal, or in Authentic Movement. Even in solitude, I often feel an inner witness whose presence sharpens awareness. We often assume sharing is the final step, but sometimes it is not. **Ask:**

- Would this work lose something if it were seen?
- Is its power in the making rather than the showing?
- Am I seeking validation, or is visibility integral to the form itself?
- If no one ever saw this, would it still feel complete?

Some works are conversations with the self, with memory, with process, with God, with the body. An audience can deepen a work—but it can also distort it. Not every seed wants public soil.

If, after asking these questions, the work still feels unfinished without witnesses, then the audience becomes an *essential* ingredient.

I have a mantra I repeat when I'm overthinking: **I am not responsible for my audience's needs, expectations, or assumptions.** Being *not responsible* does not mean being *unaware*. This looks like: "This choice may not be for everyone. It may offend, bore, or intimidate some. And I love it, and I'm doing it."

milkdreams was a profound departure from previous work and brought this into focus. It was a long, slow arc of subtle vocabulary requiring deep audience attention. I feared some would hate it, but I couldn't make choices from that feeling. I had to judge its *rightness* based on my own body. And my body said, "Yes, this is it. This is what I am trying to say." The responses to that work were stronger than previous ones. Some loved it, and I suspect some hated it. But neither potential response dictated my decisions.

Mutuality and Consent

Every audience member arrives carrying their own story. No two are the same, and none will ever fully align with mine. Mutuality is not about *sameness* but about *coexistence*—our different accounts overlapping, contradicting, and refracting each other, but both having space to exist. I do not need them to recognize my exact history. Their stories, layered alongside mine, are what make the relationship alive.

Consent lives inside this recognition. To create a healthy relationship with an audience is to allow them the freedom to meet the work on their own terms: to be moved, to resist, to misunderstand, even to disengage. It is also to allow myself the freedom to create from my own needs and urgencies, without bending toward pleasing or caretaking. Mutuality only exists when both sides honor that autonomy.

This is why intimacy onstage must be *earned*, and world-building is critical. Too often, I see two performers leap straight into weight-sharing and touch without having established who they are to each other or why that closeness matters, dropping it at the end of the duet, both seemingly unchanged. The moment lands as false because the director skipped the groundwork of intimacy: a shared reality. The details matter. When we gloss over them, we ask the audience to do the work we should have done: to fill in the gaps and make the leap of belief unearned.

The opposite is true in the Netflix series *The Diplomat*,[6] a political drama centered on a high-stakes ambassadorial appointment and a long, strained marriage. There, the marriage is revealed through the smallest gestures, like her consistent denial of hunger and his quiet habit of adding extra food to his plate, knowing she will eat from it. These details carry the weight of invisible time. They let us trust the bond because we glimpse its history. The writers and actors did the work of layering clues, and the audience feels that work as *depth*.

Both examples point to the same principle: relationship with the audience falters when we assume too much, and flourishes when we attend to the details. Trust is built through continuity, care, and the willingness to let stories unfold in parallel, sometimes aligned, sometimes divergent, but necessarily truthful.

Takeaway: Your relationship with the audience is an open dialogue: clear boundaries honor their sovereignty.

---

[6] *The Diplomat*, created by Debora Cahn, season 1, Netflix, 2023.

In Practice: Tips About Relationship

1. **Name the edge.**
   Clarify the boundaries where self meets other: performer and audience, body and space, lived story and interpreted story.

2. **Signal, don't state.**
   Send your work outward as an invitation. Let the "echo" return on its own terms rather than trying to script it.

3. **Release control, but maintain clarity.**
   Make purposeful choices, but don't try to engineer the audience's reaction. Consent thrives when autonomy is honored.

4. **Avoid false intimacy.**
   Don't demand closeness without building trust. Intimacy, between performers or with an audience, is earned through detail and continuity.

5. **Respect multiplicity.**
   Remember that every audience member arrives with their own story. Expect divergence, not sameness, and design with that plurality in mind.

6. **Check your own needs.**
   Notice where your desire for acceptance, control, or validation is affecting the work. Ask if those impulses serve the relationship.

7. **Distinguish manipulation from invitation.**
   Be wary of coercive moves (the swelling score, the show-off virtuosity) that push audiences toward a specific feeling instead of letting them respond authentically.

8. **Notice what changes *you*.**
   The audience doesn't just *receive* the work; they *alter* it. Pay attention to how their energy, silence, laughter, or resistance shifts your choices.

9. **Test for volatility.**
   Put the work in different rooms. Notice how identity, history, or temperament change the "chemistry" of the response and adjust your awareness accordingly.

10. **Stay curious about presence.**
    Ask whether a work truly *needs* an audience. If yes, why? If no, let it live privately. Either way, curiosity—not obligation—keeps the relationship alive.

Frameworks: A Temperature Check for Relationships in Your Work

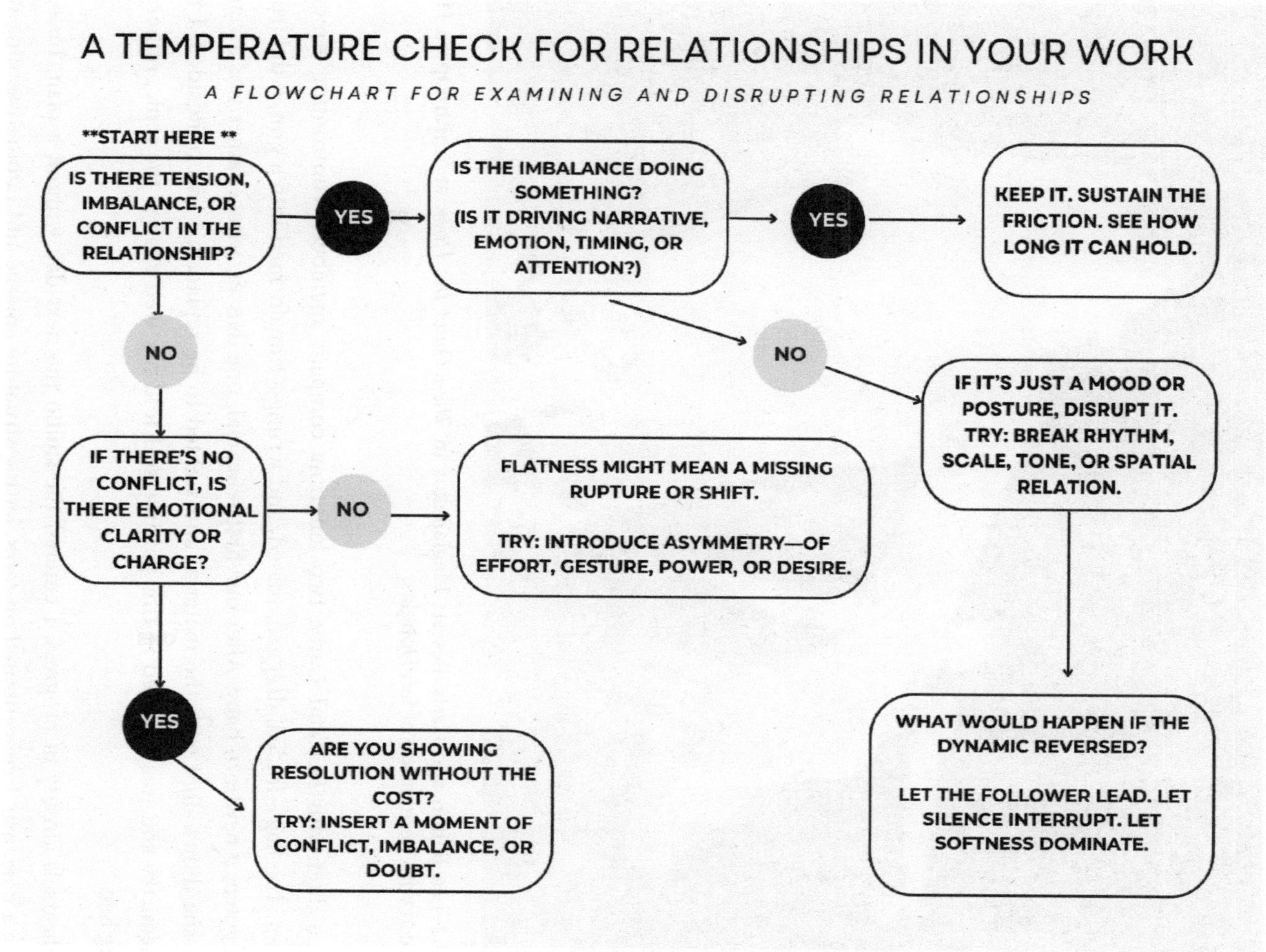

Figure 3.1 *A Temperature Check for Relationships in Your Work.* Flowchart for analyzing imbalance, tension, and resolution within artistic relationships.

From the Field: *Then Quiet the Hook*

Figure 3.2 Lea Fulton and Carly Berrett Plagianakos in *Then Quiet the Hook* at Smith Opera House. Reproduced with permission of Ian Douglas.

I began a duet with Lea and Carly, two longtime company members, confronting American patriotism. The flag—folded, dragged, tossed, and wrung—transformed into a gun, a tightrope, a pageant gown, a newborn baby. After our first rehearsal, one dancer, whose father was a veteran, told me she didn't align with the material and wanted to be replaced. I was blindsided. I loved their chemistry and was attached to this pairing, so I told her we'd change the topic, rather than recasting her.

With rehearsals already in progress, I entered the studio the next day without a plan. Instead of following a narrative, I concentrated on *form*, letting structure emerge and hoping meaning would follow. I was terrified. I poured myself into making evocative movement—partnering sequences, floorwork, intricate phrasing—hoping vocabulary would signal meaning. I devised a rondo structure (A–B–C–D–E–D–C–B–A). The movement was compelling and their dancing, beautiful. They performed complex partnering, weight-sharing, and kinesthetic response. The structure had symmetry and variation with diverse dynamics and spatial patterns. On paper, I'd checked every choreographic box. But it was boring; I was unmoved. I'd put no thought into their bond, assuming proximity, touch, and responsiveness would be enough to create a relationship.

One day, I gave them a new task: Keep everything we'd built, but transition, over the course of the piece, from *interdependence* to *independence*. At first, every move, look, and step they took was a direct reaction to the other. Slowly, they stopped responding to each other. They didn't wait for cues, even for partnering. The touch and weight-sharing from the beginning became partnerships with the floor or air because their partner was missing: two solos retracing the empty scene of their former partnership. By the end, they moved only for themselves. Tenderness and intimacy eroded, shifting from shared meaning to prioritizing *themselves*.

Over dinner one night, Lea casually said, "You know this piece is about your marriage, right?" **I had no idea.** I thought I was crafting "tension" and "arc," but the loneliness and longing in my currently dissolving marriage were clearly visible. While I wanted the work to feel explicitly relatable, I did not want to reveal the details of my story or expose my partner. Luckily, the audience didn't need me to explicitly name my story, only to create a relationship specific enough to evoke their own memories. What I learned was that specificity does not require confession.

Guidance: Cultivating Connection and Community

> In the studio, it's less about how they might fulfill my vision, and more of, "How do we come together with a strategy that translates in some way? How do all of these deep, as well as superficial, observations and fascinations come together into a form that is performed in front of people?"
>
> (Bebe Miller)[7]

We hear romantic stories of writers locking themselves in attic apartments, emerging after a year, bedraggled and jaundiced, with their soon-to-be-famous novel. But in embodied art, isolation is rarely fertile ground. Community in art is like mycelium: an unseen network linking trees and plants, sustaining growth, sharing resources, and fostering resilience. Without these networks, we risk creative isolation, which starves even the most inspired ideas.

Community looks different for each of us. For some, it's a face-to-face exchange. For others, a dialogue with history and the artists who built our field. For many, it's being witnessed, sharing work, or staying current with the field's evolution.

Whatever its shape, community requires investment. What do you *need*, and what are you willing to *give*? Do you show up to performances, readings, and sharings? Invite trusted allies into your process? Celebrate others' work? Connection takes vulnerability, courage, and the willingness to navigate conflicting needs. It requires that we know our boundaries, desires, shame, fear, habits, capabilities, and resources. We curate communities to meet us, and we challenge ourselves to meet the needs of others. With curiosity and empathy, these differences enrich rather than divide us.

Here are a few ways to invest in meaningful artistic connections:

- Attend one local or virtual art event per month, even outside your comfort zone.
- Check in regularly with an artist friend or mentor to reciprocally discuss process and challenges.
- Create a micro-community—a small feedback group, book club reading current research, or somatic group taking turns leading.
- Celebrate others' work: write about it, promote it, or share what moved you.

[7]Bebe Miller, interview by Harriet Jennings, *The Creative Independent*, October 14, 2018, https://thecreativeindependent.com/people/choreographer-bebe-miller-on-allowing-your-creative-process-to-age-along-with-you/.

- Curate your own "witness circle" (even asynchronous)—choose two or three trusted people to engage with your work at key moments.
- Find ways to engage that don't require masking or shrinking: ingesting art, reading artist biographies, or coworking online with your camera off.
- Be intentional about what you need—mentorship, accountability, inspiration—and seek those connections carefully. Do not linger in spaces that don't accept or celebrate you as you are.

Tuning In: Attuning to Space, Boundaries, and Connection

This practice invites you to explore the quiet, foundational relationships with what is.

1. **Attune to your presence.**
   Begin standing, sitting, or lying in a neutral position. Close your eyes and take slow, deep breaths.

   With eyes still closed, begin moving safely. Feel the boundaries of your body, as if all of space were contained within your skin.

   Keeping eyes closed, bring awareness to the space around your body—your kinesphere. Shift your weight, feel your equilibrium.

   Open your eyes and begin taking in the space around you, a duet between what is *you* and *not you.*

2. **Explore proximity and gaze.**
   Move through the space. Identify a fixed object (wall, chair, window, doorway) to act as your partner. Move toward it at different speeds, observing how the approach changes your sensations.

   Do you feel magnetized, hesitant, neutral, or something else? Do you notice more agency at one speed or another?

   Stop at varying distances—far, medium, and very close. At each stopping point, notice: Does your breath, focus, or balance change?

   Leave the object. Do you feel relief or disconnection? Is there longing or freedom?

   Finally, dance with the object as your witness. Let yourself tell it a story, hide a secret, or try to evoke a response from it.

3. **Engage with contact and weight exchange.**
   Choose a wall, chair, railing, or table as your partner. Offer weight—lean a hand, shoulder, leg, or back lightly, then with more force. Experiment with withdrawing weight, slowly peeling yourself away from the surface. Shift between *offering* and *withholding* weight multiple times. Notice the qualities that emerge:

   - Grounding/flying
   - Withholding/offering
   - Controlling/yielding
   - Absence/presence

4. **Integrate.**
    - Did any objects feel more compelling or resistant than others?
    - Where did you feel the push, pull, or negotiation with the room?
    - Where did the room feel empty? Where did it feel alive or mysterious?
    - How did your relationship with this space mirror how you navigate connection and separation in life and art?
        - Did your bodily actions—such as offering, withholding, moving toward, or pulling away—mirror how you relate to others in your creative process or performance?
        - Did autonomy change when partnering with the room instead of a person?
        - Did any memories or associations arise?

Studio Lab: Mapping Power, Connection, and Boundaries

Notice the invisible structures in relationships—power, agency, control, and agenda—and play with how they can be reinforced, disrupted, or reversed.

1. **Choose a relationship.**
   Pick a relationship between two performers or characters. Keep it simple: two people, one dynamic. **Ask:**
   - What draws them together?
   - What separates them?
   - Is the relationship explicit, implied, or undefined?

2. **Map the current dynamics.**
   Observe or imagine how this relationship shows up in the body. Write or sketch what you notice:
   - **Space:** nearness, distance, orbiting
   - **Touch:** weight-sharing, withholding, absent
   - **Gaze:** direct, averted, withheld, avoided
   - **Timing:** Who initiates? Who follows? Do they ignore invitations from one another?
   - **Agenda:** What seems to matter most to each of them?

   Contradictions are important. Moving in unison does not always reflect closeness, and separation in space does not always indicate rupture.

3. **Identify the story beneath.**
   Ask: What does this dynamic suggest?
   - Dependency? Rivalry? Familiarity? Replaceability?
   - Do they want the same thing? Different things? Nothing at all?
   - Is one holding power or do they share it unevenly?

   Remember: The story doesn't need to be neat. It may be fractured, contradictory, or unresolved.

4. **Devise a score to shift it.**
   Create an intervention. Choose one dynamic and either **amplify** or **subvert** it. For example:
   - If they orbit each other at a distance, push them into sudden contact.
   - If one always leads, ask the other to initiate.
   - If eye contact is random, insist on it—or forbid it.
   - If they move in unison, fracture the timing.

   Keep the score simple, repeatable, and open-ended.
5. **Test and reflect.**
   Run the score. Then ask:
   - How did the shift affect the balance of power or agency?
   - Did any new dynamics emerge? Contradictions?
   - Did this alter your perception of their relationship?
   - Might the audience now read it differently?

Pagework: Writing into Relationship

Freewrite on some or all of these questions.

1. **How do you define "community" in your creative work?**
   How do witnessing, feedback, and shared experience create meaning?
2. **At what stages of your process do you *most* crave company?**
   What actions (brainstorming, feedback, co-creating) bring you the most vital and generative connections?
3. **How do you nurture relationships with collaborators, peers, and audience?**
   Are there actions, like attending live art, giving feedback, or open rehearsals, that would deepen those connections?
4. **How does your introversion/extroversion influence your solitude or collaboration?**
   Do you prefer one-on-one collaboration, group settings, or working alone?
5. **Imagine your perfect creative environment—who is there and what are they doing?**
   How can you build or expand this ideal ecosystem with your current reality? What step can you take *today* to move closer to it?

Movements + Maps: Where Boundaries, Power, and Meaning Meet

This score invites you to shift power, proximity, or attention to redefine meaning.

1. **Create a conflict.**

   Choose a tension that does not resolve immediately. It might be between performers, between performer and audience, or between performer and objects/space.

2. **Define a specific relationship with the audience.**

   Decide how you want to acknowledge, include, ignore, or challenge them. **Consider:**

   - Spatial logic (focus, proximity, angle).
   - Awareness (fourth wall vs. direct engagement).
   - Dynamics.
   - Arc (change over time).

3. **Define three relational rules.** Examples:

   - Every movement must be initiated by one and completed by another.
   - They must share weight in each phrase.
   - No eye contact is allowed.

4. **Generate a phrase.** Using the three rules above, create thirty to forty-five seconds of set movement.

5. **Shift the relationship.** Alter one rule at a time:

   - If one held power, give it to the other.
   - If proximity was far, move it close.
   - If gaze was withheld, let it seek.

   Create a **second phrase** from these altered terms. Keep what feels compelling.

6. **Compose through relationship.**

   Decide how the two phrases live together: alternate, overlap, or collapse? Use contrast to build a short study (two to three minutes) where **meaning arises from the shifts in relationship**.

Contributor's Note: Living in Chaos

by Liz Lerman

Let's consider the Big Bang as a fable. In an instant, not even an instant, we are all born. All of it. Yet it is nothing. It's a swirling, entirely unpredictable, intense amount of energy forming and falling apart and forming again. In fact, there is no shape. Nothing sticks together. After all, nothing is nothing.

But then, a very long time later, somehow there is *stuff*. Tiny bits of stuff that emerge because gravity has discovered itself and can exert enough pressure for a thing to be seen. But still nothing sticks together. It takes thousands of what we now call years for any of this stuff to stay in relation. It does come together, but it falls away quickly.

Amazingly, stuff learns to form some kind of bond, and the parts decide to stay in relationship. Together, in a new shape, they become something like a molecule, and then more of them join the same shape or form new ones. And so something new begins to happen. There is more than one way to be a connected shape, more ways to be in relation.

What makes the stuff stick together long enough to form a relationship? Initially, what holds is the vibration, the sensing, the sound making, the motion, the communicating—all the things we now call creativity. That's what it is. It is the elements of creativity that hold us through the joys, miseries, troubles, mysteries, and challenges that come with relationships.

It would be thousands of years before we name some of the ways that creativity works through repetition and innovation. We might call those elements "artists." Artists whose lives are made up of coming together in relation, making all kinds of things, and then falling away into a new pattern. People who make the vibration, the sensing, the sound, the motion, the communication their life's work.

In 2025, as I write this, we are once again living in chaos. Let us understand that our work is to bring people, animals, environment into relation and try to sustain that long enough to learn how to see the inevitable joy, misery, trouble, mystery, and challenges that come with so many ideas, ideals, and institutions falling apart. We are called back to the essence of who we are and what we know, and how to continue as gravity rearranges itself. We construct new molecules and learn to careen in fresh ways as we live with ourselves, our communities, and our big dreams. The world we are making requires our two constants: creativity and relationship.

Studio Provocations: Questioning Relationship

We had better share our bewilderments. By hiding them from each other we should not hide them from ourselves.

(C. S. Lewis, *Letters to Malcom: Chiefly on Prayer*)[8]

Identity and Ecosystems

How do gender, race, or sexuality show up in the relationships?

Do size, age, or ability shape the dynamics?

Where is power visible? Where is it hidden?

Is culture made *visible*, or is it *implied*?

Is *your* identity legible in the work?

Are your collaborators' identities visible in the work?

Who do you feel responsible for in your process? Is that useful?

- If not, could you shift expectations, clarify agreements, or delegate?

Emotion and Affective Connections

How does the work negotiate emotion?

- Are they expressed by performers or left to the audience?
- Do you hope *specific* emotions will emerge?

Is there dependency?

- Who relies on whom?

How do performers affect one another—emotionally, physically, energetically?

Which qualities drive the relationships? Consider:

- Sympathy/Generosity
- Tension/Resistance

[8]C. S. Lewis, *Letters to Malcolm: Chiefly on Prayer* (Harcourt, Brace & World, 1964).

- Longing/Love/Lust
- Yielding/Abandon
- Nostalgia/Retrospection
- Objectification/Manipulation
- Listening/Intimacy/Connection
- Fatigue/Hopelessness
- Goals/Desire
- Aggression/Violence
- Survival/Need
- Spirituality/Prayer
- Mystery/Curiosity

Does sexuality appear? How is it expressed?

Strategic and Relational Dynamics

What are the power dynamics between the performers?

Do the relationships change?

- Are there shifts in rules, tone, reality, perspective, motive, or tactics?

Does the process confront or explore embarrassment and vulnerability?[9]

Narrative and Character

How would you describe the beginning? Is it a(n)

- Invitation
- Plea
- Offering
- Challenge

[9]This chapter by Anne Bogart explores how confronting and embracing embarrassment is a vital part of the creative process, fostering vulnerability and presence that enrich theatrical work. See Anne Bogart, "Embarrassment," in *A Director Prepares: Seven Essays on Art and Theatre* (Routledge, 2001), 113–37.

- Rejection
- Surrender
- Undoing

How would you describe the ending?

- Release
- Acknowledgment
- Dismissal
- Refusal
- Apology
- Reckoning
- A portal

Do the rules of relationship mirror real life?

- Are greetings, departures, and intimacy earned or assumed?

Who counts as a "character"?

- Could it include objects, light, sound, space, or text?

Where is the conflict?

- Is it resolved, open, or transformed?

How does repetition or change in relationships add meaning?

Collaboration and Process

How invested are your collaborators right now?

Try: If one person is more passive, try assigning them control of time, space, or initiation for a section.

Where do power dynamics show up physically?

Try: Who lifts? Who speaks? Who sets the tempo? Who takes focus? Reverse or exaggerate that pattern.

Whose ideas shape the material most?

Try: Swap roles: Have someone else edit, cue, or structure a section. Notice what shifts.

How do you invite input?

Try: Change the mode: Replace verbal direction with physical demonstration, or vice versa, and see how that alters collaboration.

What happens if one collaborator refuses or resists?

Try: Build a task around that resistance as part of the score.

What access differences shape the room? (Stamina, range, training, time.)

Try: Highlight, instead of hiding, them. Give each difference its own choreographic weight.

Audience Engagement

Where do you want the audience's attention?

Try: Stage a section toward them, then away. Compare.

Are you inviting pleasure, challenge, or provocation?

Try: Pick one and exaggerate it.

What if the audience dislikes this moment?

Try: Keep the material, but adjust tone or pacing.

How much control do you want over interpretation?

Try: Make a version where you advance a specific narrative purposefully, and another where you leave the narrative highly flexible. What do you learn from each version? Make a third version using the gems from each.

What assumptions are you making about who is in the audience?

Try: Swap to a different imagined audience. What do they elicit from you?

Which rule of "audience relationship" would be useful to break?

Try: Never turning your back on, or never facing, the audience. Speaking to the audience without looking at them, or having an internal monologue facing them.

Technical and Formal Relationships

Have you considered these relationships:

- Bodies and space
- Space and light
- Light and sound
- Sound and movement
- Light and audience
- Costumes and space

Is there tension or harmony between the technical and performative materials?

Are any technical elements personified or treated as characters within the work?

Power, Consent, and Boundaries

How is consent crafted?

- Are agreements explicit or implicit?

Do collaborative relationships feel mutual, hierarchical, or conflicted?

Through what channels can the performers communicate boundaries, needs, and issues?

- How might the production designate clear lines of communication (for example, check-ins with an intimacy director or stage management, established "pause button" language, and reporting pathways) so that performers can revise boundaries over time?[10]

Is the audience a consensual partner? Do they have agency?

Try: Find a moment engineered for reaction. Trace the mechanics behind it. Then alter one variable—timing, scale, gaze, duration—and observe how agency redistributes between you and the audience.

[10]Chelsea Pace, *Staging Sex: Best Practices, Tools, and Techniques for Theatrical Intimacy* (Routledge, 2020).

Relational Dynamics

Are the relationships unfolding linearly, cyclically, or in fragments?

Try: Retell the same relationship in a different temporal structure—if it unfolds linearly, restructure it as a cycle; if fragmented, reorder it chronologically. What shifts in meaning?

Do changes in spacing alter the emotional tone?

Try: Shift the spacing. Reverse when people are distant, near, and intersecting. How does that alter emotion?

Does silence or stillness heighten or soften tension?

Try: Insert silence or stillness into the score. Does tension rise or dissolve?

If you define the performers' relationship in one sentence, does the material reflect it?

4

Meaning

Before You Begin: Priming Curiosity About Meaning

Take a breath. Consider these questions. Let them settle in your body before moving forward. They are not for solving, but for sensing.

Who am I when I stop doing, producing, and helping?

Where do I reach for meaning when I am at my lowest?

What do I keep doing even when it no longer feels right?

When do I feel most alive, most creative, most like myself?

How did I learn which stories to tell—and which ones to hide?

Why do I need things to mean something, and what happens when I don't?

Groundwork: Becoming Meaning

> You cannot expect other people to create meaning for you. You cannot wait for someone else to define your life. You make meaning by forging it with your own hands. It requires sweat and commitment. Working toward the creation of meaning is the point. It is action that forges the meaning and significance of a life.
>
> (Anne Bogart, *And Then, You Act*)[1]

Naming the World, Naming Ourselves

Every semester at Princeton, I gathered the students' choreography into a thirty-minute piece for our end-of-semester showing. It became a delicious exercise in craft. Most of the twenty-five students had never danced before, much less choreographed. In about three hours of rehearsal, I shaped a semester's worth of wildly different studies into a single offering for an audience.

This is a place where I distinguish *craft*—functionality, logistics, and technique— from the meaningful work of *art* that moves through it.

The semester leading to this showing had each student create short studies from a range of assignments. Some tilted political, others personal, mathematical, or abstract. We kept a handful of the strongest outcomes, leaving us with a patchwork of solos, duets, trios, quartets, and group projects—material made for different purposes, on different topics, without any obvious relationship.

In the genre of class showings and recitals, it is easy to let the work become a parade of what students made and learned—no thread, no arc, just the evidence of practice. That kind of presentation has its place. But when the students taste meaning—when they feel a dance move beyond display into something that resonates—the sum transcends its parts. *Craft* starts to yield *art*.

In our brief rehearsal, I stitch their fragments together. Their material is the fabric I use to drape, cut, and stitch until form is revealed.

Even though this is a showing, not a polished performance, I want it to carry meaning. For many students, it is their first time performing. I hope their friends will feel the courage it took and meet that bravery with awe and care.

How to make sense of so many fragments?

---

[1]Anne Bogart, *And Then, You Act: Making Art in an Unpredictable World* (Routledge, 2007).

I often posed this question directly to the students. "Start feeling into the work as you run it," I'd said. "Listen for meaning." A student sometimes protested: "But… we didn't *make* a meaning." "The audience will," I would answer. "They will piece together stories from what they see. Those clues are already in the work. Our job is to hear what the piece wants to say and help it speak more clearly. Maybe we are speaking together as a group. Maybe it's the collision of your individual wants, needs, and experiences. Maybe it's the imprint of this political and social moment."

This is the eternal tug-of-war between craft and art. On one side, the deliberate choices: engaging technical skill and field-tested methods for effect. On the other side, the intuition: letting emotion and metaphor emerge organically. I don't believe this is a dichotomy. Meaning arises through both *function* and *expression*. When craft steadies expression and expression leans on craft for coherence, meaning often arrives without force. We can resist meaning, but it will surface. We may as well be complicit in its unfolding.

That instinct to find meaning can be honed like a muscle. When I need to warm up meaning-making, I do an exercise I call "The Unexpected Gallery." We pick one face of the room and see it as a gallery installation. Every dust bunny, gum wrapper, scratch in the paint, and abandoned sock becomes an intentional artistic choice. We are museum visitors, deciphering the meaning of this artwork. It shocks me how easily we narrativize and assign intention. A cynical view says we are inventing reality. After all, there is no artist behind this wall of objects. I prefer the optimism that we create meaning out of everything as a way to root ourselves in a shared reality, the bedrock of intimacy. As artists, we harness this superpower of *creating sense* through the ways we notice, shape, and, eventually, name what we see.

The Instinct to Name

We come into the world without questions or answers. Everything just *is*. Over time, the instinct to ask *who*, *what*, *when*, *where*, *why*, and *how* shapes our understanding of the world and ourselves. The questions begin in childhood, often in response to adults constantly naming things for us.

> *What is that?*
> *Where do these come from?*
> *How does this happen?*
> *Why is the—why are we—why can't I—*

Children barrage the world with questions, mapping meaning as they go. As a parent, this can be maddening. Yet, in answering them, we provide an ethical and logical framework that shapes meaning. *How* we answer these questions reveals our values, beliefs, and priorities. Do we answer with *facts* or *opinions*? Do *we* answer or invite *them* to search for their own? Do we invite them to gather data through *inner* or *outer* metrics? Are our answers offered as *absolutes*? It depends on the question, but also on what we value. Is inner wisdom as reliable as information from "experts"? There is no right or wrong way to name the world, but understanding the core of how we make meaning can help us communicate our story and connect with our audience intentionally.

Once we learn language, we reach for words the way we once reached with our hands—trying to grasp what we don't yet understand. This instinct helps us survive, but it can also limit our ability to *imagine*. Once we name something, we deprive it of all other potential identities. Calling a scene "an argument" limits its future. The label quietly dictates tone, assigns roles, and predicts an outcome before the scene has had a chance to unfold.

Our satisfaction with *answers* can eclipse our *questions*, and with them our curiosity. What happens when an audience responds to our work with a question rather than an answer? What makes us, both artists and audiences, so resistant to staying with an unanswered question?

Humans are often described as "meaning-making machines." My years in rehearsal rooms confirm this: Audiences make sense from fragments, even when none was intended. This is what "The Unexpected Gallery" lays bare: Even in a wall of accidents, the brain hungers for coherence. Cognitive psychology echoes this instinct, calling it our brain's pattern-recognition system.[2]

We may have stopped asking out loud, but inside we are still asking, *Why is this like this? Why is that there? Why can't I just… ?* When we view art, we make up the *why* through an elaborate series of assumptions, theories, or guesses. We name things. "That part is about emotional isolation. That part is discharging grief."

Sometimes we don't just seek meaning—we wield it defensively, naming things quickly to escape uncertainty. In doing so, we block immediacy, empathy, and adaptability. This is true not only in the art world but in religion, dating, social structures, and politics. "Oh… I know *that* type (of lover, artist, friend, boss, art)." We are relieved to feel we *know*. Then we can *plan*. We know what to *expect*. We are safe from *surprise*.

Of course, we *don't* know. Answers create a compelling illusion built on assumptions. Questions, though, reveal meaning. I return to *how* we seek information. Do we probe with our intellect, our emotions, or our gut? If we ask, "What *is* this?," and answer from emotion, the answer will differ from when we answer from science. Neither is wrong, but the answers will differ. We sometimes hear

---

[2]Humans are often described as "meaning-making machines," highlighting our innate drive to construct narratives and find significance in experience. This concept underpins much of creative thought and psychological understanding of human cognition and storytelling (see, e.g., Jennifer Carlston, interview by Ben Johnson, "Meaning Making Machines," *Hired Thought* podcast, December 2, 2020, https://hiredthought.com/2020/12/03/meaning-making-machines-jennifer-carlston/).

a friend lament, "My *mind* wants one thing, but my *heart* wants another.... What should I *do*?" The question exposes the architecture of our knowing—reason, emotion, instinct—each shaping meaning in its own way.

The Fear Behind Not Knowing

Meaning is shaped by our desire to be understood and our fear of being misunderstood. *Naming* shields us from the discomfort of not knowing and soothes our fear of *ambiguity*. It becomes armor against the chaos of the undefined. Leaving room for the unknown means we may be misunderstood, even judged. The fear of invisibility, rejection, or isolation drives us to define ourselves—to contain rather than explore. This is true not only for those of us *creating* the art but also for those *watching* it. An audience member who feels lost—or even stupid—becomes isolated from our work. They don't "get it" and decide they don't like our work, or even art itself. Sometimes we judge them for wanting to be entertained, "spoon-fed," or pandered to. We say, "You don't need to *understand* art; you need to *feel* it." The art lover urges the doubter, "Forget right and wrong! What did you feel?"

When we ask this, we risk dismissing their experience. When an audience member says, "I don't get it! What does it mean?" I hear fear. They are worried they seem "stupid." We can approach their fear with understanding, or let it spark our *own* fear of being misunderstood. Both of us are grappling with our need to belong. Relating meaningfully requires empathy; having contempt creates a rupture we cannot afford.

The fear of not knowing what a dance is about is just a portal to the real fear: not knowing why we're here. This existential question drives space travel, meditation, mindfulness, and religious rites. "Answers" may quiet the panic that life is unknowable and uncontrollable. But answers often reveal how much we *do not know*. Even the most "proven" scientific "facts"—like gravity and relativity—remain theories, waiting to be unsettled by new evidence. Becoming comfortable with *not knowing* is the artist's hidden strength.

How does *your* comfort with not knowing help an audience stay with *their* not knowing?

Jung's functions of the mind offer a map for creating meaning. Thinking is a necessary container, essential to art-making, but is often overprioritized. The other three functions—sensing, feeling, and intuiting—lay the groundwork for a *different* type of awareness. Consider the visceral sensation of *knowing* something. I urge choreography students to seek that sensation of seeing/hearing/tasting that you've landed on exactly the right paint color, tempo for the movement, amount of salt in the soup. You immediately *know*: **Yes, that's *it*.** That visceral sensation of knowing something enterically[3] is

[3]For more information on the enteric nervous system, see Jackie D. Wood, *The Enteric Nervous System* (Oxford University Press, 2011).

instinctual and definitive. I ask students to tap into animal instinct, to be less concerned with *making sense* and more attuned to what they *feel*. It also builds audiences able to meet our work.

Embodied Knowing

The body can bypass logic to tune into visceral intelligence. In *milkdreams*, I sought a dance untouched by language—a vocabulary drawn from the movements of my infant sons. Their bodily expression revealed that meaning does not always require words. As Antonio Damasio writes,

> Consciousness is the feeling of what happens—our mind noticing the body's reaction to the world and responding to that experience. Without our bodies there can be no consciousness, which is at heart a mechanism for survival that engages body, emotion, and mind in the glorious spiral of human life.[4]

Mirror neurons[5] fire when we move *or* watch someone else move. When we use the body as our primary communicator, the audience doesn't just *see* the movement; they physically *experience* it. It's the same reason you hold your breath when a movie character goes underwater: The body echoes what it sees. This power comes alive only when our bodies are paying attention and when what we are watching mirrors the authentic human experience.

Watching my babies dance made me wonder what tiny bodies—incapable of speech—wanted, needed, knew. *Did I still know those things?* Ivo (fourteen months) had just learned to walk, and Lucas (five years) had never had a dance class, so there were no "steps." Learning unnamable dances required meticulous analysis. The usual verbs for movement felt useless. Inhibiting patterns like abdominal support, vestibular balance, and cross-body connectivity required intense *thought*. It was frightening for the dancers to surrender control and return to reflex.

---

[4]Antonio R. Damasio, *The Feeling of What Happens: Body and Emotion in the Making of Consciousness* (Harcourt, 1999), 27.

[5]Mirror neuron theory proposes that certain brain cells activate both when we perform an action and when we observe others performing the same action. Though this phenomenon was first discovered in monkeys, neuroimaging shows analogous human brain regions, such as the inferior frontal gyrus and inferior parietal lobule, engage similarly during action observation and execution. However, direct, single-neuron evidence in healthy humans remains limited. See "Mirror Neurons and Their Functions," *Simply Psychology*, July 7, 2025, https://www.simplypsychology.org/mirror-neurons-function.html.

We embraced disequilibrium and cultivated fearlessness. The details of weight shift, directionality, impetus, and initiation were pivotal. At first, the piece became an intricate reconstruction of every move. But we lost its *why*. Stepping back to see the gestalt, I remembered disequilibrium was not about physics alone but about being unguarded, just *being* with no plan, no goal, no predetermination, embracing the very *not knowing* that often unsettles us.

Literal Versus Imaginative Meaning

Meaning depends on how we navigate the literal, metaphorical, and abstract. **Literal** meaning gives us certainty and correctness. Dictionary definitions include: *precise, actual, simple, direct, true,* and *faithful.*

Let's pause to consider what comes to mind as the opposite of literal. Published antonyms lean toward distortion: *false, exaggerated, unclear, inaccurate, dishonest.*

The opposite of literal is not false; it is figurative—layered, symbolic, expansive. Imaginative meaning is the stuff of art. To honor that spectrum, I began imagining my own antonyms: *fantastical, metaphorical, dreamed, imagined, open-ended, undefined, porous, intangible, possible, magical.*

I would be gratified to have my art described by both sets of words. I don't play favorites between the literal and the metaphorical, but I *do* resist the myth that literality rules meaning. I believe it is a reflex to protect us from uncertainty, and that overusing the literal diminishes imagination. Art lives where the literal meets the figurative—where what is named and what is imagined remain in dialogue.

Takeaway: Instead of asking what your work means, ask what it invites. Meaning will meet you there.

In Practice: Tips About Meaning

1. **Lead with questions, not answers.**
   Shape meaning as inquiry. Let your work provoke wonder rather than deliver conclusions.

2. **Layer entry points.**
   Offer multiple ways in—through image, sound, space, or emotion—so meaning becomes plural, not singular.

3. **Notice when meaning becomes armor.**
   Pay attention to moments when you rush to define something. Ask whether naming too soon is a defense against ambiguity.

4. **Sit inside uncertainty.**
   Let some passages resist explanation. Meaning often emerges when we wait inside the unresolved spaces.

5. **Let the body *be* the message.**
   Allow weight, touch, breath, or proximity to carry meaning. The body communicates before words.

6. **Invite mirror neurons to fire.**
   Remember that audiences have the neurological framework to feel what they see, if crafted with embodied authenticity. A breath held, a balance teetering, a collapse—their nervous systems echo yours.

7. **Shift between literal and imaginative.**
   Restage what feels literal as metaphor. Ground what feels abstract in the concrete. Notice how each frame opens new meaning.

8. **Change the function you lead with.**
   Thinking, sensing, feeling, and intuiting each generate meaning differently. Notice your default, then try leading from a less familiar mind function.

9. **Interrupt habitual patterns.**
   Find the moment that feels predictable, habitual, or overused. Alter its rhythm, scale, or body parts to disrupt the habit. Layer another action on top (add text while using familiar movement vocabulary), obscure it (perform it behind a set piece so only fragments are visible), or transpose it (keep the dynamics but apply them to text or lighting; keep the body parts but change the direction).

10. **Delay the name.**
    Hold off on titles, labels, and explanations. Let movement or sensation exist without naming them.

Frameworks: A Venn Diagram of Verbal and Embodied Language Goals

This list is neither exhaustive nor definitive, but these are examples of how we might observe the goals of verbal language to either match with or contradict it. By analyzing what the verbal language is doing, we can make clearer decisions about how body language might amplify or engage with it.

Linguistic Strategy	Function/Intent	Embodied Equivalent
Declarative	Stating a fact or observation	Firm stance, stillness, frontal gaze
Interrogative	Asking a question	Tilted head, reaching, shifting weight
Exclamatory	Expressing intensity or emotion	Sudden burst, expansive movement
Imperative	Commanding or directing action	Pointing, leaning, lunging, and stepping toward
Conditional	Suggesting hypothetical or future possibilities	Hovering, partial gesture, spiraling, circling
Subtext/Implied Speech	Meaning behind or beneath words	Microgestures, indirect focus, gesture layered with incongruence.
Silence	Absence, pause, withholding	Suspension, withdrawal, contraction
Poetic/Metaphorical	Language that symbolizes, implies, or evokes	Repetition, transformation, abstraction, and symbolic spatial use
Performative Speech	Language that *acts* (e.g., "I promise," "I resign")	Gestures that enact change—e.g., offering, surrendering, sealing, opening
Emphatic/Redundant	Reinforcing meaning through repetition	Echo gestures, rhythmical repetition, and mirroring
Dialogic/Relational	Meaning shaped by dialogue or response	Counterpoint, call-and-response, mirroring, interruption
Disruptive/Disjunctive	Fragmented, contradictory, or deliberately incoherent	Abrupt shifts, misalignment between gesture and tone, tension between voice and body
Metacommunicative	Speaking about speaking (e.g., "Let me explain…")	Framing gestures, "resetting" postures, pausing movement to reorient
Storytelling/Chronological	Sequencing, causal language, and narrative flow	Linear travel through space, evolving shape sequences, build-and-release phrasing

From the Field: *Sense and Sensibility*

Figure 4.1 *Sense and Sensibility* Off-Broadway at Judson Gym. Photographer unknown.

One of my favorite choreographic projects was Bedlam Theater Company's staging of Kate Hamill's *Sense and Sensibility*.[6] That production revealed how profoundly movement can provide meaning. Kate's script was the skeleton, keeping us oriented, while movement was the muscle, revealing the subtext to drive the deeper meaning. The angle of a head, the length of a pause, and particularly the movement of furniture became ways to reveal the unspoken story.

One scene made this especially vivid: a brittle, polite sparring between Elinor Dashwood and Lucy Steele, a scene with enormous secret emotional stakes. They both sat in wheeled chairs, steered by fellow actors. The chair choreography exposing their deeper agendas and private inner experiences. A sharp turn away revealed when a character felt threatened; a slow circling disclosed that they were

[6]Kate Hamill, *Sense and Sensibility*, dir. Eric Tucker, Bedlam Theater Company, world premiere Off-Broadway at the Gym at Judson, New York, November 9, 2014.

stalking; confrontation lived in the stillness. The body's dialogue was as robust as the spoken one. The audience didn't need an explanation; they *felt* the tension in their bodies.

In a modern staging of a period piece, we occupy two worlds at once. We invite the audience to enter the imagined past as if it were real, while also viewing it through contemporary eyes. Kate's plays heighten this duality, always amplifying the social commentary embedded in the original. Movement often holds the reins of that subtext, steering us toward *feeling*, a place where both eras can coexist in the body.

That production clarified a method for working with metaphor. I begin by listening for openings in the text. Sometimes the opening is structural—the exact beat where power shifts, focus reverses, rhythm changes, or intention turns. Sometimes it's linguistic: a word that doubles as a physical cue, suggesting a bodily state or action. Sometimes the movement prompt is culled from what is *unsaid*.

Once I understand the movement's goal ("to reveal that this brash, overconfident character is experiencing remorse"), I work in this sequence: feeling, body, space, and objects.

I start by noticing the subtextual feelings. What clues has the playwright embedded in stage directions or text that point to an inner experience? Then I ask how that feeling lives in the body: Where is it, and what does it do to the character's tone, breath, weight, or phrasing? From there, I consider space: How does that internal sensation want to direct the body in terms of proximity, direction, scale, or focus? Finally, I look at objects: Does anything onstage physically support this metaphor? (Do the curtains want to be blowing? Should the character be toying with a set of keys?) I move from the most subjective to the most tangible.

I am not trying to *illustrate* the text. If the feeling is "lost," I don't mime searching. But I might build movement that carries the sensation beneath the word, perhaps disorientation, scanning, or suspension. Movement should not *mirror* text, but expose the unwritten ideas that want to be communicated. When done well, the body advances the narrative as a layer of meaning that the audience feels before they can name.

Years later, at the Folger Shakespeare Library, I was teaching the opening dance. An actor turned to me and asked, "So this all happens before any of the language comes in?"

I paused, faced him, smiled, and said, "This *is* the language."

Guidance: Motivation as Meaning in Motion

We often confuse *motivation* with *inspiration*. **Inspiration** draws us toward ideas; **motivation** is the force that *bridges* idea and action. Inspiration alerts us to what matters; motivation is the willingness to stay with it long enough to act. But even that is not enough. For motivation to translate into action, the conditions must support it.

Inspiration Is Not Motivation

I was *inspired* to write this book years ago and *motivated* enough to finish two-thirds of it. Why did it take so long to publish? Not because I lacked inspiration or drive; I was excited by the content and found meaningful pleasure in the creation. The book remained unfinished because, in the scheme of my life—artistic, academic, parental, romantic, political, financial—I had not implemented a support system to maintain motivation.

Motivation doesn't spring from sheer will alone. It's shaped by what our brain needs, who we're with, and what we have. Studies show that when our senses of autonomy, belonging, and competence are intact, motivation is far easier to access.[7] Acknowledging these influences gives space to attune to what *we* need in order to "just do it." This often means rejecting the propaganda around motivation.

Most Motivational Quotes Miss the Point

I take issue with 95 percent of motivational quotes because of their dark implications:

- Absolutism
- Lack of empathy
- One-size-fits-all approach to the creative spirit
- Toxic positivity

Quotes like, "Winners never quit, and quitters never win," leave no room for context, complexity, or consent. Messages meant to "motivate" us instead often overwhelm or alienate us. Rather than action, they inspire exhaustion, shame, and loneliness.

There is nothing wrong with you for lacking motivation. The gap isn't laziness but a deficiency in the conditions that allow motivation to surface.

---

[7] Richard M. Ryan and Edward L. Deci, "Self-Determination Theory and the Facilitation of Intrinsic Motivation, Social Development, and Well-Being," *American Psychologist* 55, no. 1 (2000): 68–78.

Motivation Is Scalable

One handful. That was my partner's way into the impossible task of clearing the yard of leaves. He had been inspired by the idea of making the space inviting, but inspiration didn't move the rake. Work, parenting, and the churn of daily life kept stalling him.

Then one afternoon, he came inside, sweaty and grinning: "I cleared all the leaves!"

"How?" I asked.

"I just told myself I'd take one handful. And be satisfied with that."

One handful led to two, then five, then twenty. The ground began to show itself again—the soil, the path. Each glimpse of change made the next step inevitable. Momentum had arrived.

One handful is craft: small, grounded, repeatable. Repetition makes space for art to gather.

Motivation is not just what we do; it's how we relate to ourselves in the doing. Releasing perfectionism and the drive toward specific outcomes makes room for motivation to grow, one small act at a time. A single handful of leaves can clear a path. Likewise, a small act—one sentence, one movement, one moment of presence—can lead to profound transformation. The "handful" metaphor isn't just about action; it's about cultivating a forgiving, flexible, and sustainable relationship with your work.

I often forget this. If I don't have time to plan my entire syllabus, why bother? If I can't read the whole play, why read a few pages?

Because of inertia. In physics, inertia is the tendency for a body to continue what it's doing until something shifts it. We often default to thinking of inertia as stasis, but it can just as easily be ongoingness. One small act tips the balance, turning inaction into consistent action.[8]

Because of accumulation. Each small act compounds. One more day of journaling, sticky note on the wall, page read before bed. These small marks of persistence stack until they shift your practice and your sense of yourself.[9] They also quite literally accumulate into a book, script, phrase, or show.

[8]Thema Bryant, *Homecoming: Overcome Fear and Trauma to Reclaim Your Whole, Authentic Self* (Penguin Random House, 2022), 124. This work explores how purposeful attention and repeated actions shape behavior and motivation, relevant to the concept of inertia in psychological change.

[9]James Clear, *Atomic Habits: An Easy and Proven Way to Build Good Habits and Break Bad Ones* (Avery, 2018), 35. This work explores how small, consistent actions compound over time, creating significant and lasting change through the accumulation of tiny daily improvements.

Micro-Movements Spark Meaning

Instead of pressuring yourself to complete a monumental task, ask: What's one small thing I'm *genuinely* curious about right now? It might not be what you think you "should" do. Curiosity, novelty, and intuition have a way of breaking stuck patterns.[10]

What's your handful today? Can you try the following:

- Five minutes of movement?
- One line of writing?
- A single mindful breath?
- A text to a friend to reconnect?
- Two pages of reading or five minutes of research?
- A short performance video?
- Journaling for seven minutes?
- Ten minutes of daydreaming?
- An "artist date"?[11]

Motivation Is Relational

Motivation, like meaning, is rarely solitary; it emerges in connection with a clever collaborator, an engaged audience, or in a rehearsal where you collectively feel it land. It thrives when our meaning becomes meaningful to others. This book is in your hands because I invited others into the process—cowriting, coworking, and letting deadlines involve more than myself. Creating community does not require you to be an extrovert. Ask yourself: Where in your creative ecosystem does being in relationship create more fertile, actionable circumstances?

---

[10]Madeleine E. Gross, Claire M. Zedelius, and Jonathan W. Schooler, "Cultivating an Understanding of Curiosity as a Seed for Creativity," *Current Opinion in Behavioral Sciences* 35 (2020): 77–82, https://doi.org/10.1016/j.cobeha.2020.06.004. This article explores how curiosity motivates exploratory behavior and creative idea generation by encouraging individuals to seek novel information and break routine cognitive patterns.

[11]Julia Cameron, *The Artist's Way: A Spiritual Path to Higher Creativity* (TarcherPerigee, 1992), 37. Cameron introduces the "artist date" as a dedicated weekly solo excursion designed to nurture creativity and inspire new ideas through playful, exploratory experiences undertaken alone.

And the most profound *relationship* is always with ourselves. Self-talk can offer empathy and curiosity, or spiral into judgment and shame. Motivation retreats from contempt but flourishes with enthusiasm.

So take a moment to ask:

- What small step can I take **today** that would feel meaningful, not monumental?
- What self-talk has been impeding my motivation and how can I make a different choice?
- Who can I invite—collaborators, friends, audiences—to support my next step today?

Tuning In: The Body as a Question

This practice shifts from interpreting to inhabiting, letting the body become a question—felt but not defined.

1. **Enter the unknown.**
   Find a space where you feel comfortable moving freely. Soften your gaze or close your eyes. Find a position—standing, sitting, or lying down—that feels sustainable. Take three slow breaths and let your attention settle into your body. Notice sensations—tension, ease, curiosity, boredom, resistance.

2. **Move without meaning.**
   Begin to move with attention but without a goal. Let movement arise from sensation or impulse. If it feels familiar or rehearsed, pause. Break, blur, or unravel before moving again. Replace "What am I *doing*?" with "What am I *noticing*?" Let movement *live* before it is *labeled*.

3. **Find meaning viscerally.**
   Bring awareness to pressure, flow, and weight without diagnosing or naming anything. Imagine your body is responding to a question you can't quite hear. Try movements that are definite and intentional. Then try ones that are dissolving or unresolved. Notice the difference. Which is easier? Which feels more charged?

4. **Witness meaning in real time.**
   Choose one movement that feels resonant, not because you *understand* it but because it holds *charge*. Repeat that movement as if asking a question. Meet it with your breath, weight, and awareness. Stay with it without naming or explaining. Let its meaning change in relation to you.

5. **Integrate.**
   - What surprised you?
   - Did any gestures feel especially meaningful?
   - Was ambiguity challenging or relieving?
   - Notice if anything shifted in your attention or body.

Studio Lab: Building Meaning Through Small Connections

Build meaning through subtle accumulation, letting a small action become charged through variation, relationship, and response.

1. **Create a small gesture or phrase.**
   Choose one simple action. It could be one of these:
   - A physical gesture (place a hand on your shoulder, turn your head, begin a rhythm).
   - A repeated word, short phrase, or humming pattern.
   - A spatial decision (standing in a corner, moving toward or away from a point).

   Perform the action neutrally, without assigning meaning.

2. **Change the context.**
   Repeat the action in new contexts:
   - Shift your location in space.
   - Alter speed, scale, or dynamic quality.
   - Introduce a variable (someone watching, eyes closed).

   After each variation, **ask:**
   - Did the meaning shift?
   - What feelings, associations, or memories emerged?
   - Does the action now feel more personal, universal, or ambiguous?

3. **Introduce an external influence.** It could be
   - A soundscape or music.
   - A found object (a chair, fabric scrap, book).
   - Text (an article, poem, or your own writing).

   Perform your gesture alongside or in response to the stimulus. **Notice:** Does the meaning intensify, dissolve, or transform?

4. **Share with a witness.**
   Try the sequence in front of a witness (or imagine one). Notice how the presence of another sharpens, expands, or alters meaning.

5. **Reflect.**

   Return to your original neutral action without the added contexts or influences. Notice what lingers.

   - Has its meaning changed?
   - Did layering deepen or complicate it?
   - Was there a moment when meaning "landed" unexpectedly through sensation, emotion, or recognition?

Pagework: Writing into Meaning

Freewrite on some or all of these questions.

1. **Describe a time you felt fully engaged in your creative work.**
   - What made it feel alive, connected, or clear? What conditions can you re-create?
2. **What is something you feel *motivated* to do, but struggle to act on?**
   - Does your motivation stem from real meaning, or is obligation or expectation driving it?
3. **Think of a project or idea you've been avoiding.**
   - Is your hesitation telling you to wait or to pay closer attention?
4. **When have you created purely for yourself? When have you made work for a specific audience, institution, or commission?**
   - How did your motivation shift in each case?
5. **What is one small action you could take to align inspiration, motivation, and action today?**
   - What if that were enough?

Movements + Maps: Listening for Meaning

In this score, resist the urge to define meaning too quickly. Let meaning arise through action, perception, and embodiment.

1. **Create a phrase of eight to ten movements where each gesture feels as tangible as an object.**[12]
   There should be density, weight, texture, shape, and volume for each movement. Think of each as a favorite object displayed on your mantle: "This is a vintage sailboat." "This is green glass from the beach."

2. **Choose a word with personal resonance** (like *climate change, childbirth, freedom*).
   Use it as source material to create three to six movements that convey its essence. Start literal—even mimetic. Then strip away literal meaning. Shift quality, direction, or body part until the word dissolves into sensation.

3. **Watch an animal interaction** (in nature, a video, or a pet).
   Observe their communication. Borrow their rhythm, spacing, and dynamic. Let their movement language speak to your body before your mind. Create a short sequence from this.

4. **Build two short sequences from these pieces.**
   Use these three phrases (*object, association, animal*) and **build a phrase totally intuitively.** Try not to analyze. Reorder, delete, repeat, reframe. You don't have to use everything you made. Record the phrase.

   Using the same material, start over with **a meaning, purpose, or goal**. This could be:

   - "This solo is a story about my feeling of being trapped by my insecurity."
   - "This solo is a statement about feminism and sexiness."

   Again, reorder, delete, repeat, reframe. But this time, **choose with intent**. Record the phrase.

5. **DJ the two outcomes.**
   Find the gems from each phrase and DJ the two outcomes—cut, mix, repeat, and layer to build a third phrase. Create an order and arc.

6. **Optional: Erase and rebuild.**
   Remove a key moment, shift its context, or blur its structure to see what meaning survives or transforms.

---

[12]Prompt adapted from Susan Rethorst, workshop instructions, New York City, 2005; see also Susan Rethorst, *A Choreographic Mind: Autobodygraphical Writings* (Theatre Academy Helsinki, 2012).

Contributor's Note: Capital-M Meaning

by Katherine Profeta

We think about meaning, and we think about meaning for whom? And sometimes—not always, but often enough we go straight to the audience—we hope what we make will have meaning for them. If it doesn't, what the hell are we doing?

But, obviously, it can't mean anything for them until it first means something for us.

So how do we negotiate these two ideas of meaning, the ***for us*** and the ***for them***?

We know what's deadly—the simple equation. We, the artists, have meaning A in mind; we translate it into the medium B of performance. The audience views this medium B of performance and retranslates it back into an articulated meaning, which they spit back out on demand during the post-show Q&A. Huzzah! Both sides of the equation match, so communication occurred!

And how boring—ugh. If that were all we needed, why don't we just skip the performance part, sit down with a beverage, and chat about A?

(We are talking about meaning in dance, after all, and dance and words are not the same. Let's make sure we are conjuring an expansive definition of meaning: the kind that can be slippery, or fleshy, or slant, or hovering just below the conscious mind.)

On the other hand, I suspect we've all been witness to performances where the artists didn't seem to give a damn about what the audience could and couldn't see, did or didn't feel, to such an extent it felt ungenerous. No kind of meaning was traveling through the room to new body-minds; nothing was electrified or felt as a shared possibility. This is unsatisfying too, and does not seem to deliver on the foundational promise of performance.

As a choreographer and director, you are creating meaning for yourself, but you do it through the medium of performance, which means that the act of sharing is where it takes place. Your chosen artistic language shares the existence of other human beings written right into it. It means that some of your tools might include things like surprises, or very slow shifts, or working the edge of a sight line—all things that create a sense of discovery for someone who, temporarily, knows less than you know, does not yet know where you are going, and wants to be taken for a ride into some combination of what they *recognize* and *don't yet recognize* (adjust ratio as appropriate—that is your choice).

But if you *only* think about the act of presentation, you're in danger of selling both yourself and your audience short. You're in danger of predisposing yourself to give an audience only meanings it already recognizes (which means, only meanings you already recognize). Nowhere new to go.

So there's a tension here. That tension is what we all need to dive into.

Studio Provocations: Questioning Meaning

In a good play, the questions are more important than any answers the playwright might offer. The questions remain with you long after you've left the theater, disrupting easy patterns of thought, expanding your sense of possibility.

(Sarah Ruhl, *100 Essays I Don't Have Time to Write*)[13]

Dramaturgical

Describe your beginning.

- Is it decisive, tentative, or something else?
- What would the *opposite* of this beginning be?

Describe your transitions.

- Cross-fades? Hard cuts? Slow evolutions?
- Do you use the same method for transition throughout? Is it working in every section?

Does everything that you begin, end?

- If not, what happens to it?

What would we guess about the middle if we put the beginning and end side by side?

- What does that tell you?

Are there sections?

- Are there any rules or devices that define a section?
- Have you reordered them?

Try: Write each section on an index card. On the front write only a name ("Devon solo"). On the back, create a coding system, a visual key of meaningful elements. You can add coding (color, symbols, etc.) for dynamics ("fast-paced" "languid"), duration, number of performers, and any aspects that feel substantive. You should end up with a little drawing on the back that equates to a matrix of descriptions ("wild and chaotic," "under two minutes," "two to three people," "movement,

[13] Sarah Ruhl, *100 Essays I Don't Have Time to Write: On Umbrellas and Sword Fights, Parades and Dogs, Fire Alarms, Children, and Theater* (Faber & Faber, 2014).

no text," "silence"). Using the backs only, create an order based on alternating the visuals as much as possible. Flip them over to see your new order. Make cursory transitions just to temporarily hold it together, and try a messy run.

What are the rules in this world? (For example: Who initiates movement? Does unison imply agreement? Does eye contact signal intimacy? Does music dictate timing? Do scenes begin and end cleanly?)

- Are the rules visible or invisible? Named or simply assumed?
- Are they inherited from theatrical convention (face front, build to a climax, resolve the conflict)?
- Do the performers explicitly agree to them, or are they operating inside habit?
- What happens when a rule is broken?
- If your piece doesn't name its rules, how are you building the world so we understand them?

Is there a turning point?

What have you named?

- Can any of it be renamed?
- What wants to be unnamable?

Does anything get broken?

- Have you considered breaking something?

Where is the contradiction?

- How might you lean further into contradiction?

What elements *must* remain clear, and where might ambiguity thrive *more*?

What accumulates?

- **Has anything been accumulating without you realizing it?**

What have you thrown away?

- Can you throw one more thing away?

What do you want your audience to leave with?

Narrative

What stories emerge when you zoom in on detail or out to arc?

- Do they align or conflict?

Does your work have any explicit stories?

- Can you say them as if narrating a synopsis?*

* This does not suggest you need a *literal* story. Even a completely abstract work can have a beginning, middle, end, and key movements, like exposition, inciting incident, rising action, climax, falling action, and resolution.

If there are multiple stories, how do they intersect?

What is the *origin story* of this piece, and how has it changed?

How literal do you want to be?

- What have you designed to transmit facts?

What metaphors or symbols are you using?

- Are there images or gestures that seem to gather meaning without your planning?
- How much are you ***guiding*** the audience, and how much are you leaving meaning-making up to them?

Personal History/Memory

Is this describing a personal or collective memory?

What might an audience guess about your priorities in making *this* work?

Is there anything personal you've *deliberately* omitted?

Social

Write your dream review from the perspective of an artist you admire, a child, or a stranger.

- What parts of your work conflict with the description?

Write your most devastating, soul-crushing review. (Only if you know how to protect your heart within this experiment.)

- Is the fear of this response keeping you from making any specific choices?

Try: Create a short section or beat that *deserves* that review. Make the thing you're afraid they'll hate. Is there any information there?

What is the tension between how this looks/feels in your mind and what you see?

- What is not happening that you want to happen? Do you know why?

Relationship

Who would be your dream person to advise you?

- What would you ask?
- Take a guess as to what they'd say. Speak it aloud if you can.

In the rehearsal process, how is power organized?

- Is that working for everyone?

Is there conflict?

- Is that useful?

Are there any ways your ethics are not implemented in this art-making?

How does your work invite or resist multiple interpretations?

Emotional and Relational Dynamics

Do you want more or less

- Empathy?
- Betrayal?
- Loss?
- Love?
- Fear?

- Fatigue?
- Hope?
- Rigor?
- Danger?
- Tension?
- Freedom?
- Trust?
- Mystery?
- Community?

5

Environment

Before You Begin: Priming Curiosity About Environment

Take a breath. Consider these questions. Let them settle in your body before moving forward. They are not for solving, but for sensing.

When do I let my surroundings shape me?

Who do I become in unfamiliar surroundings?

Where do I feel most whole, creative, fed, or nurtured?

How do old places still shape how I feel and move today?

Why does one environment invite me to open—and another to shrink?

What do I often notice first in a new environment, and what do I often overlook?

Groundwork: Co-Creating with Environment

> No settled family or community has ever called its home place an "environment." None has ever called its feeling for its home place "biocentric" or "anthropocentric." None has ever thought of its connection to its home place as "ecological," deep or shallow. The concepts and insights of the ecologists are of great usefulness in our predicament, and we can hardly escape the need to speak of "ecology" and "ecosystems." But the terms themselves are culturally sterile. They come from the juiceless, abstract intellectuality of the universities which was invented to disconnect, displace, and disembody the mind. The real names of the environment are the names of rivers and river valleys; creeks, ridges, and mountains; towns and cities; lakes, woodlands, lanes, roads, creatures, and people.
>
> (Wendell Berry, *The Art of the Commonplace*)[1]

The Art of Context

In 2001, two weeks after leaving my seven-year performance career with Bill T. Jones/Arnie Zane, I began my first professional choreography job. In early September, I arrived at Bates College to create a twenty-minute group work. Having left the company to both begin my choreographic career and find love, the rollercoaster of mating and dating was a natural theme for *The Shark Attack and Other Dating Rituals.*[2]

During the first two rehearsals, we played with irony and kitsch, taking a sarcastic, playful approach to dysfunctional communication. It was hyperbolic and brash; we laughed out loud countless times.

The third day of my residency was September 11, but that rehearsal would not happen. I saw no one that day, staying holed up in a dorm room, glued to the news. When we returned to the studio on September 12, the environment had changed, not only in our studio, but globally.

Listening as an Act of Leadership

If this situation happened today, I would facilitate an authentic process. We would talk, move, cry, and dialogue with our feelings, letting them shape us and the work. We would recognize that we were no longer in the same environment. We would release what we thought we were making and let this moment catalyze a new work. Perhaps some of our earlier material would still be usable, but I

---

[1]Wendell Berry, *The Art of the Commonplace: The Agrarian Essays of Wendell Berry*, ed. Norman Wirzba (Counterpoint, 2002).
[2]Alexandra Beller, *The Shark Attack and Other Dating Rituals*, student work, Bates College, 2001.

wouldn't force it. I would prioritize the authenticity of the performers over the piece, and stay attuned to our resources, mental health, and healing.

But as a new choreographer, I had not yet gained this adaptability or presence. I was clinging to a version of professionalism I believed I had to prove—one that prized form, commitment, and continuity over interruption. I didn't yet know how to let the ground shift under us and stay balanced. I heaved us forward, mistaking momentum for steadiness.

The work suffered.

Grief weighed us down. Humor only amplified it. It was untimely, disconnected, and out of place. The failure offered a profound lesson. Environment, I learned, is not a backdrop but a condition, participant, and co-author.

What Is Environment?

What lives inside the word *environment*?

Synonyms like *climate*, *habitat*, *setting*, *ambiance*, *context*, and *terrain* reveal how layered the term has become. Environment is emotional, social, biological, and dynamic. If space gives us the geography, environment gives us the weather, the conditions we move through, the pressures and invitations at play. Space might be the architecture, but environment holds the atmosphere. Two artists can rent the same studio, but their environments differ drastically if one is grieving and the other, in love. Environment holds not only *where* but *how it feels to be there*, and *why it matters*.

We often speak of environment as something *outside* us—something that *frames* us. But breath crosses the boundary with every inhale, and again with every exhale. Sensation floods in; attention and action stream out. The body is not a container but a membrane—porous, receptive, expressive. Environment doesn't merely surround us; it moves through us, shaped by what we notice, resist, allow, and ignore. And just as we're shaped by it, the environment takes on the charge of our presence—our energy, our judgments, our ways of seeing.

In systems thinking, this dynamic is called *reciprocal influence*[3]—a feedback loop in which parts continually shape and are shaped by the whole. In somatic practice, it's the dialogue between inner and outer experience. The boundary, then, is not our skin but our attention. As tree rings register cycles of drought and abundance, our bodies accumulate the environments we've moved through, reflecting

[3]Brenda J. Zimmerman, "Some Emerging Principles for Managing in a Complex Adaptive System," working paper, Plexus Institute, 2000. Zimmerman is a pioneering scholar in organizational systems theory, focusing on complexity, continuous change, and feedback loops.

them in our posture, breath, tone, and phrasing. We are not passive participants in our environments; we're sculptors in conversation, continually attuning to both the visible and the unseen, felt, imagined, and sensed.

Of course, environment is not an objective fact. Is an open field *expansive* or *threatening*? Is a crowded city street *overwhelming* or *captivating*? Our emotional, cultural, familial, and geographic histories co-create how we perceive an environment, and how it, in turn, responds to us.

One performer's anxiety changes how the room feels. A charged room changes how *I* feel. It's more than cause and effect; it's a shared field. The environment is not a container but a condition. It changes when someone enters or leaves, when a window opens, when silence extends beyond our expectation. Environment is dynamic, shared, and responsive, always becoming, but also holding *what was.*

What Shapes an Environment?

If environment is composed of so many parts, how can we possibly affect it?

Let's look at some of the forces that shape environment.

The body is an environment. What happens there ripples through our emotional, spiritual, and relational systems, and the reverse is also true. Work, relationships, and trauma are digested by the body, sometimes long before they're fully understood. The inner landscape is a powerful force in activating, softening, or shifting its environment. When we urge the body toward a particular quality, presence, or intention, it reshapes our attitude, mood, and experience. In turn, this alters any space we inhabit.

Often, the shifts we hope to see in a room begin in the body. When clients report that they "can't figure out what step to take next," I often give them a walking pattern. When students describe feeling "ungrounded," I cue more yield and push. **The body always holds the clues—and often, the keys—to transformation.**

The physical world—what we can touch, see, hear, smell, and taste—offers constant stimuli. Recognizing, acknowledging, and adapting to this shift is critical. When I am facilitating, I always discuss the overhead lights. As a neuro-spicy brain, they sap my creativity. For someone else, a dim space depletes their energy. We negotiate to shape an environment where we can all thrive. This requires noticing how stimuli affect you and others, and what world you want to co-create.

The personal, communal, national, and global environments—emotional, social, political, and historical climates—shape perception and experience. An artist working in a gentrified neighborhood, a war zone, or a climate-affected region cannot ignore how these larger forces shape the container of their work.

These forces also enter the room with us. I often ask students entering a class, "What do you hope to pick up and what do you want to put down today?" We enter a shared space holding a lot of invisible material. Feelings, beliefs, habits, and wounds come in with us. Owning, even naming, these substances can shift their impact on our shared environment. Sometimes it's as simple as saying, "FYI, I'm feeling impatient and edgy right now," to my kids or my partner. The room shifts because I've named the thing we're all feeling as *mine*. Others are free to leave it with me rather than absorb it, take it personally, or spin stories about it. This can also be a regulating tactic in a rehearsal room.

How we understand environment determines how we move inside it. In many traditions, land is not a backdrop or resource but a living being with rights. This changes how space is choreographed, inhabited, and listened to. What if the rehearsal room were approached in this way—as a **living field** with its own presence and voice?

I wish I had known that on September 12, 2001, when I walked into rehearsal. I hadn't yet learned that environment isn't just context; it's co-author. When the world shifted, our piece did not. I clung to my old plan, ignoring the new collaborator: our feelings, the shared global trauma, our communal authenticity.

The Skill of Shifting Perspectives

The first step in collaborating with our environment is *attunement*: noticing ourselves within the context of the space, the moment, and our collaborators. The next is collaboration. That begins with adjusting our aperture: zooming in and out to reveal layers of meaning.

If you walked into a new room, glanced around, and left, you might say, "There were a lot of books and a table. It was a library."

Or if you walked in with the narrow lens of a pinhole camera and saw only a shelf of cookbooks, you might say, "I think it was a kitchen."

Both interpretations come from partial vision—one too broad to see detail, the other too narrow to see context. Neither view tells the truth, and both miss what the room actually is: the bedroom of a political dissident under house arrest in a fascist regime.

When we don't shift our perspective, we risk erasing what's most vital. The same is true in the studio. If we stay too wide, we overlook the floor's hardness, the flicker of a light, the way one performer avoids another's gaze. If we stay too narrow, we forget the larger intention, the dynamic of the group, the context of the audience, or the world outside the doors.

A child's crumpled drawing in a pile of papers feels different when framed and displayed in a museum. The environment shifts the meaning. Change the frame, and we change the story we tell about it, the value we place on it, and the feelings it carries.

The same is true in our work. A rehearsal or performance takes on a different weight depending on the frame around it. Are we working on colonized land? In a rapidly gentrifying district? On an artist's colony or in a repurposed gun factory?

With the rise of immersive theater, we've become more conscious of how the environment offers more than a container, but a map of meaning. The audience is part of the frame, and every detail is constructed or considered. But what if all work is immersive, whether we admit it or not? What would you do differently if you treated every environment as site specific?

Dynamics and Design

I choreographed for the play *A Midsummer Night's Dream* at the National Museum Building in Washington, DC. It was a beautiful, intimate set built inside a cavernous space with a vaulted ceiling. The director imagined the fairies as deeply animal. The costume designer, however, leaned toward spectacle—endless trains, stiletto heels, silhouettes made for a runway. The set designer pulled in the opposite direction, crafting a detailed, intimate stage nestled inside the yawning expanse. The acoustics introduced another element: Voices clashed with recorded sound, each fighting for clarity in the echoing space.

This was the ecosystem of the play: scale against intimacy, animality against artifice, detail against vastness. My first instinct was to meet the cavernous space with expansive movement, but together with the costumes, this tipped toward caricature. What was missing was animality—not in costume or concept but in the body itself: weight, instinct, breath. Layering subtlety and authenticity against exaggeration helped restore balance. Sometimes the chemistry of environmental elements calls not for more of the same but for contradiction, so the work can achieve balance.

Whether in process or production, attuning to environment makes the work responsive, responsible, and alive.

Takeaway: Environment is a living, changing character in our work. Ignoring it risks us losing a crucial collaborator.

In Practice: Tips About Environment

1. **Shift your aperture.**
   Zoom all the way in, then all the way out. Notice a single detail (a dancer's breath, a crack in the floor). Then step back to the entire field (the group's rhythm, the city outside the window). What new stories emerge when you hold both scales?

2. **Name the charge.**
   Before starting, name one personal current you're bringing into the room ("I feel restless," "I'm grieving"). Let the group know it's yours to hold. Notice how naming shifts the atmosphere.

3. **Negotiate the space.**
   Play with the environment's physical givens: lights, temperature, acoustics, seating, smell. Don't just endure them—adjust, swap, or redesign together. What thresholds of comfort or agitation change the work?

4. **Attend to the missing element.**
   When the environment feels unbalanced, ask: What's absent? What's dominating? Temper what's loud. Use contrast to restore coherence.

5. **Play with thresholds.**
   Mark the threshold into the studio—doorway, curtain, stairwell. Create a ritual of arrival. What shifts when you cross consciously into the environment of the work?

6. **Rehearse with the audience present.**
   Even if no one's there, imagine the audience in the room. How do the details change when you sense their bodies, attention, and stakes as part of the environment?

7. **Let the environment lead.**
   For one section of rehearsal, let the environment co-author. Respond only to cues from the space: a sound outside, the weight of air, the room's scale. Track what emerges when you stop steering.

8. **Frame the audience's experience.**
   Determine the audience's proximity and exposure. Are they inside the action, or observing from afar? How does that frame shift what you highlight and what you minimize?

9. **Rehearse in shifting environments.**
   Take the work into varied contexts: studio, street, home, landscape. Track what holds steady and what transforms. Which environments crack open new possibilities?

10. **Consider the environment's memory.**
    Ask what stories this place carries: celebration, trauma, labor, resistance. How might those memories echo in the present work?

Frameworks: Adapt, Interrupt, or Align with Your Environment

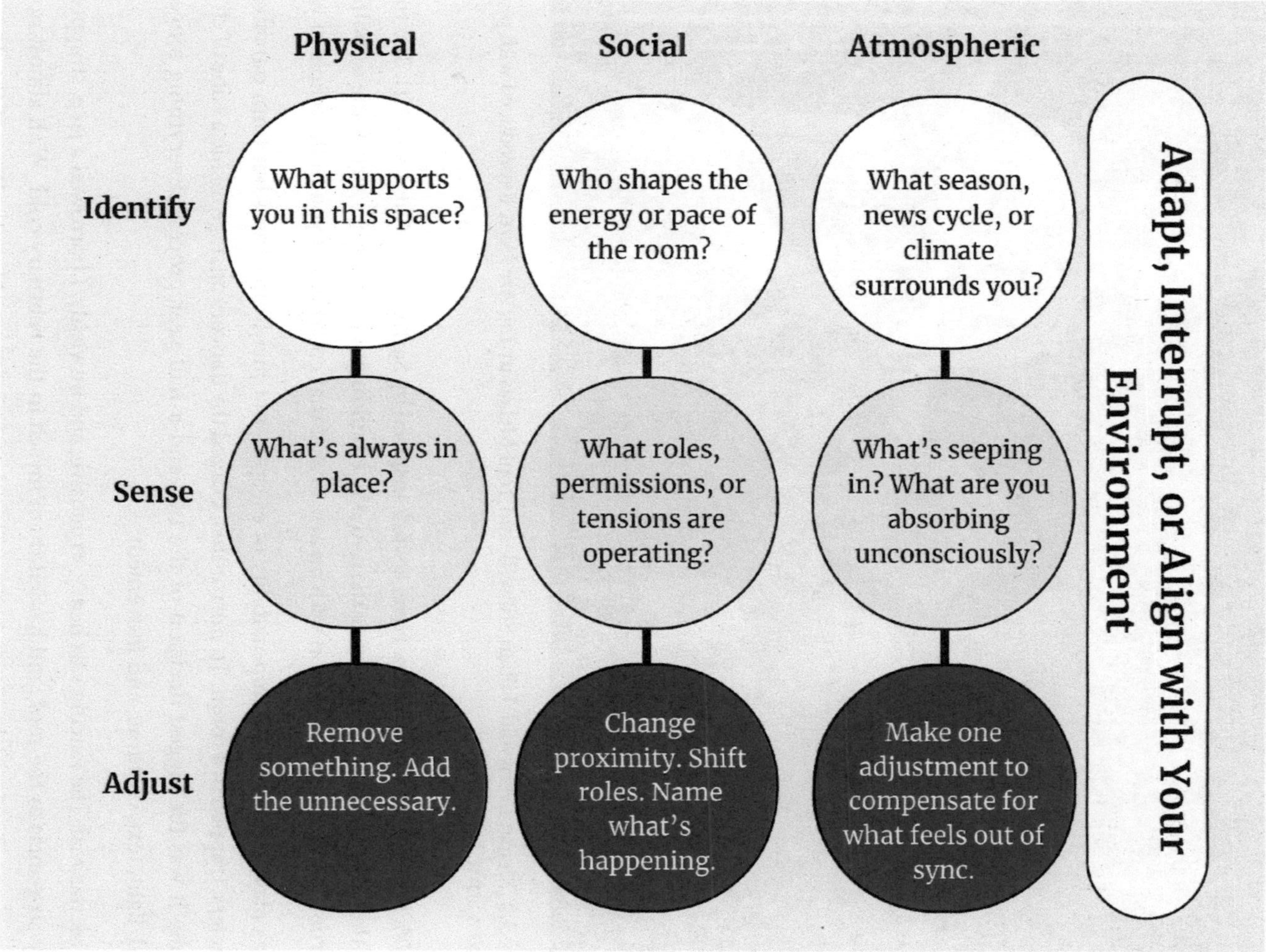

Figure 5.1 *Adapt, Interrupt, or Align with Your Environment*. Diagram tracing how physical, social, and atmospheric environments shape creative attention and choice.

From the Field: *You Are Here*

Figure 5.2 Megan Brunsvold, Lillian Stillwell, and Toni Melaas in *You Are Here*. Reproduced with permission of Steven Schreiber.

In 2006, I began creating *You Are Here*, a work inspired by Sartre's *Huis Clos* (*No Exit*). The title came from the "You Are Here" maps in malls and office buildings. They always struck me as both absurd and true—declaring your location with an arrow, as if that could orient you to the whole of your life.

Sartre's play centers on the impossibility of escape—not just from others but from ourselves. Four characters, trapped in a room. To mirror this, I caged the dancers onstage inside a cube of chain-link fencing. It was the biggest decision of the two-and-a-half-year process. Everything hinged on it: sound, light, text, costume, and movement.

The risk was real. The fencing was heavy, expensive, and unwieldy. I borrowed a jeep, strapped twelve six-by-six panels to the roof, and hauled them myself in the February cold. With almost no staff or budget, every step was laborious. And I still had no proof it would work. What if the dancers were subsumed by the cage, the lighting cast constant shadows, or the acoustics collapsed? But for me, the environment *was* the story. I couldn't make the piece without it, so I committed. The cage wasn't just scenery; it was the condition necessary to generate the work.

When the cage finally arrived in the studio, everything shifted. We improvised endlessly, adapting to its demands. It didn't just *restrict* movement; it also *provoked* it. Each performer's relationship to the walls was distinct—some resisted, some surrendered, some treated the fence like a partner. Movements toward or away from the fence became charged with desperation, resistance, tenderness. The text spoken through the metal took on new weight. The solid, square, reflective frame became a metaphor for their world, and the claustrophobia it induced in the audience brought embodied fear into the room—shaping the work from the outside in.

Despite carrying the cage in my imagination for years, I couldn't have choreographed what we made until it was there. The environment wasn't a scenic element, but a collaborator, a provocateur, and a question. One I couldn't answer for the dancers or the audience. We had to live inside of it together.

Guidance: The Choice Between Doing and Pausing

Recently, I hit a real low. I was exhausted, apathetic, and uncomfortable in my life. A pile of work (including this book) loomed over me, and I spent the entire day trying to muster motivation to minimal effect. By the end of the day, I had neither worked nor rested. I felt awful about myself and slipped into a real funk.

Looking back, the problem wasn't the hard day; it was my failure to choose. I let myself remain in an uncomfortable inner environment instead of recognizing what was off and choosing to remodel it.

I could have said, "I'm taking the day off. I'll do things that feel restful, joyful, and recuperative, then handle my work tomorrow." Or, "I'm having a tough day, but getting through this pile will feel good. I'll shower, have an iced coffee, ask a friend to co-work, and knock this stuff out. Tonight, I'll focus on deep rest."

Either could have been the right choice. The stuckness came from refusing to choose.

Sometimes, we check in and realize: *I don't want to create.* That realization is not a dead end; it's the moment to commit. From here, there are two paths: **forward momentum** or **restorative practice**.

Forward Momentum: When you decide to create but don't feel creative, adjust your expectations. Release a singular definition of "productive" and widen the frame. **Ask:** Can I *analyze* instead of *invent*? Is there something to clean, organize, or edit? Would tasks, games, or obstacles help? What brain functions *are* available right now, and what can I do with what I have? This kind of self-awareness is freeing. It shifts the goal from forcing inspiration to working with what's present. Maybe you finish a grant proposal, email collaborators, research costumes, or watch rehearsal footage. Respecting your energy and flow doesn't have to mean doing *nothing*, but it *does* require aligning your expectations with your resources.

Restorative Practice: When you realize you need rest but feel guilt or anxiety about it, approach yourself with the curiosity and tenderness you would a grieving friend or disregulated child. **Ask:** What part of me is asking to be heard? Is there a tempo that might help me locate my aliveness? What if this pause is an essential part of the process? Replenishment is where curiosity reenters. Take a walk without a destination, doodle for no one, write a letter you won't send, lie on the floor, and let your weight return to gravity. These are not detours from progress; they are how the body metabolizes experience. A fractured self lacks the flow for creativity to emerge organically. This kind of attunement is neither indulgent nor idle. It reorients the process toward presence, reminding us that sensation, desire, and pleasure are not distractions but vital data.

Rest is not a break from creativity; it is a condition of its possibility, inviting joy as a method, not a reward.

Work and rest are both crucial energies in our creativity. But we need to know *which* we are committing to and invest in it. The act of *choosing* is inherently creative. What kept me stuck that day was not my mood, lack of resources, or burnout. It was not making a *choice*. Practicing clear decisions is part of the same intentionality we need to make art. Whether you choose rest or action, select it with clarity.

The energy you honor today will fuel your work tomorrow.

Tuning In: Finding the Art Already Here

This practice invites you to notice attention as a form of movement.

1. **Arrive in your space.**
   Stand, sit, or lie down in a safe space. Close your eyes and take a few deep breaths. Notice the **feeling** of your inner body first. Yield your weight. Feel your breath entering and exiting, the body growing and shrinking around your breath.

2. **Expand your senses.**
   Keeping your eyes closed, shift your focus to **sound**. What do you hear in the distance? What do you hear nearby? Can you hear any part of your body (breath, heart)?

   Move to **temperature**. Where do you feel warmth or coolness? Do the air and ground have different temperatures?

   Explore **touch**. How does your clothing sit on your skin? What textures are touching you—fabric, floor, air? Where do you feel weight? Is there a **scent** you notice? Is there any **taste** in your mouth?

   Open your eyes and scan the space. Without fixating, notice the quality of light, the textures, objects, lines, angles, and the distance of each part of the room from your body.

3. **Make micro-adjustments.**
   Shift from observation to participation. Begin with the smallest possible adjustments.

   Allow the distances between you and various parts of the room to grow and shrink, leaning toward or away from a mark on the wall, a chair, a shaft of light. Let yourself be moved by curiosity about the environment.

4. **Play with the self and the space.**
   Begin walking, shifting, or moving slowly, responding to what you encounter. Sense the presence and even character of walls, furniture, and objects before touching them. Feel how your proximity shapes your feeling toward them.

   Experiment with interaction. Press against a surface. Sit on a chair. Glide your shoulder over an object. Begin a contact improvisation with the space, considering what the consent of the object or surface would require from you.

5. **Create meaning.**
   Take a pause. Place an imaginary audience in the space with you. Start the same contact improvisation, finding a clear beginning. Imagine this improvisation as a performance. Craft a mystery, an arc, a conflict in the room. Feel the tension of time as a driver toward meaning.

6. **Reflect.**
   What tools from this practice—attunement, micro-adjustments, dialogue, meaning—could I bring into my daily studio work?

Studio Lab: Choreographing the Environment

This practice invites you to shift your perception of space from passive setting to active partner, letting place shape presence.

1. **Uncover your spatial defaults.**
   Walk through the space naturally. Let yourself walk, run, jog, tumble, lean. Take two to three minutes to consistently locomote through the space, letting your body make the decisions. Don't override any instincts or instruct yourself. Without changing, notice where in the space you move freely, what areas you ignore, and which magnetize you. Do any places hold charge, pull, or invitation? Do any summon repulsion or the impulse to retreat?

2. **Identify and mark three spaces:**
   - **Comfort Zone:** A familiar, habitual area.
   - **Neglected Space:** A spot you rarely engage with.
   - **Metaphorical Space:** A location that feels ripe for metaphor or story—somewhere that seems to hold symbolic, cinematic, or emotional potential. This could be a doorway, window, corner, or an architectural feature that sparks your imagination.

3. **Disrupt your comfort zone.**
   Return to the **Comfort Zone** and challenge its familiarity:
   - **Change your orientation.** Get into an upside-down or inverted position, look at it from the floor, or bring a chair to look at it from above.
   - **Shrink or expand.** Take up as little or as much space as possible.
   - **Move in a way that feels unnatural here.** Become grotesque, stylized, primal, or abstract—anything but your usual way of moving.
   - **Improvise as a creature, presence, or powerful force.** How does this ordinary place frame something extraordinary?

4. **Animate the neglected space.**
   Engage with the **neglected space**—a corner, a blank wall, or a space that previously felt insignificant:
   - **Linger here.** Let your skin, ears, and breath register the environment.
   - **Move deliberately.** Allow the space to shape your posture, breath, and pacing.

- **Imagine this place holds personal significance.** What if this were a childhood bedroom? A birthing room? A place where something ended or began?
- **Improvise here.** What happens when you treat this overlooked space as the emotional core of a scene?

5. **Activate the metaphorical space.**
   Step into your **Metaphorical space**—a place that feels charged with potential. This is where the architect, choreographer, and storyteller in you meet. Become a **director or set designer**. Move through the space as if you are inside this imagined scene.
   - What story could take place here?
   - Is this a balcony from *Romeo and Juliet*? A prison cell in a sci-fi film? A sacred ritual site?

   Let the space dictate how you move. How does its architecture, restrictions, or expansiveness shape your choices? Let it act on you. Let it change your timing, tension, and intent.
6. **Reflect:**
   - What changed in your perception of space?
   - Did any area reveal unexpected emotional weight?
   - How did your body's response shift as you reframed each location?
   - How might this exercise influence your creative work?

Pagework: Writing into Environment

Freewrite on some or all of these questions.

1. **Describe the space where you most often create.**
   Is it a creaky old loft filled with idiosyncratic furniture, or a sleek corporate tower with glass, marble, and a security desk? Do you enter a rehearsal building buzzing with other classes and artists, or a solitary room that belongs only to you and your collaborators? How do these conditions affect you? Do they influence how you warm up, where you put your bag, how you speak, what feels possible in your body? In what ways does this space support your process, and in what ways does it inhibit you?

2. **What parts of your environment do you habitually ignore?**
   Do you track the emotional tone of the group and attempt to regulate it? Do you adjust the lighting, temperature, or acoustics? Do you register the weather outside, or the neighborhood around the studio? What other forces are shaping the environment that you tend to miss?
   Choose one neglected aspect—a corner of the room, a sound you tune out, an atmosphere you avoid—and write about what might happen if you treated it as central.

3. **Think of a time when the environment reshaped your work.**
   Maybe the floor was too slick, the room too small, the acoustics impossible, or the weather uncooperative. At first, it may have felt like an obstacle or a deficit. But recall the moment you stopped fighting and let those conditions enter the piece. How did your energy shift once the environment had agency? What new choices, meanings, or textures emerged that would not have existed otherwise? Are you currently facing any similar obstacles?

4. **Choose a well-known work—your own or another creator's—and imagine it in a radically different environment (*The Odyssey* in a prison cell; *Little Red Riding Hood* in a high-rise building).**
   How do the new environmental constraints shift the potential vocabulary, relationships, metaphors, or tone? What unexpected meanings or tensions emerge when the same work is placed in a different world?

5. **Imagine the environment your current project longs for.**
   Would it thrive in a bare warehouse with concrete floors, a wooded clearing at dusk, a crowded street corner, or an intimate living room? What qualities—light, sound, temperature, background, anonymity—would let the work find itself? If the piece could choose its own conditions, what would it ask for? And with the resources you have now, how might you create even a fragment of that atmosphere?

Movements + Maps: The Space That Shapes You

This score invites you to engage with the environment as a driver. What changes when you let the environment lead?

1. **Phrase 1: Local Environment.**
   Be still for a few minutes. Notice the smallest details: temperature, floor texture, shadows, sounds. Translate observation into movement. Let the environment choreograph for you—a creaky floorboard inspires a repeated weight shift, the flicker of light sparks a gesture. Shape these responses into a thirty- to forty-five-second phrase.

2. **Phrase 2: Global Environment.**
   Reflect on the larger forces surrounding you—political climate, family, weather, relationships. Translate these into movement: a series of gestures, shifts of dynamic, or traveling patterns. Shape these into a thirty- to forty-five-second phrase.

3. **Phrase 3: Intersection.**
   Choose one restriction from your physical environment. Stay within a six-foot area, only move when you hear a sound, avoid contact with walls—whatever feels alive. Combine the two phrases inside this restriction. Let them overlap, collide, interrupt, or echo each other. Break your restriction once, at a moment that feels pivotal.

Contributor's Note: Immersive Theater: Sculpting the Environment

by Kelly Bartnik

My background in immersive theater began with the original production of *Sleep No More* in Boston in 2009. I later joined the New York production when it opened in 2011 and performed in it for nearly two years. That experience transformed me—as both performer and maker—and raised essential questions about how environments shape audience connection. I had never encountered a world so all-encompassing. The detailed, immersive environments helped me access character in deeply fulfilling ways.

After leaving the show, I worked across many immersive projects—as a movement director, choreographer, writer, director, and rehearsal lead—gaining experience in every facet of development within a form that continued to captivate me.

In 2019, I simultaneously developed two immersive works that explored contrasting aspects of the form—allowing me to interrogate some of the questions *Sleep No More* had left me with. These two projects—*HERE* and *Re:*—became a way to continue that exploration. Together, they taught me that space can act as either collaborator or constraint—and that it fundamentally shapes both narrative and performance strategy.

In the case of *HERE*, the space existed in a fully decorated state before any narrative was developed. The location was a small, five-room apartment-style basement in Chinatown, fully designed and furnished by Jae Lee and Yvonne Chang. Although I wasn't aiming to root the work in a particular time period, I recognized an opportunity—immersive spaces are difficult and expensive to build, and this one already existed. That prompted a different kind of creative question: How do I "explain away" the space, rather than design a narrative that fits it?

We began rehearsals by treating the space's objects as generative material—each item became a prompt for narrative and character creation. Actors explored relationships with these items, developing short narratives that helped us construct their characters. Once the individual character identities emerged, we began linking them to form interpersonal dynamics. In this way, a narrative emerged organically—rooted not in concept but in the space as it already existed. That constraint sparked unexpected discoveries we never would have reached without the space's preexisting limitations.

By contrast, *Re:* was an entirely different kind of undertaking. It was an experiment in distilling immersive theater down to its most essential elements. Inspired by the intimacy I'd experienced in

Sleep No More, I wondered: What remains when all the theatrical elements are stripped away? What remains without moody lighting, cinematic scenery, stylized costuming, or atmospheric sound?

I created a performance in which I cast the audience member in a defined role—without offering any of the usual clues of environmental storytelling—and explored whether connection could still emerge. The piece unfolded over twelve hours, with one audience member at a time, each participating in twenty-minute increments—inviting intimacy through repetition and duration. This format echoed the physical demands of *Sleep No More* and invited the subtle shifts that arise through repeated, structured choreography.

It was staged in an unadorned Brooklyn rehearsal studio—white walls, hardwood floors—a space that, while not neutral, offered a relatively blank canvas. This minimal setting allowed for a more intimate and distilled form of immersion, helping me focus on the core elements of character and audience engagement.

Whether we name it or not, environment is always part of the creative equation. Every work exists in space. So the real question isn't whether to consider environment—but how, and from what point of view.

Studio Provocations: Questioning Environment

> To make sense is to enliven the senses. A story that makes sense is one that stirs the senses from their slumber, one that opens the eyes and the ears to their real surroundings, tuning the tongue to the actual tastes in the air and sending chills of recognition along the surface of the skin. To make sense is to release the body from the constraints imposed by outworn ways of speaking, and hence to renew and rejuvenate one's felt awareness of the world. It is to make the senses wake up to where they are.
>
> (David Abrams, *The Spell of the Sensuous*)[4]

Emotional Environment

What's your current emotional weather, and how is it affecting your art?

What feelings might you be leaking into shared spaces without meaning to?

What changes if you let the room's mood set the tempo?

Social Environment

Whose attention in this room feels most alive to you right now?

Try: Let what excites them most become the driver of your next rehearsal.

What role are you unconsciously playing in the group dynamic—leader, anchor, resister, spark?

- Is that serving the work, or just familiar?

If you traded places with someone else in this room, what would you notice immediately?

- What would feel harder? What would feel easier?

Who in this room is carrying the most responsibility? How would redistributing it shift the dynamic?

What agreement is operating here that no one has named?

Try: Say it out loud. Does the room shift?

---

[4]David Abram, *The Spell of the Sensuous: Perception and Language in a More-than-Human World* (Vintage, 1996), 51.

Physical Environment

What part of this space are you avoiding? What happens if you move straight into it?

- Place something there now. What changes?

Which corner, object, or threshold in the room is holding the most charge?

- Begin the next phrase or section there.

How is the architecture choreographing you—inviting, restricting, echoing, resisting?

- Are you moving with it or against it? Try the opposite once.

What happens if you let light, sound, or temperature set your rhythm?

Try: Choose one and follow it for two minutes.

If this room decided where the work begins, where would it start?

- Start there.

Cultural and Historical Environment

What stories already live in this space?

- Which ones are you amplifying right now? Which ones are disappearing?

If the land beneath this room could speak, what would it ask of this piece?

How is the neighborhood outside these walls pressing on your work?

What traces of history (celebration, trauma, resistance) are shaping what's possible here?

How does this environment frame your audience as insiders or outsiders?

What cultural or political forces are co-authoring your choices right now?

- If you named them in the room, would anything feel different?

Inner/Personal Environment

What shift in your own body would most alter the environment?

- Make that adjustment once.

How is your current state influencing the tempo of this rehearsal?

- What happens if you alter your tempo?

What change in light, sound, proximity, or structure would help your brain engage differently?

Is your nervous system settled, activated, scattered, focused?

- How is that shaping the room?

How does this environment meet your neurotype?

- What do you need more or less of—quiet, texture, structure, movement, dimness?

What are you asking this work to hold for you that you haven't named?

- What would change if you named it?

6

Process

Before You Begin: Priming Curiosity About Process

Take a breath. Consider these questions. Let them settle in your body before moving forward. They are not for solving, but for sensing.

Who am I when I stop trying to *figure it out*?

When do I stop reaching for the answer and listen instead?

How do I know when my inner voice is intuition or the inner critic?

Where do I go—mentally, emotionally, or physically—when I'm stuck?

Why is it sometimes easier to begin and other times nearly impossible?

What habits support me, and which ones are familiar but limiting my view?

Groundwork: The Laboratory of Process

The scientist is not a person who gives the right answers, he's one who asks the right questions.
(Claude Lévi-Strauss, *A Confrontation*)[1]

The Unseen Shape of Our Work

We talk a lot about *what* we make. Less often do we witness *how* we make it. Yet when we attend closely, process is *everything*: our thoughts before we enter the studio, the habits we lean on, the way we talk to ourselves when we're stuck.

Process is what we do, what we avoid, and what unfolds in between.

It reflects our values. We may *aspire* to make bold, ethical, poetic, or surprising work; observing our process reveals whether or not they live in our praxis. A choreographer may value collaboration, yet mostly works alone. Another may describe risk, but leave little room for surprise or vulnerability. If our values and our process don't align, the work will inevitably carry that tension. If we want to understand our process, we have to look at our habits. Staying in relationship with both habit and curiosity allows our process to mirror the artist we are—beyond training, beyond descriptions, beyond what we *wish* we were.

Try: Ask yourself:

What do I do first, almost without thinking, when I begin to create?
Which parts of my process feel automatic rather than chosen?
What in my practice feels so natural that I rarely question it?

These questions bring us to the skeleton of our process: the habits that shape the conditions under which our work takes root.

Habit as Compass

Writing about process is like explaining how to tie your shoes or pour a glass of water. These acts are automatic, usually unexamined. Each artist develops an ecosystem of process—patterns so ingrained they no longer feel like choices. **This is the terrain of habit.**

[1]Claude Lévi-Strauss, *A Confrontation* (New Left Review, 1970).

Habits often get a bad rap. Yet without repetition and familiar rhythms, our attention would drown in minutiae, leaving little space for invention. It is habit that lets us walk to the subway while our imagination drifts to relationships, materials, or tomorrow's rehearsal.

Personal process means living in relationship with our habits. The artistry lies in sensing when they scaffold us and when they numb us. Habit is not the enemy, and disruption is not a cure. When left unexamined, habits can harden into rigidity—into identities that mask us, even from ourselves. When disrupted without intention, we lose depth, continuity, and the chance to build trust with our own way of working.

Habits scaffold creativity the way a skeleton supports the body: not as a cage, but as a framework. They let us pour curiosity, risk, and wild invention into a stable vessel. Through the Laban/Bartenieff lens of **Stability/Mobility**,[2] we recognize that only with grounding and anchoring can expansion and elasticity flourish. Habits offer that grounding.

Habits are not only behaviors but architectures of safety, identity, and survival.

- Do I rehearse at night because I feel more creative when everyone else's needs have been met?
- Do I need a structured warm-up before I play because my body craves the known before the unexpected?

Our habits reveal not only *how* we work, but *why*. They expose unconscious needs—what we fear, trust, and may not yet feel ready to face.

We often view habits as shameful. We may fear being seen as boring, unimaginative, or lazy. We inherit myths that a "real" artist must be endlessly inventive, allergic to repetition, fueled only by inspiration. Yet repetition carries *wisdom*. It points to where our creative pulse already lives. Many habits exist not to *stifle* creativity but to *protect* it. Rituals of warm-up, daily practice, or working at a particular hour can anchor the body and mind, creating the safety from which risk becomes possible.

Habits are often as much about care as they are about craft. Sometimes what a process needs is not novelty but repetition, depth, and long investment. Investing in our habits *can* be an act of loyalty, and a signal of faith in ourselves.

---

[2]Irmgard Bartenieff and Dori Lewis, *Body Movement: Coping with the Environment* (Gordon and Breach Science, 1980), 32–6. In Laban/Bartenieff Movement Analysis (LBMA), stability and mobility are interdependent themes: Stability provides grounding and support, enabling mobility, which allows for expressive and adaptive movement; both are essential to dynamic, functional, and creative motion. For more on Laban/Bartenieff, see appendix A.

Habits can be grounding and stabilizing, or numbing and avoidant. When treated as messengers, they sharpen responsiveness, helping us sense when to stay anchored and when to veer.

Try: Choose one habit in your current practice. Trace it back. When did it begin? What did it protect or allow? What might it be asking you to risk now?

Disrupting the Familiar

If habits are our compass, disruption is the gust of wind that shifts the needle.

Destabilizing our patterns uncovers treasures hidden beneath the familiar. Breaking conventions and tendencies lets new intelligence emerge. Breaking something arbitrarily, though, is needless chaos. This is not upheaval for its own sake but focused curiosity. We often hear the advice to "try something new, break your habits, change it up." But disruption for its own sake can become its own kind of rut, a reflex that assumes *breaking* is always better than *building*. Disruption is powerful when it arises from the needs of the *work*; otherwise, it risks leaving us unmoored.

What if this were entirely different? When the patterns I lean on feel rigid or the material predictable, I return to this question. If routine anchors my process, disruption breathes life into it. **Not every habit is worth breaking.** The art lies in choosing the ones whose disruption will enliven, illuminate, and redefine.

Try: Take one small, repeatable behavior—where you sit, how you warm up, the order of your rehearsal tasks—and flip it for a single session. Notice what surfaces.

Disruption often reveals itself most vividly at the start. **Beginnings**, fragile and electric, hold the entire seed of what follows.

Beginnings Shape Everything

I run a workshop called "Immediate Dances." Each week, eight choreographers and twenty-four dancers arrive with no plan. They receive a score, a studio, and ninety minutes to devise a short original work. The pieces are videotaped, and afterward we discuss the *process* rather than the *product*.

One year, I witnessed something remarkable: eight choreographers, surrounded by a group of unfamiliar dancers, with nothing planned, **beginning**. Each process was utterly distinct. One sat in a circle, speaking in hushed tones, gesturing gently. Another played a video to show the dancers. Across the room, a group started improvising in pairs. Another began dancing vigorously, accumulating choreography as the dancers followed. None resembled another. Each beginning carried the seed of everything that came after.

The body offers a parallel. Early in embryonic development, a cluster of cells begins contracting. That first cell, mysteriously pulsing, attracts nearby cells, eventually pulsing in unison. At this stage, the brain has not formed. The process is cellular, a programmed sequence of conductivity. From this spark, rhythm emerges, a pulse that may one day sustain life.[3] If development continues, these cells become heart tissue, and that pulse can mark the entire arc from the first beat to the final one.

Creative rhythms begin in the same way: from an inner intelligence, a mysterious pulse asking us to listen. Sometimes faint, uneven, nearly inaudible, but alive. Each beginning carries the rhythm of what it may become.

Try: Instead of pushing forward with the next idea, create a series of beginnings. Don't worry about what they'll become. Begin, and begin again.

If beginnings are seeds, the conditions around them determine what grows. Process flourishes not only through what we do but through the environments, rhythms, and pressures that shape it.

Building the Conditions for Growth

Process is more than what we do. It's how we think, dream, resist, prioritize, and recalibrate. It is the gardener's restless vision of what might grow, the decision to buy the seed, the seed itself, and the eventual fruit. It is also the gardener's to-do list: the tools chosen, the clothes worn, the daily tending, the procrastination. Even staring out a window as insights creep in belongs to process.

Many of my own revelations arrive on the subway, and I *hate* the subway. But, as an introvert, watching strangers move through their lives, share an environment, and form micro-relationships, always awakens my pattern recognition and meaning-making. What can feel like wasted time—waiting, wandering, staring out the window—often becomes the terrain where connections surface. My mind, relieved of pressure to produce, can *process*.

Try: Ask yourself:

- Where do ideas actually surface for me?
- What environments tend to nourish them?
- When insight comes at an inconvenient time, how do I respond?

We often imagine process as the vessel and our work as its contents. Yet the vessel *shapes* what it holds. A riverbed directs water differently than a dam or a canal. A clay pot preserves, a sieve filters, a basket breathes. So, the architecture of our process alters the work inside it—its texture, flow, and eventual form.

---

[3] A. F. Moorman and V. M. Christoffels, "Cardiac Chamber Formation: Development, Genes, and Evolution," *Physiological Reviews* 83, no. 4 (2003): 1223–67.

Try: Ask yourself:

- What kind of home does this work need?
- What rhythm does it want?
- What conditions help it breathe?
- Who belongs in the room?
- What pressure makes it come alive?

Just as vessels differ, **processes** themselves generate radically different outcomes.

Different Process, Different Outcome

Some artists commit to a single process across works. Their pieces vary in tone, topic, or design, but share a consistent structure and ethos. Others invent a new process for each creation, letting each piece demand its own architecture. One choice tends toward a **signature style**, the other toward **novelty**. Most of us live somewhere in between, repeating certain rituals while inventing others anew. Neither model is superior. What matters is alignment with your vision and this particular work.

Try: Map the architecture of your last three creative processes.

- What choices shaped the outcomes?
- What patterns repeat across projects?
- What seems to anchor your process each time?

Notice how your process generated the outcome, and whether you *liked* that outcome.

Constraints—spatial, temporal, sensory, logistical—act as provocations. I once asked dancers to move only within a tiny kinesphere, which amplified intimacy and made the text crystalline. Another time, we rehearsed in silence for weeks, which revealed hidden rhythms. When funding, collaborators, or venues vanish, survival instincts emerge.

Sometimes the work thrives because of these conditions, not despite them. Creativity begins as problem-solving. Before we ever call ourselves artists, we are inventors. A baby reaching for a toy experiments with distance, coordination, and persistence. Learning to walk is an ongoing negotiation with gravity and equilibrium. Falling becomes data. Adjustment becomes instinct. We are wired to meet friction with adaptation.

When we give ourselves constraints—limited space, missing funding, an unexpected collaborator—we activate that same neurological orientation. A "problem" is not an obstacle to creativity; it is often the ignition of it. Constraint narrows the field just enough for invention to spark.

Playwright Ntozake Shange used poetic form itself as a constraint. In her choreopoems—most famously *for colored girls who have considered suicide / when the rainbow is enuf*—she restricted linear plot and conventional character, allowing rhythm, movement, and voice to carry the story. The very limits she set became the architecture for radical invention.[4]

Try: Introduce one deliberate constraint that creates a problem your body must solve.Limit your space. Remove sound. Eliminate repetition. Restrict yourself to one gesture or one text fragment. Stay with the constraint long enough for frustration to turn into invention. Notice what strategies your body develops.

Amid habits, beginnings, and constraints, process also demands *faith*. **Mystery** holds a place inside creation, one that resists control.

Trusting the Mystery

Not every creation needs to prove brilliance, win awards, or leave a legacy. Sometimes it can simply exist. This requires stepping into a process without judgment, goals, or expectation—trusting the flow.

When my kids make art, I cheer them on.

"What is that yellow monster doing to the ship?" I ask my son about his picture.

"I don't know..."

"A mystery! How fun!"

I have never said, "How can you not know where this is going?"

Yet we speak to ourselves this way constantly.

Do I frame every picture my children create? Of course not. Do I consider their drawing wasted time if it doesn't end up framed? That's laughable. They nourished themselves with imagination and practice. They learned something for the future. That's a huge success.

What if we treated ourselves with the same encouragement? The playful, uninhibited process of a child—the one not yet filtered through judgment—is a holy grail.[5] Paired with analysis, craft, education, and research, it becomes a potent combination.

---

[4]Ntozake Shange, *For Colored Girls Who Have Considered Suicide / When the Rainbow Is Enuf* (Scribner Poetry, 1977).

[5]Mihaly Csikszentmihalyi, *Creativity: Flow and the Psychology of Discovery and Invention* (HarperCollins, 1996), 110–13. Csikszentmihalyi's research shows that engaging deeply in a creative process—without self-judgment or fixed expectations—produces states of intrinsic enjoyment and learning, regardless of outcome.

Try: Carry a notebook, voice recorder, or phone app. Capture every passing idea with respect. Treat each as a potential seed, knowing it may never be planted—and that this, too, is part of the process.

Trusting the mystery also means trusting others. **Feedback**, when woven with care, can deepen process without dissolving its wildness.

Choreographing Feedback into the Process

Every artist needs feedback. But each process requests it differently—its timing, form, and sources must adapt to the art, the artists, and the context. Feedback is not something that merely happens *to* the work; it is part of the work's *becoming*. It can clarify or confuse, affirm or derail.

Choosing *how* feedback enters is a powerful part of crafting our process. Who do you invite, and when? What kind of input is useful, and what might be premature or harmful? Do you need embodied responses, metaphors, silence, advice, neutrality, or disruption? Early in a creative process, strong opinions can spark defensiveness. Later, overly cautious feedback can obscure what's needed. Consider the stage you're in:

- What mode of feedback supports you best—verbal, physical, visual, written, or silent?
- Whose insights matter most right now?
- What parameters, rules, or conditions help you stay open and receptive?
- How do you want to feel after receiving feedback—clearer, affirmed, challenged, curious?

There is no universal answer. But naming these conditions helps you honor feedback as a tool rather than a verdict.

The best feedback doesn't end with the conversation. Reflection afterward—slow, selective, in your own time—helps you hear *your* voice alongside *theirs*. Sometimes a comment that stung yields insight days later. Sometimes the most valuable note gets metabolized quietly, absorbed before you even realize it. You can keep a single phrase, a gesture, or a question and discard the rest. Let your nervous system and curiosity decide what feedback carries forward in your process.

Try: Sketch a "feedback map" for your current or next project. List who, when, and what kind of feedback would serve you best at each stage. (For more feedback tools and forms, see appendix B.)

Feedback becomes one more rhythm inside process, an interplay between instinct and response. **Accepting** this interplay leads us toward the larger picture of what process itself teaches us.

Devising and Accepting Our Process

Process is a means to an end but also its own journey, where **instinct** meets **intention**, **habit** meets **disruption**, and the work finds its **momentum**. What we get out of our process is not always immediately visible. If we judge it only by its outcome, we have missed the point. I've made countless choices that seemed to have failed, only to return later as the solution. I've gone off on tangents that have ended up being the scenic route to the heart of the work. Each success and failure brings me closer to myself as a creator. Resisting risk, absurdity, and embarrassment inhibits creativity.

Of course, not every detour feels scenic. Some stretches of process feel flat, repetitive, or like dead ends. Those moments of exhaustion belong too—another rhythm inside the larger one. They don't signal failure so much as another phase of the journey—the body or the work pausing, circling, or waiting for conditions to shift.

Process is an investment in the unknown. Each process teaches us something new about the work and ourselves. If we listen closely, those lessons become the heartbeat that sustains our creative lives. Notice what the work demands. Interrogate your habits. Release judgment. Say yes. Let your process define the work *and* reveal you to yourself.

Takeaway: By listening to what the work demands, interrogating habit, releasing judgment, and saying yes, the process will define the work and reveal us to ourselves.

In Practice: Tips About Process

1. **Reveal what the work needs.**
   Each piece has its own logic. Your job is to find the one it's asking for.
   Try: Ask your piece: What kind of conditions do you need? Silence? Urgency? More time alone? A crowd of collaborators?

2. **Begin like you've never begun.**
   Beginning the same way each time may train the work to follow old paths.
   Try: Change the beginning of your process. Begin with light, costume, or laughter. Let the unfamiliar reroute you.

3. **Let the environment collaborate.**
   Let the room, light, sound, and surfaces become partners in the process.
   Try: Choose a space that disrupts your norm—too small, too public, too echoey, too quiet. Let the unfamiliar shape your next rehearsal.

4. **Map the consequences.**
   Your creative decisions ripple. Trace them. The tempo you set, the tools you use, and the conditions you allow all lead to outcomes—intended or not.
   Try: Choose a recent piece. Trace three process choices you made and name the direct result of each one in the final work. What would you tweak next time?

5. **Interrupt the loop.**
   Habits form for good reasons, but can quietly limit what's possible.
   Try: Identify a repeated behavior in your process. Instead of removing it, shift one element: time of day, collaborators, or the order of tasks. What happens when you bend the pattern?

6. **Slow down feedback.**
   Feedback can clarify or derail. If it comes too soon or from the wrong source, it can distort the work's pulse. Find the tempo and format that suits *you.*
   Try: Make a feedback map for your current project. Who do you want to hear from? When? And what kind of input—emotional, structural, technical—serves the work at each stage?

7. **Notice the pulse.**
   Rushing to resolution can tidy the work before it has ripened. Waiting too long to shape it can blur its edge.
   Try: Ask yourself: Am I resolving this to relieve uncertainty? Or postponing structure out of doubt? What does the work need—pressure, patience, or tension?

8. **Balance work with rest.**
   Insight often comes from pause. Avoiding the work might not be laziness—it might be digestion.
   Try: Walk away on purpose. Put your piece down for three days. Let the nervous system catch up. Notice what surfaces in the quiet.

9. **Embrace the ineffable.**
   Not everything in your process will (or should) make sense. The inexplicable is often what makes a work magnetic.
   Try: Let one part of your process stay unexplainable. Trust it. Don't name it, frame it, or fix it. Let it stay wild.

10. **Let the process teach you.**
    Your process is speaking, even when the piece isn't. Instead of interpreting your ideas, investigate the methods that shaped them.
    Try: Mid-process, choose one decision—how you entered, what you repeated, what you avoided. Follow it like a clue. Make one new choice that contradicts it. Let that tension lead the next decision.

From the Field: *Give Up, or A Bird Lying on Its Back*

Figure 6.1 Lea Fulton and Christina Robson in *Give Up, or A Bird Lying on Its Back*. Reproduced with permission of Anton Martynov.

Some choreographers thrive on a consistent process, finding stability and freedom in repetition. For me, repeating the same method dulls my imagination. I can't make something *new* with a known process.

I invent a process for each new work. That doesn't mean working without *form*. In fact, over time, I've come to recognize that my process follows an arc of phases: imagination, research, exploration/experimentation, creation, analysis, editing, destroying, recalibrating, designing, presenting, processing. I move in waves through these, doubling back and skipping forward, but these stages are always present.

One piece, *Give Up, or A Bird, Lying on Its Back*,[6] asked whether language can ever fully describe dance. I wanted the audience to see the figurative tip into the literal, to press words through the sieve of movement and see what got stuck.

---

[6]Alexandra Beller/Dances, *Give Up, or A Bird Lying on Its Back*, premiere, the Green Building NYC, 2013.

The process:

- I choreographed a phrase and taught it to students, capturing my verbal descriptions.
- I asked my company to choreograph from the written description without showing them my phrase.
- The dancers and I redescribed each dancer's phrase verbally, using pop culture images, creating "songs" that paralleled the rhythm of the movement.
- I gave each dancer another dancer's song and asked them to create a small hand-based movement study from it.
- A sign language interpreter joined us, translating their gestures into ASL signs, creating a word bank.
- A poet devised writing from the constraint of the word bank.
- I used these multiple materials (texts and movement phrases) to craft the piece.

The piece operated as a scientific inquiry, each step a hypothesis. Inviting a sign language interpreter, for example, was a shot in the dark. I was prepared for her to say, "None of this is sign language." Instead, it pushed the work in a direction I couldn't have designed. No other process could have made this piece. Every participant was a translator, shaping the material with their perspective. The piece let the audience witness meaning-making as it fractured, reassembled, and reappeared.

Eventually, this became a flexible framework I now use at universities—not as a finished method, but as a living inquiry that reshapes itself with each group. Each time, the choreography, text, number of dancers, and design shift—but the structure holds. The score gives me something rare: a process I can depend on that still surprises me.

For me, each work demands a structure that responds to specific questions. For some, having a reliable process offers continuity and stability that supports creativity. For me, it risks erasing the raw edges I rely on to meet new work with urgency and openness. Reinventing my process each time helps me step outside my patterns and stay in a space I find endlessly generative: *the unknown*. The point isn't whether *you* should invent a new process for every piece; it's whether you've asked the question.

Ultimately, the piece wasn't only about a polished result—it was about building a system of observation that held confusion, dissonance, and multiple truths, yet still produced a rigorous work. It reminded me that process is less a destination than a map: Its purpose is not arrival but revelation.

Guidance: Balancing Effort and Renewal

As I write this, I am burned out, a place I know well. What usually feels juicy is dry, what normally feels joyful is dull. Burnout arrives for many reasons—financial limits, caregiving, illness, unrest, family tangles. Burnout disrupts the rhythm and flow of creativity, alarming for artists because our passion, and often our livelihood, depends on creative vitality. Recognizing when and how to recuperate is essential to sustaining artistic rhythm.

The LBMA theme of Exertion/Recuperation becomes transformative when creativity stalls. What do these words mean to you, in your body, in your work?

"Work and rest!" is the quick answer I often hear—shaped by capitalism, exceptionalism, and a culture that devalues rest. We overwork, overstimulate, then collapse, treating rest like a crash landing instead of an intentional act. LBMA defines exertion/recuperation as forces that respond to and stabilize one another, rather than a binary.

Exertion is effort toward an outcome. Recuperation is effort too—just redirected. Imagine spinning to the right until dizzy. The best reset isn't sitting down but spinning left until equilibrium is restored. Exerting ourselves in opposing ways balances our bodies, energy, mind, heart, and relationships, creating stability and recuperation.

Picture an office worker under fluorescent light, surrounded by screens. For this office worker, training for a marathon becomes recuperative—not because it is "restful" but because it balances their particular fatigue. It is, of course, an exertion. **But still, it heals them.** They sleep better, enjoy food more, and have more patience for their kids. Despite the arduous activity, they feel less burned out than if they opted for traditional "rest."

Wrestling with dramaturgy might be "spinning right"—dense, analytic, detail driven. Recuperation might be freewriting, improvising, or letting accidents interrupt. Being in deep experimentation and improvisation might be "spinning left"—intuitive, impulsive, and spontaneous. Recuperation might be editing the sound, drilling directions in a phrase, or developing specific gestures in a scene. A change of rhythm, task, or perspective can restore energy, allowing us the stamina to continue.

Recuperation isn't only what happens *after* the work; it can be designed *into* the work. I work on spreadsheets sitting on a physioball, to add *flow*, but I plant myself firmly in the studio when watching a new section develop, for *stability*. Being able to analyze what *type* of energy would offer balance is critical. **Ask:**

What *kind* of energy is being depleted? Is it analytical or improvisational? Focused or diffuse attention? Controlled or wild?

What kind of *action* could replenish it, either *while* you are in it, or as a follow-up?

While I resist rigid binaries, *contrast* has value here—naming one exertion allows us to discover its balancing energy. What is something in your art-making that exhausts you? Trying to assess the big picture, the relationship arcs? Coaching text/phrase material? Grant writing? What activities or dynamics would balance these?

Stuck on a decision? **Freewrite** about the seed of your idea. **Overwhelmed** by the big picture? **Drill** the footwork, edit a monologue, design the postcard. Working **alone**? Invite **community** to an informal showing. Too much **masking**? Go somewhere familiar and **hibernate**.

Use the following framework to consider your current process and how to recover from it. It's not easy! Seeking balance *is* exertion itself. **Self-care is radical work.**

When we honor these cycles in our process, we create space for new ideas, perspectives, and engagement. We design our process for sustainability, not just productivity. Process becomes a rhythm we live inside, not a race we run through.

Frameworks: A Diagnostic Tool for Recuperative Design

Instructions: Identify an emotionally, mentally, physically, socially, or creatively depleting activity. It could be part of artistic practice, a relationship, a professional task, or a daily obligation that leaves you off-center.

This activity is not "bad." We're identifying the aspects that drain you to find counterbalance—an activity, environment, or rhythm that recuperates.

You do *not* need to answer every question. Notice those that feel *resonant or revealing.*

Once you've identified the exhausting aspects, consider their opposites. This builds a **recuperative practice** that restores the energy, attention, or capacity that's been overdrawn. Once you've answered the meaningful questions from the left, describe a reversal on the right. For example, if "Does it require constant decision-making or multitasking?" felt crucial, write, "Requires NO decision-making or multitasking" on the right. You are not trying to *find* the recuperative activity but *describing* it. There will be numerous activities that fulfill the description.

Finally, use the descriptions in column three to find one or more quick, accessible, low-cost interventions. Try to incorporate one on days you do the original activity.

Questions to Ask	**Original Activity**		**Description of Recuperative Activity**
Relational and Social Dynamics			
Are you alone or with others during this activity? **If with others:**			
How big a group?			
Are they familiar or strangers?			
Must you socially mask?			
Do you feel emotionally safe?			
Are you leading, collaborating, or following?			
How much emotional caretaking is required?			
Cognitive and Emotional Processing			
Does this require logical, analytical thinking?			
Creative, divergent thinking?			
Emotional sensitivity or empathy?			

Questions to Ask	**Original Activity**		**Description of Recuperative Activity**
Constant decision-making or multitasking?			
Are you responsible for others' experience or outcome?			
Is there time pressure or urgency?			
Do you experience self-doubt, criticism, or perfectionism?			
Environmental and Sensory Experience			
Are you indoors or outdoors?			
Is the environment noisy, quiet, bright, dim, cluttered, sterile, etc.?			
Are you over- or understimulated?			
Do the temperature, lighting, sound, or smell affect you?			
Do you have bodily autonomy?			
Are you confined or able to move freely?			
Kinesthetic and Somatic Impact			
Are you sitting, standing, walking, or in motion?			
How much physical exertion is required? **If a lot:**			
What type of physical exertion: cardio, weight-bearing, repetitive?			
Are the movements forceful or gentle?			
Do you feel free-flowing or tightly controlled?			
Are you attuned to breath, posture, energy?			
Are you sudden or sustained?			
Is there much focus on your surroundings? Detailed or diffuse attention?			
Time, Rhythm, and Structure			
Is the activity structured or open-ended?			

Questions to Ask	Original Activity		Description of Recuperative Activity
Are you following someone else's schedule or your own?			
Can you reflect/reset between phases?			
Do you feel rushed or dragged by the pace?			
Agency and Consent			
Did you choose this activity or was it assigned?			
How much control do you have over outcomes?			
Are your boundaries respected?			
Inner Orientation			
Is this driven more by intuition or logic?			
Are your strengths being used?			
Are you "seen"?			
Meaning and Motivation			
Do you believe in the purpose or value of the task?			
Is there a clear outcome, or little closure?			

Example:

What is the social dynamic?	I feel censored, controlled, overly visible, claustrophobic.	Alone or with trusted friends. Improvisational, free, or hidden, protected.
What physical dynamics does it require?	Controlled, detailed, focused, tight.	Free, general, diffuse or unfocused, relaxed.

Based on this example, what activities would serve this description?

Here are a few:

- Rolling slowly on the floor
- Swinging on a swing
- Drawing with the nondominant hand
- Walking aimlessly in a park

Tuning In: Sensing the Cycles of Process

This practice invites you to experience how exertion and recuperation create rhythm, the same rhythm that shapes process.

1. **Begin with exertion.**
   Choose a simple, repeatable action. It could be tapping, circling, humming, pacing, swaying. Stay with it. Allow the action to grow—bigger, faster, heavier, more insistent—until your body feels saturated. Notice the moment when effort shifts from energizing to tiring, from alive to too much.

2. **Let recuperation arrive.**
   Without stopping, allow your body to choose its own counteraction. Notice how the shift emerges as a response, not a decision. Stay with this recuperation and let yourself fully experience it.

3. **Return and repeat.**
   Come back to your first action. Stay with it until your body again tips toward change. Follow whatever recuperation arrives now. Is it the same as before? Different?

4. **Allow the cycle to continue.**
   Keep moving. Let exertion and recuperation keep trading places. You don't need to return to your original action unless your body asks for it. Allow movement, energy, space, or focus to keep shifting whenever change is requested, noticing how each new state arises in conversation with the last.

5. **Connect to process.**
   Notice how the unfolding cycle mirrors the creative process. Exertion and recuperation don't always alternate in neat pairs—sometimes we return to the familiar, and at other times we catalyze something unexpected. Process, too, carries this rhythm: repetition and change, stability and surprise, each state arising in dialogue with what came before.

6. **Reflect.**
   - Where do I often exert past my resilience?
   - What do I organically do to recalibrate?
   - What changes if I trust the timing of my own rhythm?

Studio Lab: Generating Through Oppositional Tension

(This exercise was created in collaboration with Katherine Profeta)

This exercise invites you to hold contrasting forces, letting their friction generate movement and unexpected synthesis. What emerges when contradiction is generative, not a problem to solve?

1. **Identify core words.**
   Write a list of words vital to your artistic voice or current project. These could be values, emotions, or themes (expansion, precision, chaos, surrender).
   Write their opposites. Trust your instincts about what feels like an energetic or conceptual opposition.

2. **Translate words into movement.**
   Create two movement events. Keep them distinct in quality, letting the physicality hold metaphorical meaning, not literality.
   - One phrase from the original list (A).
   - One phrase from the opposites (B).

3. **Refine the opposition.**
   Perform phrase A, then phrase B. Repeat several times. Notice how they inform or pressurize each other.
   - **Play with time:** Elongate one, sharpen the other.
   - **Play with space:** Make one expansive, the other condensed.

4. **Feel *the call for* C.**
   After working with A and B, sense what would triangulate them. What third phrase (C) could make both A and B feel more charged—by creating context, contrast, tension, or flow?

   Phrase C doesn't need to reconcile them; it might sharpen their differences, tilt the balance, or open an unexpected pathway.

5. **Test the orders.**
   Experiment with all six possible sequences. Notice how the meaning, rhythm, and resonance shift in each arrangement. Which feels inevitable? Which unsettles? Which surprises you?
   - **ABC, ACB, BAC, BCA, CAB, CBA**

6. **Reflect.**
   - What did C reveal about A and B?
   - Did it change how you experienced them?
   - Did C create harmony, escalation, or rupture?
   - Which sequence asked the most of you? Which gave you the most?

Pagework: Writing into Process

Freewrite on some or all of these questions.

Exertion and Recuperation

1. **Consider your recent creative projects.**
   Identify one that felt **exhausting** and one that felt **restorative**. What made them draining or energizing—environment, physicality, socialization, or mental load?

2. **Identify where you currently feel stuck, drained, or overly exerted.**
   Write about it (e.g., "My meetings with the lighting designer feel tight, controlling, and tense") **Consider:** what would "spinning in the other direction" look like? What environmental, relational, or structural elements do you need for balance? How might you bring those qualities to the same event (e.g., "I am going to do LD zoom meetings while walking/bouncing/swinging in a hammock").

3. **Describe your typical creative rhythm.** ("Bursts of inspiration" vs. "methodical effort.") Notice the EKG, the ebb and flow. Where can you build recuperation *directly into* the process?

4. **Reflect on when creating feels *restorative*. What conditions make this happen?**

5. **What part of your process is the most emotionally, physically, or intellectually taxing?**
   Imagine an observer watching you do this taxing part. Where might they identify imbalance or inefficiency? What systems could you introduce to make this easier?

Writing from Inside Your Process

1. **What are your default tools?**
   Do you begin with research? Physical generation? Concept generation?

2. **Choose one predictable element in your process and imagine its opposite.**
   If you start alone, imagine beginning collaboratively. If you generate movement first, consider starting with text, soundscape, found objects.

3. **Reflect on a time when a limitation (space, time, resources, or collaborators) forced you to adapt.**

   Did that constraint hinder creativity or manifest something unexpected? What limitation in your current work could become a catalyst?

4. **If your current project had a voice, what would it ask for?**

   More time? More risk? Less perfectionism? More witnessing?

Movements + Maps: Trusting the Unknown You

This score invites you to break habits, invite chance, and embrace discomfort. Instead of seeking control, lean into curiosity. Allow the process to become your collaborator. Alter your usual rhythm; relinquish control.

1. **Change your landscape.**
   Choose an unfamiliar space for creation. Try a library, park, or hallway. Let your surroundings influence your choices. Try a kitchen if you're usually locomotive, a stairwell if you need verticality. Let the space invite an unusual **scale** or **tempo**.

2. **Reshape time.**
   Adjust your rehearsal duration and schedule. If you usually rehearse for two hours, try five; if evenings, try mornings.

3. **Interrogate your habits.**
   Identify three deeply ingrained artistic habits. Write them down. Then:
   - Break two.
   - Invest in the third more intentionally than ever.

4. **Introduce chance.**
   Incorporate a randomizing element—a dice roll, shuffled playlist, or random words as movement prompts. Let chaos design your creation.

5. **Flip your instinct/analysis cycle.**
   If you typically create by intuition, use a structured methodology (mathematical patterning, timed improvisations, or movement scoring). If you bias toward analysis, use sense memory, improvisation, or free association.

6. **Invite friction.**
   Collaborate with someone whose aesthetic, process, or approach contrasts with yours. Integrate an unfamiliar material or movement technique. Allow tension to push your work in unexpected directions.

7. **Begin in response.**
   Tell someone your title. Let them guess what that looks like. Create what they describe, letting their interpretation become your beginning.

8. **Invite interruption.**

   Set a timer at irregular intervals. Stop what you're doing when it rings and start something completely different. Let interruption rewire your flow to show you what you cling to or avoid.

9. **Leave a trace.**

   Document one image, phrase, or gesture that captures the feeling of your process that day. Don't explain it. Accumulate them. Start each day by revisiting them. Let them seed what's next.

Contributor's Note: Site of Construction

by Janet Wong

I feel a little overwhelmed as I recall the past thirty years of making work alongside Bill T. Jones. Each work seemed to have demanded its own process. I'll share one.

In 2006 we premiered a work called *Chapel/Chapter* during the inaugural season of the reconstructed Gatehouse at Harlem Stage. It remains one of my favorite pieces. The process was a complex one as we were generating the script, the music, and the choreography concurrently, and often together in the same room. There was a sense of urgency, agency, and purpose from the beginning to the end, which is not always the case. The initial idea for the work came during a visit to the construction site.

As we walked, wearing hard hats, through the gutted neo-Gothic structure with stained-glass windows, Bill decided on the title of the work, and with that the seed of intention for the piece. The ideas started floating in right there and then—the audience will sit in church pews on four sides with projections on the floor; there will be stories that may explore judgment, redemption, forgiveness, and more. Oh, that initial spark of inspiration!

On the first day of rehearsal, the phrase "the road to hell was paved with good intentions" was introduced into the room, and it opened doors, windows, and cracks. Language played a big part in the work, not only in the storytelling, the music, and the projections but also in creating the very specific movement vocabulary. The three stories that became the spine and purpose of the work were culled from the news, a court transcript of a trial, and a personal story of a dancer. We worked with a dramaturg to help us weave together the stories, but he was not a good fit. He had come from the theater world and did not quite understand how dance can serve the narrative. Our disagreements forced us to analyze and defend our ideas, which in hindsight was beneficial to the process. I strongly believe that the power of dance begins where words fail.

By the time we premiered *Chapel/Chapter* in December, the Gatehouse was still a construction site. Building material was everywhere offstage, there was a layer of construction dust on everything, and heating had to be pumped in through a hole in the wall from an HVAC truck parked outside the building. Every single piece of equipment had to be brought in. We discussed postponing the premiere by a few months, but the work insisted on being born. And who were we to stop it?

Studio Provocations: Questioning Process

For every fact, there is an infinity of hypotheses.
The more you look, the more you see.
(Robert Pirsig, *Zen and the Art of Motorcycle Maintenance*)[7]

Habit and Change

Name a creative habit. ("I come into the studio with a plan.")

Try: Remove it for one work session.

What limit or constraint are you facing? ("The rehearsal space is noisy.")

Try: Next rehearsal, use this as the main driver.

When do you usually depend on instinct versus analysis?

Try: If you usually begin with intuition, start with form. If you begin structurally, start with sensation.

Identity and Introspection

Do you have "a creative process"?

- Describe it. What works about it? What are its limitations? What is one pattern you see in the outcome?
- What would its *opposite* look like? Can you try one rehearsal, or a whole piece using this method?

What are you avoiding?

- What would be one way to turn toward it?

How are you balancing control and surrender?

Try: Next rehearsal, try leading with the one you use less.

[7]Robert M. Pirsig, *Zen and the Art of Motorcycle Maintenance: An Inquiry into Values* (HarperCollins, 1974).

How much do you *not know* in this work?

How supported do you feel?

- What would support you more?

How often do you interrupt your defaults?

Try: Choose one to test for a day:

- Have more fun
- Work faster
- Work slower
- Release control; let it *become*
- Enter the space with **no expectations**

Try: Create a table with three columns:

1. **Task/phase** of your artistic process (e.g., rehearsal, writing, email outreach)
2. What **brain function** it requires (clarity, stamina, vulnerability, precision, patience)
3. How you **respond** to it (avoidance, urgency, excitement)

Example:

Task/Phase	Brain Function	Response/Feelings
Grant writing	Analytical, clear-headed, big-picture thinking, but detail-oriented, executive function.	Disheartened, avoidant, depressed, resistant.

4. **Ask:** Where are you **overgiving** or **underresourced**?
5. **Create a modification. *Example*:** "I could co-work with my bestie, with a five-minute improv jam as a break."

Is the concept of *healing* in your process?

What distracts you?

- Is that sometimes/never/always helpful?
- If it is rarely helpful, what can you change to shift it?

How do you plan? Has that been working?

Try: In your next session, work differently (chance, collaboration, hour-by-hour structure, no plan). What changed?

Where is *comfort* in your process?

- What contributes?
- How can you increase it?
- When does comfort become complacency?

What is the role of anxiety?

- Does it feel useful? Inhibit you?
- Do you have strategies to get yourself out of it?

What feels divine or magical to you?

- How could you invite more of this?

What is the role of chance?

- Do you want more or less chance/accident/discovery/serendipity?

Try: Design a rehearsal where chance leads.

Collaboration and Influence

Ask a collaborator to describe your process.

- What description would you hope for? How does this compare?

How much authority do you give your collaborators?

Try: Shift the authority for one session.

What would the audience *guess* about your process based on this work?

How would your favorite artist solve the most significant problem in your work?

Who offers you guidance—directly or indirectly?

- Is there a mentorship you could initiate?

What are you borrowing?

- Have you truly made it *yours*?

Exertion/Recuperation

What part feels most taxing right now?

Try: Identify the most exhausting part. How could you lighten that?

How do you recover from different phases—research, rehearsal, editing?

- What else could you try?

When do you take breaks, and what do you do?

Try: Shift the timing, duration, or activity of your breaks.

How do you balance critical observation and loving celebration of your work?

How do you define a mistake?

- How do you recover emotionally and creatively when something goes "wrong"?

What happens if you intentionally destroy or erase?

Try: Delete something at the top of a rehearsal. What does it provoke or reveal?

Fear and Courage

Note: *Use these prompts gently.*
What is the greatest fear you have about yourself as an artist? (There is an exercise to work with this in chapter 8, "Faith.")

What are you most afraid will happen in this process?

- What do you do when that fear shows up?
- Have you explored working *from* that fear?

Try: Do the "Dialoguing with Your Inner Critic" exercise in chapter 8, "Faith."

Where do you most want answers?

Try: Linger in that uncertainty. Create from that place without trying to solve anything.

Practicality and Structure

What is your ideal *time* and *duration* for a creative session?

Try: Map your energy across the day or week.

- When do you feel most open, intuitive, grounded, or alert in your body?

***Where* do you do your best creative work?**

Try: Work in a contrasting environment. What felt disorienting? What sparked something new?

- What spaces make you feel bold, curious, or open? Is there a way to be in one more often?

What physical, social, or emotional environment supports your process most?

- How might you create that environment more?

What agreements have you made about your process (with yourself, collaborators, funders, or audiences)?

- Are they serving the work?

What rituals, comforts, or setups support your creativity? (A clean desk, green juice, chocolate, Post-it notes?)

- Do you invest in them?

Reflection and Growth

What was the moment this work first sparked?

- What excited you most?
- Is that still there?

What is part of your process you've never questioned?

Try: Use the opposite strategy for a day or more.

Where in your body do you feel when it's *right*?

Try: Spend a rehearsal methodically checking in with that place as you create.

What is one thing this process has taught you that no other has?

Metacognition and Rules

Does your process have a purpose/goal unrelated to the outcome (e.g., community building, trauma release)?

Is your process research based?

- How do you research? Are there other methods you might try?

Try: Research through a new mode: interviews, somatics, crowdsourcing. What changes?

How transparent are you with your performers?

- Would changing that be useful?

How do these operate? Are they working?

- Ritual
- Repetition
- Writing
- Talking
- Habit
- Expectation
- Watching
- Dreaming

Try: Choose two. Enhance one; interrupt the other.

What are the rules in your process?

- Who are they serving?
- When do you break them?

Try: Reverse something.

- Delete something that feels important.
- Watch separate sections simultaneously.
- Create a mystery.
- Interrupt a habit.
- Be durational. Let it go "too long."
- Shock yourself.
- Give away power.

Choose three. Integrate them into a rehearsal. What emerges?

Sensation and the Body

How much distance can you get?

Try:

- Take a break.
- Watch it from farther away.
- Listen but don't watch.
- Watch with no sound.

How do discipline and rigor scaffold your process?

- Would you benefit from more or less?

Try: If you need more rigor, build yourself a tight plan and stick to it. If you need less, add chance, games, and intuitive exploration to your next rehearsal.

When do you destroy things?

Try: Destroy a fragment you're attached to. Watch what emerges in its absence. Make something different to replace it. (You can have it back afterward!)

Is there violence?

- What feels violent, and is it useful?

Can you differentiate between valuable discomfort and toxic discomfort?

- Where do you feel these in your body?
- When you notice harmful discomfort, what is your strategy to recalibrate? Does it work?

Perspective and Play

How difficult do choices feel?

Try: When stuck, create a simple version of both options.

How do you balance productivity and play?

Write your process as a list of verbs. ("Research, build, adjust, collaborate, refine, share.")

- What patterns do you see? What verbs are missing that you would you *like* in your process?

Try: In your next rehearsal, create from the missing verbs.

What if you made work as someone in another profession?

Try: Create a score, sketch, concept, or movement study as someone more

- **Rational** (engineer, mathematician, architect)
- **Sensorial** (chef, potter, gardener)
- **Intuitive/emotional** (psychic, child, addict)
- **Didactic/technical** (teacher, surgeon)

Aesthetics

What do you consider beautiful?

- What is the *opposite* of beautiful?
- What is ugly?
- What aesthetic risks scare you?

Try: If you often create with beauty in mind, make something "ugly." If you avoid beauty as a goal, create something "beautiful."

What happens if you strip your work down to the bone?

Try: Present its most minimal form. What do you notice without additional elements? What do you miss most?

What never belongs?

Try: Add one element you've always rejected. What does it challenge or clarify?

How do you use the following:

- **Form/structure:** lines, simplicity, layers, repetition
- **Tactility/emotionality:** pleasure, softness, hardness, viscerality
- **Dynamicism/tempo:** momentum, arc, duration

Try: Create from one you rarely use.

7

Facts

Before You Begin: Priming Curiosity About Facts

Take a breath. Consider these questions. Let them settle in your body before moving forward. They are not for solving, but for sensing.

Who do I trust most to offer me facts?

How do I distinguish between a fact and a belief?

What have I made up to make things feel more certain?

When do I realize I've filled in the blanks without knowing it?

Why does *not knowing* feel scary in some moments and spacious in others?

Where do I feel grounded in what I know, and where do I feel insecure about my knowledge?

Groundwork: Thinking, Feeling, and Sensing with Facts

> Very few beings really seek knowledge in this world. Mortal or immortal, few really ask. On the contrary, they try to wring from the unknown the answers they have already shaped in their own minds—justifications, confirmations, forms of consolation without which they can't go on. To really ask is to open the door to the whirlwind. The answer may annihilate the question and the questioner.
>
> (Anne Rice, *The Vampire Lestat*)[1]

Owning Our Fiction

Facts are slippery, subjective, and sometimes betray us. They can conflict with imagination, fantasy, and intuition—the stuff of art—yet art cannot be made without them. They *claim* objectivity, but facts are often curated and cherry-picked to confirm bias. They can stabilize a moment or destabilize a relationship. They can ground us in shared reality or be weaponized to sow chaos. Facts are places we meet, like a sunset, season, or shared experience, but also the territory of miscommunication, dispute, and violence, like a boundary between countries or scientific disagreements. Facts can be deeply personal or universal to a species.

These tensions lead us to question our perception, reality, and meaning.

If we approach facts not as *conclusions* but *provocations*, we leave space to negotiate meaning, transforming the stasis of *certainty* into the movement of *curiosity*. We can start by asking the following:

- How can we use facts to leverage our imagination?
- How can facts reveal our agendas, opinions, and fears?
- How can facts map where we end and the world begins?
- How do we learn to value our inner matrix of facts as much as traditional metrics?

First, let's define a "fact."

What Is a Fact?

A fact is assumed to be definitive and unchanging. But what qualifies as fact depends on the field. In **science**, it must be observable and repeatable; in **law**, it must hold up in court; in **journalism**, it needs corroboration; in **philosophy**, there is disagreement on what counts as a fact. It can be independent of observation (analytic philosophy), negotiated through language and power (constructivism), or

[1] Anne Rice, *The Vampire Lestat* (Ballantine Books, 1985).

something personally felt or witnessed (phenomenology). Even a fact depends on context. This frees us to self-determine how to define facts in our creative process. What definition gives us stability *and* mobility, function *and* expression, the whole *and* its parts?

Are *memories* facts? Are *feelings* facts? What of **somatics, oral tradition, and inherited trauma**? What of a body's recoil, a tremor in the voice, a gut churning? Are these facts? They don't come with citations but with breath rate, pulse, and lived knowledge. Believing any fact requires faith in the source—and when the source is *us*, others must trust our perception. If you say your breath is shallow, *you* are the evidence.

In medicine, this plays out with devastating consequences, where the facts described by patients of color, women, fat, and disabled people are routinely disbelieved because these are not considered reliable narrators by the medical industry. Without agreement, a fact withers. Without shared facts, shared reality dissolves, and we lose the ground on which intimacy and communication stand.

When performers describe pain, discomfort, or resistance, do we *honor* or *judge* them? When we speak from the body, saying, "I need to move slower," "This doesn't feel consensual," or "I'm numb," do we take these as *facts*, or gaslight ourselves? For **somatic facts** to create action, we must trust the body's wisdom as a sacred site of information. When that trust is broken, by ourselves or others, it stagnates momentum.

So, whose facts are we using? How did we arrive at them? And what stories, opinions, and assumptions have been hitching a ride inside them?

Facts are points of contact with reality—what can be observed, sensed, or verified in shared experience. They give us coordinates, something stable enough to move around. Even personal or somatic facts, though invisible to others, arise from lived perception and can be tested against attention and repetition.

Some "facts" are not facts at all, but norms, metrics, hierarchies, and inherited agreements that have calcified into inevitability. They gain authority through repetition, not foundation. When we see them clearly, we discover they are choices—not laws. The work, then, is learning to distinguish between what is *verifiable*, what is *embodied*, and what is merely *rehearsed*.

Facts in the Body and the Senses

Bonnie Bainbridge Cohen describes a fact as a fixed point you can move around.[2] Facts create stability. My twelve-year-old asked me, "Why don't they do time zones in increments of ten minutes?" The

[2]Bonnie Bainbridge Cohen describes facts as stable reference points that enable movement and exploration, extending in somatics to include "felt truths," or embodied personal facts. See *Sensing, Feeling, and Action: The Experiential Anatomy of Body-Mind Centering* (Contact Editions, 2008).

answer is: we could—but we've agreed not to. Our construction of time (clocks, calendars, seasons) provides a shared reality. This allows us the stability to cross time zones, state lines, and still find one another. We also have deeply personal facts. In somatics, a "felt truth" is a fact.

Felt truth: What happens in your nervous system, muscles, breath, or gut is real, regardless of whether it can be proven or measured externally. Somatic educators emphasize felt senses, proprioception, equilibrium, and interoception as the primary sources of embodied data.

Consider:

- What in your process is truly observable or felt—and what is inherited, assumed, or rehearsed?
- When you say "that's just how it is," whose agreement are you relying on?
- What facts live in your body that you have dismissed because they lack external proof?
- Which forms of evidence do you privilege—and who taught you to privilege them?

Facts locate us in space, culture, and experience. A **somatic fact** ("My body flinches when I hear a loud noise") is no less real than my temperature; it just emerges from internal perception rather than external measurement. **External** facts can be used to erase our lived truth. My temperature runs a full degree low. When I have a 101 temperature, it is 102 compared to "normal." If a doctor dismisses that personal fact, their diagnosis will be wrong. And when institutional metrics override lived experience often enough, we begin to doubt our own bodies—in medicine, and in art. The inner critic is often born there.

While it is tempting to see facts as inviolable and unchangeable, they are actually contextual, mobile, and relational. Scientific facts often begin as hunches or intuitions tested over time. Dancers relied on proprioception long before it was named by neuroscience.[3] Yogic breathing shaped somatic wisdom before research confirmed its effects.[4] Midwives located fetal positioning through touch before ultrasound visualized the same truths.[5] Embodied knowledge has frequently preceded scientific "discovery." This gap between what is sensed and what is proven is where faith enters: trust in the body, experience, and each other.

---

[3]Charles S. Sherrington, "On the Proprioceptive System, Especially in Its Reflex Aspect," *Brain* 29 (1906): 467–82.

[4]M. Pal et al., "Assessment of the Effects of Pranayama/Alternate Nostril Breathing on Parasympathetic Nervous System," *Journal of Clinical and Diagnostic Research* 7, no. 5 (2013): 821–3.

[5]Anne Katrine Klemmensen et al., "Abdominal Palpation to Determine Fetal Position at Labor Onset: A Test of Accuracy," *Acta Obstetricia et Gynecologica Scandinavica* 90, no. 6 (2011): 728–34.

How we define "fact" depends on who we are and what systems we trust. In a cultural moment rife with misinformation and institutional distrust, how we treat facts in our creative process becomes not just **philosophical** but **ethical**.

For this chapter, I am valuing the underdog of facts: **sensed, lived, and felt experiences**. Some of these are shared: sounds, objects, physics. Others are deeply personal: tight shoulders, a churning gut, shallow breath. Turning to the body as both metric and lacks checks and balances, but centers the human—which art demands. However, we do not simply believe everything we see, hear, feel, or think without interrogation. Separating fact from assumption, association, and adherence is key.

Sensory Facts

Our senses provide a small but reliable kinesphere of facts. I *see* my computer on a table. I *hear* birdlike sounds outside my window. These sensory details form my immediate, provable reality. Someone might enter the scene and say, "It must be nice to work to the birds singing." "It must be nice" is *projection*—a story layered onto the scene. "The birds are singing" is an assumption; perhaps it's a recording. "Work" is a guess, leaping from object to function.

Isolating what is observed from what is assumed trains us to see where interpretation has slipped in—a crucial practice in art-making. I may *assume* the sound is live birds. Knowing when I am *interpreting*, rather than *observing*, is a crucial skill; practicing it in daily life repatterns attention so it becomes automatic in art-making.[6]

Sensory facts ground us. We can observe a dancer's foot pressing strongly into the floor and their partner exhaling vigorously. These are **facts**. When we mistake interpretation for fact, we create art—and relationships—on unstable ground.

If we decide the force meant anger, and the exhale frustration, we've **interpreted**. There is no harm in interpretation if we know we're doing it. It is when we jump from observation to interpretation unconsciously that we fall into *assumption*. This collapse between observation and interpretation shows up constantly in the studio:

[6]Sarah Mae Sincero, "Bottom-Up Processing in Psychology: Definition and Examples," *Simply Psychology*, September 6, 2023, https://www.simplypsychology.org/bottom-up-processing.html. This article clearly explains the difference between bottom-up (data-driven, sensory-based) and top-down (schema-driven, knowledge-based) processing in perception, referencing key theorists James J. Gibson and Richard Gregory. It reviews supporting neuroscience and psychological research, showing how immediate sensory facts are built into reality via sensation, while context and prior experience shape perception through interpretation.

- "If they did *x*, that means they feel *y*."
- The performer who starts nodding at the note without metabolizing it.
- The designer who doesn't ask for details, believing "everything will be fine."

Interpreting sensed experience requires rigor. Are we observing—or reacting from training, bias, or fear? Are we seeing what is there, or what we expect to see?

Feelings as Facts

Feelings can be facts—and they can be examined. Emotion and accuracy are not mutually exclusive. The feeling is a fact; the story we tell about it is a construction that often attaches itself unconsciously.

"I am sad" is a statement derived from sensation but also a place for inquiry. My feeling is proven by my body, which feels heavy, listless, and heartsick. Weight, lethargy, fatigue, and emotional tenderness are my coordinates. I feel like crying and have an instinct to curl into a protective ball. **I don't need a story to validate it.** Blood sugar, sleep, or old wounds may contribute, but the *why* does not negate the fact. Yet we often use **stories** as metrics for **feelings**.

"Why are you sad?" you might ask.

Here is where things go awry. I feel sad, yes. This is a fact no one can dispute. The feeling is *what*; a story is *why*. When we conflate *what* with *why* in life or art, we mistake interpretation for fact, the birthplace of *assumption*.

What is the story? I may have a hormonal shift or a vitamin deficiency. The weather may be affecting me. An old emotional wound might be activated by a new injury. These are *stories*. They may be true. When people say, "You're not sad, you're hormonal," they use the story to *refute* the fact. But when we use it to stand in for the original facts, we lose valuable information and often invalidate ourselves and each other.

The desire to explain our feelings with a neat tale offers a mirage of control. If we understand why we feel something, perhaps we can avoid or inspire that feeling in the future. Recognizing *patterns* in our feelings is useful. Using the story to dismiss the feelings beneath it is dangerous.

"Why are you sad?" demands explanation. "I don't know" feels intolerable. So we offer a story and call it fact.

"My mother has cancer" is an understandable *reason*. It gives us a map. You can read a grief book, visit your mother, and research oncology. You'll repeat the story and receive validation. "That's awful!" they'll say. "Of course you're sad!" The more "credible" our story becomes, the less we see the smaller facts beneath it. Our aperture becomes so large that we no longer see the details. In art and life, this is where we lose context, inclusivity, and integrity. Consider if they asked:

"What is the saddest part?"

"The thought of her missing my wedding."

We could leave it there. But probing deeper, more material adheres to that fact. My friend is marrying her longtime girlfriend, a relationship her mother never celebrated. The wedding was a bid for acceptance but colored by anger and shame. Her mother's lack of acceptance amplified her feelings of isolation, fear, and rejection. She is also feeling grief for the mother she never had.

Anger, shame, isolation, fear, rejection, and grief. Each attached to different parts of the story. Some conflicting, others propping each other up.

If she never tells her complex story, the audience will fill in the blanks, creating a version that validates their own worldview. Their relationship with their mother will color her story and their interpretation will become "fact." This is how stories begin to masquerade as facts.

This is the same relationship we have with our audience. Sometimes we *want* them to perform the Mad Lib, adding their context and associations to create an experience that speaks directly to them. But to do this, we must leave *space*, blanks for them to fill in. We must either offer our unique details or provide room for theirs. The danger is when we do neither.

Reductive storytelling sacrifices contradiction and complexity for neatness and clarity. This denies us being fully seen. Our inner world is rarely summative; if we tidy our stories too quickly, we flatten not just our feelings but visibility. When we make space for specificity, tension, vulnerability, friction, and incongruity, we make room for our wholeness as artists and humans. When we see, and perhaps show, the threads and seams of our art, we offer the story that is truly ours, not a facsimile, placeholder, or simplistic cartoon of our truth. We reduce the space for assumption.

Untethering Facts from Assumptions

Facts that become stories too quickly smuggle in assumptions. These are *givens*, constructs, and priorities we've accepted without inspection. Some of the most persistent givens are "social facts,"[7] the norms that shape our behavior without consent. In art-making, compositional hierarchies abound. These are rules we don't question that scaffold our process. Many are shaped by whiteness, capitalism, heteronormativity, and ableism. We reproduce them mindlessly, unaware when they clash with our values.

---

[7]"A social fact is every way of acting, fixed or not, capable of exercising on the individual an external constraint… which is general over the whole of a given society while having an existence of its own, independent of its individual manifestations." Émile Durkheim, *The Rules of Sociological Method*, trans. W. D. Halls (Free Press, 1982).

A student was choreographing a solo about indecision. She wanted it to end ambiguously and vulnerably. Her movement and music ended simultaneously, followed by a blackout. The symmetry denied her an ambiguous ending. When I asked if she'd considered dancing past the music, into silence, through the darkness, she was shocked. The idea of moving past the music felt off-limits, even though no one had ever named it as a rule. She'd absorbed it through the norms of dance competition choreography. It was a significant risk to consider an unfamiliar choice, revealing options she'd never considered. She'd never allowed sensation or intuition to override inherited forms.

Social facts become ingrained in our bodies through repetition, judgment, and the avoidance of embarrassment, all at the service of *belonging*.

The desire to belong can overshadow the hunger to be seen.

When we mistake a social fact for a personal truth, the danger is not only to our innovation but to our integrity. **Art becomes less a conversation with the world and more a rehearsal of its rules.** If we only use "what we are allowed," we cannot make ourselves known. And if we remain hidden, can we really feel that holy sense of belonging?

- What assumptions are built into your creative habits?
- What do you hold as a fact about your art that might actually be a habit, tradition, or trend?

Barney O'Hanlon often discusses "un-reifying the world"—or **unnaming the known**. By renaming or unnaming, we disrupt entrenched, reactive, and unexamined thinking, making room for new meaning.

Try calling the cyclorama "the back door" or upstage "the abyss." "Head toward the back door" or "Move toward the abyss" sparks imagination. Naming the audience "the enemy," "God," or "the dungeon" radically shifts how we relate to performance.

Names carry association, and relying only on common ones dulls storytelling. In art, we don't just find truths; we stage, amplify, and sometimes distort them. That makes the responsibility for specificity even greater.

Two Case Studies in Renaming

In *Make Thick My Blood*,[8] a two-person adaptation of *Macbeth*, we decided Lady Macbeth was the dagger. When she entered, Macbeth saw a blade and responded to her as both a threat and an object. He held and used her body as if wielding a weapon. This exposed the rage within the relationship and raised the stakes. Her body became a conduit of violence, rejecting the traditional reading of her as a manipulative villain. It helped us invest in a trauma-informed, feminist interpretation.

---

[9]Make Thick My Blood, by Stephan Wolfert and Dawn Stern, directed and choreographed by Alexandra Beller, Theatre Row, New York, premiered July 29, 2022.

In my solo show *us*, I folded, wrapped, and twisted the American flag into a jump rope, tightrope, noose, and pageant gown. By recontextualizing it, the audience generated new associations. The flag activated their stories and became a portal to mine. This is how renaming shifts what feels fixed.

Renaming designs reality. *World-building* and *rule-making* are deliberate acts of authorship. When a director decides, "In *this* world, no one _______. Everyone ________. One can only _________ if they _________," they have established a shared reality with the audience, a conspiracy of facts that creates a unique environment.

Audience as Meaning Maker

Every fact we offer can be reframed, misread, or overdetermined by someone else's story. Our facts are shaped not only by *our* assumptions but also by *theirs*.

We cannot control that. **But we can account for it.**

If we present a "clean" story—"I am sad because my mother has cancer"—the audience might nod and move on. The meaning is handed to them, already digested. However, if we allow the story to remain porous, revealing contradictions, friction, or unresolved emotional knots, the audience becomes a coinvestigator.

This is the difference between closing a loop and holding it open. It is also the difference between presenting a norm as fact and inviting the audience to question both.

Closed-loop storytelling **delivers** meaning by telling the audience what to think and feel. Open-loop storytelling asks them to **participate**. It requires them to metabolize ambiguity, reflect on contradiction, and connect the work to their lived experience.

Taken to its endpoint, as in the work of Marina Abramović, the audience's perception becomes its defining force. In *Rhythm 0*,[9] for example, the premise is factual: The artist will remain passive for six hours, and the audience is free to do as they please. But that fact becomes volatile once paired with the assumptions, desires, fears, and ethics the audience brings. The artist does not deliver the meaning of the piece—it is excavated by those witnessing it, and even more so by those participating.

[9]Marina Abramović, *Rhythm 0*, performance, Galleria Studio Morra, Naples, 1974.

From Fact to Form

Once we've named our facts, we still don't own them. Facts take shape through interaction—between body and story, artist and frame, audience and moment. A fact can anchor us, but it can also mislead, especially when it's inherited, unexamined, or mistaken for a given.

This is the work:

- Notice which facts are felt, which are borrowed, and which are assumed.
- Clarify what your body is telling you, even if it cannot be externally verified.
- Name the conditions under which your facts form.
- Then decide, deliberately, how to offer them to others.

A useful process might look like this:

- **Identify:** What is the fact—sensory, somatic, or social—that you're relying on?
- **Interrogate:** Is it stable, habitual, cultural, or deeply personal?
- **Reframe:** What shifts if you treat it as assumption, interpretation, or invitation instead?
- **Apply:** Let that reframing guide a choice in structure, movement, or staging.
- **Observe:** Notice how facts mutate when embodied—what holds, dissolves, or surprises?

Every choice you make—every material, gesture, or phrase—is a fact the audience will absorb. These guide attention, frame meaning, and distort, isolate, or amplify certain elements. You are always shaping what will be believed, questioned, or missed.

You don't control interpretation, but you influence its architecture. **You shape the environment in which meaning happens.**

Consider your facts consciously. Hold them with care. Let them adapt. And when you're ready, build from them something only *you* could make.

Takeaway: Facts live in the body, in culture, and in form. Making art is not about proving what's true—it's sensing, shaping, and questioning what's already operating.

In Practice: Tips About Facts

1. **Start with the sensory.**
   Begin with what you can directly observe or feel. See, hear, smell, touch, taste—sensory information offers reliable coordinates. Let the body be a barometer. If it doesn't land in your body, it won't land in the work.
   Ask: Do I trust this sensation? Do my collaborators trust my perception?

2. **Separate *facts* from *story*.**
   Notice what is observable or felt and what is layered with narrative. A flinch is a fact. "They're hurt by me" is a story built on that fact. You don't need to discard story; just know when you're telling one.
   Ask: What do I know? What am I assuming? What else could be true?

3. **Look for the givens.**
   Many "facts" in creative processes are actually defaults, traditions, or social norms. Examine the inherited rules you're following without realizing it.
   Ask: What choices feel automatic? What would happen if I didn't do it that way?

4. **Break feelings into felt truths.**
   Overwhelm often signals a cluster of sensations and interpretations. Zoom in. Disaggregate.
   Ask: What am I actually feeling? Where is it in my body? Naming small truths can ease emotional flood.

5. **Untether facts from assumptions.**
   Facts often carry assumptions with them. That doesn't make them less useful, just heavier. We're performing in a theater; that's the fact. *Using the stage* is the assumption. What other places in the theater hold energy, tension, or surprise? Let the environment speak before assigning it meaning.
   Ask: What part of this is observable, and what part is inherited? If this weren't the default, what would I choose?

6. **Rename to reimagine.**
   Language shapes perception. What happens if "the mirror" becomes "the portal"? "The audience" becomes "the witness"? "The bed" becomes "a trap"? Try renaming spaces, objects, or roles to shift your relationship to them. Let function be *discovered*, not *dictated*.
   Ask: What changes between us when I rename it? What story becomes more likely?

7. **Leave space for the unknown.**
   Let ambiguity have a place in your work. Not everything needs to be explained or resolved. Uncertainty is fertile. Wonder aloud. Pause before answering. Let some meanings remain suspended.
   Ask: Where am I rushing to explain? What would happen if I left this unresolved?

8. **Shape meaning through detail.**
   Every material, rhythm, pause, or gesture carries meaning, whether you place it there or not. Use small, intentional facts to build the scaffolding of your world. Coherence emerges through the accumulation of choices.
   Ask: What am I reinforcing through repetition? What small fact could clarify or complicate this moment?

9. **Claim your fiction.**
   Acknowledge your authorship. Fiction isn't the *opposite* of truth; it's a structure built *from* it. Let your inventions be aware of themselves. Don't disguise interpretation as proof. Make your framing deliberate, not defensive.
   Ask: What am I presenting as fact that is actually interpretation? Where am I shaping meaning but pretending I'm not?

10. **Stay curious about certainty.**
    When something feels absolutely true, slow down. Certainty often masks assumptions.
    Ask: How did I come to know this? Is this truth, training, or desire? Let certainty become a site of inquiry, not a conclusion.

The Story You're Telling… and Another One You Could

Fact	Belief	Alternate Belief
What is observable or happening?	What interpretation or meaning are you assigning?	What else might be true (a new frame)?
Example: She turns away. Her back is visible. Her head tilts down.	She's withdrawing. She doesn't want to engage.	She's guarding something private. She's inviting us to see a new side of her.

Figure 7.1 *The Story You're Telling… and Another One You Could.* Table guiding reflection from observable fact to belief and alternate interpretation in artistic perception.

From the Field: The Career I Didn't Want—and the Life I Already Had

Figure 7.2 Alexandra Beller.
Reproduced with permission of the Ginger-B3ardsmen.

I was sitting in my living room when the call came: my Off-Broadway show might move to Broadway. The estimated fee was the exact amount I had calculated would send my two children to college. I jumped up and, alone in the room, I blurted out, "I don't want a tenure-track job!"

The words startled me. They weren't a reasoned decision but a fact my body delivered before my mind arrived. For years, I'd chased a tenure-track job. I'd earned my MFA and CMA to strengthen my candidacy, sent out applications consistently, and had convinced myself this was my ultimate dream job.

Meanwhile, my freelance life brimmed with the very things I wanted from a university position: teaching high-level thinkers, mentoring artists, choreographing, writing, and collaborating with experts. I loved my work, but I kept applying for jobs so I wouldn't get "off track." When I saw that number on the calculator, it hit me: The *tenure-track job* was a placeholder—a container that *stood in* for my desires. I had manifested everything I wanted from an academic position, except a plan for my children's education. I was already living my dream, yet I kept pursuing "my dream job."

This realization changed not only how I saw my own career but also how I mentor others. I began to notice how often we bundle multiple desires into one monolithic goal. We slap a name on it—"get into a big company," "sell a TV pilot," "lose weight," "get a grant"—and devote ourselves to chasing that *label*, not the needs. Meanwhile, the smaller truths inside often remain unspoken and therefore unreachable.

With my mentorship clients, I began dissecting their goals and examining the fragments. For example:

Client: I want to be in a big dance company.

Me: Can you name five reasons why this matters?

Client: I want to travel. I want rich, creative collaborations. I want to dance every day. I want to *say* I make my living dancing. I want to be surrounded by artists.

Once the container opens, the truth spills out. Suddenly the "big company" isn't the only answer; it's one option among many. We can brainstorm ways to meet those desires *immediately*: traveling for summer festivals, dancing daily by teaching or assisting, collaborating with an ensemble of friends. When we treat goals as facts, they harden into fixation rather than being an ongoing negotiation with our evolving future. When we unpack them, their contents come into view; more often than not, they're already within reach.

Guidance: Instinct and Analysis

> If what Picasso proposed is true, that the first stroke on the canvas is always a mistake, it is best to get on with the mistake, without delay, earlier rather than later. Write one sentence, make one choice or point at something and say "Yes." And then, as the process unfolds, and as long as I keep at it and stay attentive and resolute, making adjustments to each mistake, things eventually fall into place.
>
> (Anne Bogart, *What's the Story*)[10]

We've all heard about right- versus left-brain thinking, much of which is reductive.[11] More useful is to consider the relationship between instinct and analysis. Both are essential to the creative process, but they rarely play well together. Each has a job. Each has a danger.

Instinct is generative. It produces images, impulses, associations, and risk. It says, "What if?" It thrives in uncertainty and invention. Its danger is, when questioned too soon, it shuts down. A free flow of gut instinct, wild imaginings, and subconscious offerings is abruptly halted by questions like, "Is it good?" or "Where is this going?" Judging too soon blocks the creative currents that allow work to emerge organically. We can scold, shame, and bully our daydreamer-self into silence.

Analysis is structural. It asks what serves, what repeats, and what can be cut. It pesters us for a *why*. Without it, work lacks clarity and rigor. When we approach material analytically—asking, "Does this fit here?" or "What can I cut?"—we need a clear eye and a steady heart. Its danger is, when it arrives too early, it suffocates invention; when it arrives too late, we cling to what we love though the piece does not need it. The clear eye of analysis requires emotion to step aside.

So how do we find the flow between these two essential but conflicting forces? **Rhythm.** Instinct and analysis must take turns, showing up where they thrive. We must learn which best supports which moment of our process. This is an ecosystem unique to each artist.

I begin with **instinct**: intuition, viscerality, and uncensored imagination. I let wild, unpredictable, and indefensible imagery enter the room. I partner with absurdity, resist ascribing meaning too quickly, and allow the work to surface without defense. Keeping my inner critic at bay allows my playful, weird, intuitive side to drive, activating unexpected possibilities. Yet instinct alone is not enough. First

---

[10] Anne Bogart, *What's the Story: Essays About Art, Theater, and Storytelling* (Routledge, 2014).

[11] Sarah McKay, "The Creative-Right vs Analytical-Left Brain Myth: Debunked!," *Dr. Sarah McKay Neuroscientist Blog*, October 24, 2023. This is an accessible yet research-based blog post that dismantles the right-brain/left-brain myth and explains how creative thinking involves integrated brain activity, demonstrating how judgment can interfere with creative flow.

impulses are high in truth but also habit. Just because something comes from the body does not mean it escapes scrutiny.

So I turn to **analysis**: critical observation, tough questions, and ruthless editing. I step back. I test the structure. I cut sentimentality and people-pleasing. Analysis is not creativity's enemy; it is its sculptor. It sharpens, clarifies, and refines what instinct generates. In rehearsal, analysis asks: Does this moment serve the whole arc? Is this gesture anchored in history? Do we need stillness here instead of movement? When I step back, resisting nostalgia and attachment, I can lean into craft, architecture, feedback, and logic.

Other artists prefer to begin with analysis—researching, building text, creating image banks, outlines, and schedules. If facts spark your imagination, begin there. But eventually, intuition and divergent thinking must enter the room. The structure must be disrupted. The body must contradict the outline. An image must appear that doesn't fit the plan.

This might mean turning off the critical lens and experiencing the piece physically. Watching a run and noticing: Where am I bored? What section makes me tense? Where does my breath catch? What part of the stage pulls my eye? What moment makes me lean forward? Don't ask why. Don't fix it yet. Just register it. Let the body respond before the mind explains. Instinct taps into the subconscious, responding to images, sounds, and feelings. It asks, "What if we… ?" It teases, reveals, and invents in ways we cannot predict.

You might try the following:

- Letting performers distort the plan.
- Removing music and seeing what remains.
- Moving through the material in silence.
- Speaking the text while walking, lying down, or out of order.

The key is not choosing one over the other but keeping them distinct, giving each its own time to work. **Instinct** asks you not to overthink—to play, wander, and not know. It needs protection from criticism, rigidity, and literalism—from yourself and from others. **Analysis** asks for tough love, releasing attachment and seeing the piece with clear eyes.

Picasso's idea that "the first stroke is always a mistake" reminds me that mistakes are not failures but beginnings. Instinct frees us to make the mark; analysis refines it until it resonates. The rhythm between them—fluid, imperfect, honest—is where the real work lives.

Tuning In: The Body of Evidence

This practice invites you to notice what feels automatic, challenge what feels inevitable, and discover what emerges when movement breaks from assumption.

1. **Notice physical facts.**
   Move freely for a few minutes. Observe what repeats: shapes, qualities, rhythms, directions.
   - Do you use a wide stance?
   - Avoid backward travel?
   - Hold your ribs tightly?

   Resist naming. Let the "facts" of your habits reveal themselves.
2. **Disrupt the facts.**
   Choose one and actively contradict it.
   - Narrow your stance and explore imbalance.
   - Travel only backward.
   - Let the ribs lead a breathy dance.

   Pause: What does the disruption feel like—awkward, freeing, comical, vulnerable? What feelings surface?
3. **Test the mechanics.**
   Layer anatomical explorations:
   - **Spine:** flex, extend, side-shift, rotate. Where is there ease? Where is there avoidance?
   - **Joints:** move your hips, shoulders, and ankles through their full range. Which pathways feel habitual?
   - **Balance/Weight:** shift initiations (heel-first, toe-first, off-center). Let yourself tip, sink, teeter. What happens to your breath and focus?

   Notice which "facts" of your structure stabilize you and which limit you.
4. **Sense meaning in shifts.**
   Play with subtle postures and notice emotional or narrative tones:
   - Shoulders raised toward ears might add tension, alertness, or hesitation.
   - Head dropped, shoulders rounded might evoke grief, retreat, or boredom.

- Chest open, arms extended might invite expressiveness, exposure, invitation, or demand.
- Weight on your outer feet might signal hesitation, detachment, or lightness.

Explore micro-adjustments:

- A tilt of the chin.
- The placement of your eyes.
- Your breath volume.
- A gesture of the hands.

Ask:

- Do certain shapes evoke any archetypes or characters?
- Do any postures spark memories or emotions?

Studio Lab: Facts as Points of Leverage

This practice invites you to treat facts, ideas, and assumptions as compositional tools: something to build from, question, bend, or explode. What happens when you hold a clear idea, then stretch it to its edges?

1. **Establish your starting point.**
   Choose an idea for a piece. **Express it in a single, clear sentence:**
   - "This work explores how trauma lives in the body."
   - "This piece centralizes uncertainty by asking performers to say 'yes, and' to every prompt."
2. **Deconstruct the language.**
   What memories, sensations, contradictions, or relationships do your core concepts evoke? Zoom out beyond your initial meaning.
   Example: *For Trauma and the Body*
   - **Trauma** → rupture, repetition, protection, disassociation, imprint, alertness, absence, memory loops, freeze
   - **The Body** → flesh, threshold, breath, pulse, scars, contact, sensation, resistance, orientation, fragmentation, boundary
   - **Tensions between them** → numbness, vigilance, craving safety, slow reentry, involuntary gesture, misrecognition, mutual care, mistrust, reaching without arriving

   (You're not looking for clarity, just layers.)
3. **Translate concepts into formal elements.**
   Pick at least one lens—space, structure, relationship, or kinesphere.
   Ask: How can I translate these words into a structure? For example, using "Trauma and the Body" as the concept:
   Space
   - A solo is contained inside a taped square, while the rest of the space remains untouched.
   - Performers inhabit different light zones; when one enters another's space, they lose visibility.
   - Corners are frequented more than center; thresholds are crossed, then immediately retracted from.

Structure

- A movement sequence is taught and retaught, but never completed the same way.
- Each section ends before it resolves; music or light cuts out mid-action.
- Performers follow an external countdown that overrides their internal pacing.

Relationships

- A duet where one dancer leads without looking at the other.
- Trios form and dissolve without explanation; eye contact is avoided or overstated.
- Proximity increases across the piece but never results in touch.

Kinesphere

- Movements start with large reach but end in flinch, curl, or hesitation.
- Dancers trace lines on their own skin or repeat self-soothing gestures while navigating space.
- One arm moves expansively while the other remains inert; asymmetry accumulates.

4. **Challenge a process assumption.**
   We all inherit unspoken norms. What's one you've internalized—about rehearsal, clarity, process, or power? **Examples:**
   - "The audience must understand everything."
   - "Rehearsals should be linear and goal driven."
   - "All dancers must contribute equally."

   Flip it:
   - Make a piece where ambiguity is the *goal.*
   - Start from the end and build backward.
   - Assign roles randomly and let power imbalance shape the piece.

5. **Build a *process collage.***
   Collect the concepts, images, and provocations that have surfaced and design a process.
   - Rehearse in silence.
   - Work from text that dissolves into gesture.
   - Assign tasks via dream journaling.
   - Make a score where space dictates emotion, not the reverse.

   Let each constraint be a **fact**: something to shape, resist, or respond to.

Pagework: Writing into Facts

Freewrite on some or all of these questions.

1. **Recall a recent project or idea.**
   Write about a moment when instinct carried you. Then write about a moment when analysis shaped the outcome. What did each offer? Did they ever fight each other?

2. **Think of a creative goal you've been holding—finishing a piece, landing a commission, publishing a book.**
   Break it into smaller desires. Which parts of the goal could you begin meeting right now?

3. **Track your creative rhythm over a few days.**
   When do you notice instinct leading? When does analysis take over? Do you separate them, or do they blur? How does this rhythm support or strain your process?

4. **Write about a moment when instinct and analysis clashed.**
   What did your gut say? What did your mind argue? How did you navigate it then, and what might you try differently now?

5. **Remember a time when your idea of a "fact" shifted—about your work, your process, or yourself.**
   What triggered the change? What opened up once the truth moved?

Movements + Maps: Unraveling Facts

This score invites you to explore the interplay between facts and assumptions in your creative process. Grounding your work in simple, provable truths, then unraveling their stories, invites curiosity and ambiguity. Let the facts guide you but also question them.

1. **Choose a grounding fact.**
   Create one simple, verifiable fact. It can be physical, environmental, or conceptual. **Examples:**
   - "This dance is centered on weight shift."
   - "This piece begins with a single repeated word."
   - "The audience sees only shadows and no bodies for the entire piece."
2. **Identify attached assumptions.**
   Make up two different associations for your grounding fact—they can be emotional, symbolic, aesthetic, or conceptual. **Examples:**
   - **Fact:** "My weight shifts left to right."
   - **Assumption 1:** "This suggests indecision or imbalance."
   - **Assumption 2:** "Constant weight shift will be exciting and vigorous!"
3. **Work with the bare fact.**
   Develop a short study, through movement, text, image, or staging, that focuses *only* on the fact. Resist interpreting or embellishing. What happens when the fact stands alone?
4. **Layer the assumption.**
   Choose one assumption. First reinforce it. Then undermine it. Repeat with the other.
   - Assumption: "Indecision"
     - **Reinforce it:** Hesitate before each shift.
     - **Undermine it:** Make the shift sudden or decisive.
   - Assumption: "Exciting and vigorous"
     - **Reinforce it:** Accelerate, add percussion. Explore sweat, impact, and drive.
     - **Undermine it:** Keep the rhythm but strip it of energy—make the same shifts slow, dry, or monotone. Maintain the form but empty out the excitement.

5. **Rename and reframe.**
   Experiment with naming. Call the weight shift a "negotiation" or the shadows a "memory." How does this influence the feeling or reading of the piece?

6. **Reflect.**
   Ask:
   - What stayed true about the fact?
   - What stories did I attach, and how did they evolve?

Contributor's Note: Ongoing Excerpt

by Deborah Hay

Addressing my physical body as a multicellular, nonlinear, ephemeral entity, I eliminated the singularly coherent individual who dances. By manufacturing this being in 1970, dancing became alive and all-inclusive for the first time in my life.

To be safe in framing the language to describe my approach to dancing, I formed questions beginning with, "What if… ?" And to cover my ass further I included, "What if every cell *has the potential…* ?" My questions reflected how I translated what I was experiencing as I danced. They amazed me because I never consciously thought about the reality they suggested. For instance, "What if every cell in my body at once has the potential to perceive wisdom while remaining positionless about what wisdom is or what it looks like?" Who thinks such things? Who wouldn't want to return to how this inquiry exposed one's bodily potential daily? Making no assumptions about the validity of my experience, I tested the same question alone and with others, sometimes the same question for years.

Fifty years later, I realize how these questions have choreographed all of me. Trusting my dance is currently without question.

Studio Provocations: Questioning Facts

> The most interesting art is born out of the tension between the known and the unknown—the tension that emerges when we stop rushing toward answers and allow ourselves to dwell in the questions.
>
> (Anne Bogart, *What's the Story*)[12]

Subjectivity and Perception

What are the clearest facts about this piece right now?

- How do you know—what did you actually see, hear, or feel?

Where would another fact help you clarify, disrupt, or shift this moment?

- What concrete detail is missing?

Is this section overdetermined by facts?

- What would happen if you removed one?
- What if you added mystery, contradiction, or fantasy instead?

Experiential Inquiry

What am I asking the audience to "know" in this moment?

- Is it sensory, narrative, emotional, or ideological?

When do I want them to feel certain or uncertain?

- What have I done in the staging, rhythm, or information flow to create that?

Where do I want them to fill in the blank?

- What am I deliberately withholding?
- How can I stage it so they piece it together themselves?

What happens if the audience knows something the performers do not?

- How does that shift tension, power, or empathy?

---

[12]Bogart, *What's the Story: Essays About Art, Theater, and Storytelling.*

Facts and Assumptions

What is the most compelling fact driving this section?

- Can I point to it in the body, text, or staging?
- What assumptions might be hitching a ride?

Which "rule" or given have I accepted without questioning?

- Who taught me this rule?
- What happens if I break it for one rehearsal?

Which fact in this section is armor?

- What is it protecting?

Somatic Facts

What is my breath, weight, or pace in this moment?

Try: Change one of them. What shifts?

Which facts do I want the audience to sense?

- What in the staging, rhythm, or effort makes it legible?

What facts can be sensed through something other than sight or sound?

- Through proximity? Duration? Stillness? Effort?

Renaming/Unnaming

If I renamed the most obvious thing in this scene (the floor, the air), what new meaning would surface?

Try: Run the scene once using the new name out loud in rehearsal directions. Notice how behavior shifts.

What shifts if I call the movement the "evidence," "lie," or "confession"?

Try: Perform the phrase three times—once as evidence, once as a lie, once as a confession—without changing the choreography. Only shift intention.

Tension/Catalyst

What fact am I hiding from the audience, or from myself?

Which contradiction in this piece could be amplified rather than resolved?

What fact would change everything if it arrived incomplete—or ten seconds earlier or later?

8

Faith

Before You Begin: Priming Curiosity About Faith

Take a breath. Consider these questions. Let them settle in your body before moving forward. They are not for solving, but for sensing.

Who do I have near-total faith in right now?

What in my body lets me know it's safe to move forward?

When do I trust myself, and when do I experience self-doubt?

Where in my life have I followed my intuition, and what was the outcome?

Why is it easier to trust the unknown in some areas of my life than in others?

How do I respond to *not knowing*—shrink from it, reach toward it, or wait inside it?

Groundwork: The Compass of Faith

> All writing, all art, is an act of faith. If one tries to contribute to human understanding, how can that be called decadent? It's like saying a declaration of love is an act of decadence. Any work of art, provided it springs from a sincere motivation to further understanding between people, is an act of faith and therefore is an act of love.
>
> (Truman Capote, *Conversations with Capote*)[1]

Arriving at Yes

I trudged to the kitchen, uninspired. Though the fridge was sparse and I had no plan, I started cooking. I had leftover chicken and started making couscous, but had no other plan. I saw an onion, so I sautéed it. I added garlic and spices and deglazed the pan with chicken stock. I added the chicken and started reducing it. I saw a lemon, so I added lemon juice, which prompted me to add lemon zest to the couscous. Suddenly inspired, I poured the couscous into the chicken pan, added a bunch of Parmesan, and ended up with a delicious couscous "risotto" that has since been added to my repertoire.

I was surprised at how much I'd enjoyed making the meal. Despite starting with nothing—no plan, no inspiration—I had a spontaneous, creative experience, following the flow rather than directing it toward an outcome. This process mirrors my best experiences in art-making: starting from the unknown, trusting the process, and allowing the work to guide me. I trust that starting from *nothing* will lead to *something* and that my role is not to know everything but to *stay alert* to possibilities.

Faith is not the confidence that the meal will be delicious; it's the act of chopping the onion anyway.

Much like cooking without a recipe, art-making invites us to trust our instincts, materials, and improvisational fortitude. Faith is the thread that connects these elements, helping us transform the unknown into something profoundly nourishing.

I have stood in a silent studio with dancers awaiting my next instruction, having no idea what to say. The next step often feels like a chasm. I swallow my panic and wait, trusting the silence to bring something—a sound, a gesture, a breath. It always does. This moment, like so many others, is an act of faith. Faith, in these moments, isn't about me; it's about the process, the art, and the present moment.

This kind of lostness in the rehearsal room can feel good. Possibility is alive and awake. Anything might happen. It's different from the lostness of "I have no idea where I am or where I'm going," which can feel fraudulent, even humiliating. This uncertainty is fertile ground for faith; it requires a

---

[1]Truman Capote, *Conversations with Capote*, ed. Lawrence Grobel (New American Library, 1985).

willingness to make decisions, knowing they will lead *somewhere*, even if the destination is obscured. Faith in art requires delighting in the unknown. Where **facts** provide grounding, **faith** asks us to shed certainty, trusting that something valuable will emerge without needing a road map or clear next step.

Love and Faith

Faith is a type of unconditional love—a devotion to what has yet to emerge, without requiring proof. The question often arises: Is love a *feeling*? It certainly *activates* feeling, but I think love is bigger. Not a single feeling but the state that gives rise to many—bliss, fear, tenderness, grief. The feelings shift, but the state remains steady underneath.

And what of love that is not for a person but for our art?

There's a specific sensation to sitting in a studio or a theater, watching and loving the thing you made. It differs from romantic, platonic, or parental love; it is unlike the love of students or of country. It is uniquely tied to creation. In many ways, it's *self-love*; what we are looking at is both *of* us and *beyond* us. Through our art, we can fall in love with ourselves unabashedly and uninhibitedly, something society often shames out of us. As with all great loves, we are asked to surrender to it, to learn from it, to change because of it, to accept its flaws, and celebrate its development. Faith sustains this love, keeping us present when doubt looms. Together, faith and love create the foundation for honest, resonant art.

Faith versus Belief

Faith and belief are often conflated, but they arise from different parts of us. Belief leans on the recognition of what *has* worked, the knowledge that this will happen because it has *happened before*. **Faith lives beyond precedent.** It is what we draw on when there is no evidence yet.

This distinction is echoed across creative disciplines. Studies of highly creative individuals consistently point to tolerance for uncertainty, willingness to take risks, and the suspension of premature judgment as core capacities in novel thinking.[2] These qualities are practiced in conditions where proof does not yet exist. Faith is not mystical; it is a creative competency. Psychologist Ellen Langer describes a similar stance in her research on mindfulness: The willingness to notice novelty and embrace uncertainty, rather than rush to closure, is what allows new possibilities to emerge. She writes that when we stay open to multiple perspectives, we "become architects of possibility rather than prisoners of certainty."[3]

---

[2]Teresa M. Amabile, "Componential Theory of Creativity," Harvard Business School Working Paper 12-096 (2012), 5–6 (on "flexible cognitive styles" and "suspension of judgment").

[3]Ellen J. Langer, *Counterclockwise: Mindful Health and the Power of Possibility* (Ballantine Books, 2009).

Belief says, "I've done this before, so I can again."

Faith says, "I've never done this, and I still choose to begin."

When I feel faith, it rarely arrives as *confidence*. It comes through **gesture**: walking into the studio, opening the notebook, saying yes to a process whose outcome I can't see. It is an **act**, not a **certainty**. I have also felt belief without faith: leaning on past experience while feeling quietly disconnected from the new work. In those moments, faith must be rebuilt.

Faith partners with the unknown to yield what we cannot yet imagine. This partnership is the foundation of an artist's resilience. Doubt often walks hand in hand with faith, whispering, "What if this doesn't work?" This can be a signal to pause, listen, and recommit to the process.

Faith is a choice we make again and again in the face of uncertainty.

When convinced we're making our "worst work ever," we could lean on past metrics and reassure ourselves: "I've done this before, I'll do it again." But if the last piece's success is what carries us through this one, we're not inventing—we're repeating. And repetition does not demand faith.

Faith arises in risk. Risk disorients us: Up feels like down, direction disappears, the old coordinates no longer apply. Doubt enters not just as thought but as sensation: Where am I? What am I making? This dissonance is proof that we are in new territory. Faith doesn't resolve the dissonance but steadies us inside it, a counterweight, holding us upright when the process tilts. Like a gyroscope, faith spins quietly at the center, offering orientation when reference points vanish.

The Messy Middle: Resisting Certainty

Robert Wilson famously said, "Until it's good, it's always bad." I try to resist this binary, but it stalks me. When I'm watching a piece that isn't yet working, I feel the magnetic pull of good/bad, right/wrong, yes/no. It takes strength to stay in the messy middle and not seek certainty.

These binaries seduce us with their simplicity: If I can decide what is "good" or "bad," I'll know what to do. But the hard work is to stay in the ambiguous zone, where not knowing becomes a craft, cultivated through repetition, attention, and time. We get better at *not knowing* by sitting with it, noticing when we reach for false closure, and building tolerance for silence and friction. In the continuum between control and surrender, we ideally live in the middle.

Long-term relationships make this visible. In their research on romantic partnerships, the Gottmans[4] identify four patterns—criticism, defensiveness, contempt, and stonewalling—that predict collapse.

[4]John Gottman, *The Seven Principles for Making Marriage Work* (Orion, 2000).

These impulses arise in art-making, too: the urge to prejudge, defend, withdraw, or dismiss. Faith asks for another response. Can we stay *vulnerable* when we're scared? Can we remain *curious* when silence urges us to decide?

Think of the moment with a partner or collaborator when you've just said something vulnerable and are waiting for their response. The silence stretches. You want to fill it—finish their sentence, coax them forward. The steadier choice is to wait. To trust that what needs to emerge will emerge. Faith in the studio asks the same: presence without coercion, patience with the unknown.

The messy middle is not just temporal; it's spatial. We circle familiar pathways. We return to certain facings. We hover near habits—corners we begin from, directions we prefer, gestures we trust. The body starts repeating before the mind has decided. We can interrupt these habits, leaning into the unfamiliar as a method for summoning faith. Switch facings. Work at a diagonal. Sit when you'd usually stand. Begin from the opposite side of the room. These aren't tricks; they're choices that can rewire how possibility moves through us. Breaking a spatial pattern can shift a creative one.

The pressure to make it all mean something is heavy. There's dopamine in meaning; it feels like arrival. But forcing clarity too soon flattens the work. The metaphors become too tidy, the contradictions collapse. Faith means letting the work stay illegible longer than we want, trusting that meaning will arrive—not through assertion but through lived time.

Culture, Practice, and the Right to Choose

For many of us, the word *faith* carries memories of being shamed, coerced, or diminished for doubting. Doubt may have been framed as failure. Faith may have been invoked to override embodied knowing or silence critical thought.

The kind of faith I'm naming here lives elsewhere. It is not a test of worth, talent, or virtue. Creative faith cannot be imposed. It arises from within and returns when nourished—not as a reward but as a relationship. It is private, personal, and lived. And like any relationship, it can be nurtured through attention, ritual, and loyalty.

Across cultures, there are practices that honor this kind of faith. In Japan, the concept of *ma* (間)[5] reveres the charged interval—the pause between movements, the breath before the next sound. In art-making, *ma* is trust stretched across silence. It assumes that what has not yet appeared is still part of the composition.

In Ghanaian philosophy, *sankofa*[6] teaches that returning is part of moving forward. It invites us to retrieve what was left behind—not as retreat, but as continuity. Sometimes faith isn't ahead

---

[5]Arata Isozaki, *Ma: Space-Time in Japan* (Weatherhill, 1979).

[6]Molefi Kete Temple, "Sankofa: Rituals of Memory and Return," in *Africanisms in American Culture*, ed. Joseph E. Holloway (Indiana University Press, 2005), 127–43.

of us; it waits behind us, buried in something we left too soon: a project, a practice, a version of ourselves.

These are not metaphors but cultural technologies—living evidence that the human impulse to hold faith without certainty is ancestral.

So if the word *faith* has ever been used to wound you, you are allowed to reclaim it. Let it mean attentiveness, patience, or returning. Let it be something you define through *use* rather than *inheritance*.

The Anatomy of Your Faith

Faith isn't a mood, a trait, or a moral achievement. It is alive and responsive. It has seasons, habits, and needs. Like a body, it requires care. Like breath, it can it can shift something inside us.

It grows through experimentation, inquiry, and practice. Our faith-building mechanisms are unique, but patterns emerge. See if one—or more—resonates with your faith anatomy.

The Immersive: Thrives Surrounded by Other People's Art

Some artists remember their faith by stepping into a theater or gallery and witnessing **others at work**. They sit in the audience and remember: *Art matters. I care about this.* Their faith pulses through proximity. Saturation, conversation, and exposure nourish them.

The Solitary: Requires Space and Time to Listen Inward

For some, faith lives in **quiet**. It shows up in solitude: long walks, blank pages, and studio days without goals. They need to listen to themselves through the silence. Unpressured time restores creative trust.

The Playmaker: Revels in Silliness, Experimentation, or Sensual Immersion

For others, faith emerges through **play**: unrehearsed movement, ideas that feel "crazy," the delightful chaos of making a mess and laughing mid-process. Their faith is intuitive, sensual, and improvisational. It grows when they follow their strange and gorgeous impulses without justification.

The Structuralist: Grounds in Systems, Rituals, or Frameworks

For some, faith grows through **structure**. Repetition, consistency, and loyalty create the grounding and enough stability to take risks. That may be daily writing time, regularity in their studio praxis, or the rhythm of returning to the same questions. Roots deepen through consistency.

The Witness: Connects by Seeing the Impact Their Work Has on Others

Some are fed by the role of community. For them, faith is **relational**. It lives in the exchange. Feedback, collaboration, co-working, and ongoing artistic conversations nourish it.

None of these are fixed types. Most of us recognize all of them in some measure. But one may be vital right now—a place to focus your attention.

Finding Yes

I once believed faith would arrive like a muse or miracle. More often, it comes in sideways: through habit, patience, and the choice to stay present when doubt is loud. Learning to sit with doubt as *one* feeling among *many*—without letting it hijack attention—has become foundational to my artistry. Faith is saying yes to the relationship with art. A yes even when walking away feels easier. A yes to vulnerability, to sticking with it, to trusting that love can carry you through the hard parts.

If you find yourself lacking faith, begin with **what brings you closer to yourself**— the *listening* part that moves toward creation without demanding proof. Start with the smallest thing you believe in: the body's capacity, your training, your collaborators, or the certainty that art always reveals itself over time.

Try sitting with one of these questions:

- When was the last time you felt faith in your art? What was happening around you? Can you re-create any of these conditions?
- What kinds of activities, people, or spaces make it easier for you to trust your work?
- What conditions drain your faith or invite doubt?
- What kind of nourishment does your creative faith need right now?

Faith is not a light you carry. It's the act of walking in the dark, again and again, with your palms open.

Takeaway: Faith is alive—an ongoing relationship with what you cannot yet name. It asks for participation—attention, patience, and courage. It invites you back, again and again, to the work you love.

In Practice: Tips About Faith

1. **Begin without proof.**
   Start before you're ready. Begin even when you don't know what the piece is about, resources are thin, and you have no production booked.

2. **Pause instead of pushing.**
   In moments of friction or fog, resist the urge to force. Wait. Welcome silence or stillness as advisors. Listen for your personal rhythm of inspiration, motivation, and action.

3. **Risk something small.**
   Take a step that feels disorienting. Try a new approach, a less polished idea, a structure you don't yet understand. Risk is the condition that makes faith *necessary*.

4. **Notice your defaults.**
   Where do you tend to begin? How do you respond to *not knowing*? What do you repeat unconsciously? Noticing our defaults can illuminate where control has overtaken surrender and flow.

5. **Treat doubt as data.**
   Don't rush to resolve doubt. Ask what it might be pointing to. Doubt often signals that you're risking a new method or moving into uncharted territory.

6. **Let the work respond.**
   Let the work answer your questions. Don't complete it too quickly. Let it confuse you, be unclear, and change its mind.

7. **Find faith in the body.**
   When you can't find it in your thinking, look for faith in your breath, posture, movement, or gesture.

8. **Reflect and track.**
   After each session, ask: What helped me stay in the work? What pulled me out? Learn your creative metabolism.

Practices by Faith Architecture

The Immersive

1. Immerse yourself in others' work. Let excellence, risk, and originality spark your belief in what art can do.
2. Choose a moment from another artist's work that stirred you. Let it remind you what matters.

The Solitary

1. Simplify. Step away from external noise. Let silence amplify your voice.
2. Take a walk. Lie on the floor. Rent space without needing to produce.

The Playmaker

1. Play with materials. Make a mess. Invite absurdity, inconsistency, and contradiction.
2. Move, dance, yell, laugh. Revel in being unapologetic and uninhibited.

The Structuralist

1. Create a structure of obstacles, restrictions, and constraints. Let the shape give you a way in.
2. Use repetition to rebuild trust.

The Witness

1. Let someone into your process. Choose what kind of feedback you want and when. Ask for reflection instead of evaluation.
2. Invest in collaboration, community, and conversation. Find a mentor, join a group, create opportunities for ongoing exchange.

From the Field: *egg*

Figure 8.1 Alexandra Beller in *egg* at Abrons Art Center. Reproduced with permission of Judith Stuart.

About a year into motherhood, I woke up sweaty from a dream. I was trying to dance, and the dance felt urgent. Someone was hurling raw eggs at me, and I had to catch them—each one fragile and high stakes. It felt impossible to pause or to abandon either task. I couldn't do *both*.

The dream was a reckoning with my first year of motherhood, trying to maintain my artistic practice while protecting a newborn baby. It was about trusting that failure would seed possibility.

I choreographed the dream—a dance where failure was inevitable. It started as a love duet with a single egg, then accumulated obstacles, expectations, and restrictions until I could no longer meet them. I performed a virtuosic phrase in unison with another dancer, who berated me if I missed a step. Another performer interrogated me about my breastfeeding schedule, demanding complex mathematical responses. A third dancer handed me eggs, shoving them into my mouth and hands until I couldn't carry any more. The eggs accumulated across the stage, littering the floor with risk.

Two dancers in a duet would suddenly yell, "Falling!" and collapse. I was meant to catch them before they hit the ground.

Eventually, I would fail. Some nights I'd scream, "Stop it!" or freeze. Sometimes I cried. However it arrived, my failure would scatter everyone from the stage, leaving me with its detritus. Alone, I improvised on a floor covered in eggs.

Each night, I placed my faith in the eggs' survival. In my body's resilience. In the unknown trajectory of the dance. Failure and faith are not opposites. Faith isn't belief in our success; it's our ability to stay present, to learn something, to be changed, even by failure.

Every time I performed *egg*,[7] I had to surrender completely. I couldn't rely on what had worked before. The piece had never "succeeded," and it was never meant to. That was the point.

Faith meant trusting the audience to recognize the beauty inside collapse. Trusting my dancers as they trusted me. Trusting the structure itself to hold meaning. Trusting that a dream could become a dance.

When I premiered *egg*, I felt proud of it, certain I had made something real. The *New York Times* disagreed. The review said, "The dance, by turns sweet and poignant, feels like a private affair, a catharsis that doesn't quite work as theater."[8]

I kept performing it. Over time, *egg* became one of my signature works. It's been taught in dance history classes. Audience members still write to me about it. That review hurt, but it did not erode my faith. I continued not because I was certain the piece would be appreciated but because it mattered. It was worth making and worth staying with.

P.S. I never broke an egg!

[7]Alexandra Beller, *egg*, performance, Abrons Arts Center, Henry Street Settlement, New York, June 7–10, 2009.
[8]Claudia La Rocco, "Dancing Through a Sea of Eggs," *New York Times*, May 8, 2009.

Guidance: Asking Our Inner Critic to Take Some Personal Time

I often ask students to create at lightning speed, so fast their inner critic can't keep up. The time constraint requires faith that choices will lead somewhere, even when the path is unclear.

Art thrives on decision-making. But we often get stuck trying to get it "perfect" before "it" exists. We interrupt ourselves to ask:

- What if this idea isn't strong enough?
- Should I go back to my original plan?
- What if the audience doesn't "get it"?

Our inner critic doesn't just slow us down; they freeze us. They stop us before the first mark is made, convincing us that doubt signals a dead end.

Critique is a fundamental part of editing but the tone of our inner critic is often off. They're not just discerning; they're punishing. They micromanage and bully us.

In art, as in physics, momentum begins with movement. A body at rest resists change; the first action breaks inertia. Friction appears immediately—doubt, resistance, complication—but friction also creates traction. Action generates momentum. One choice alters the field, leaning into the next. Making decisions quickly gives us something tangible to press against and redirect.

Art only exists when it enters the world. In our head, it remains hypothetical and without consequence. We don't yet know what we'll feel until it becomes real. We can't sense its rhythm, feel its drive, or recognize its patterns. To feel anything, art must *exist* as something we can watch, shift, touch, name, or refuse.

The inner critic's job is to protect us from that visibility. It whispers, "Just think about it a little longer." It wonders, "What if they hate it?" It yells so loudly, our conversation with the work is drowned out. It wants us to *imagine* everything and *create* nothing because once the work exists, we can be seen, misunderstood, and judged. The inner critic mistakes vulnerability for danger.

Generating quickly is a way to practice trusting our instincts and letting the work exist without apology. It allows us to practice nonattachment while still caring deeply—devotion without control.

Faith means trusting that there is magic in your first answer. If your inner critic is loud, try making choices faster. A structured score, timed process, or set of obstacles can offer just enough pressure to keep you moving forward, without time for self-doubt.

Create conditions that support risk. Allow failure. Leave room to get it wrong.

A **score** is an act of faith. The deviser trusts the structure to awaken action. The artist trusts that action will generate meaning.

Try: Set a timer for ninety minutes. Choose a score from this book or invent one. Make something: movement, text, music, collage, a game. Work fast. Don't look back. Make a choice. Make another. Cut something. Replace it. Keep going. It doesn't need to be good; only to exist.

If your inner critic shows up, ask them to step outside. You're not exiling them; just rescheduling the meeting. You can speak to them later. For now, let faith lead.

And if you can, have *fun*. Fun is its own form of faith: remembering that joy is worth following even before you know where it's leading you.

Frameworks: Dialoguing with Your Inner Critic

Before beginning, check in with your body. Do you want to explore something tender? Only proceed if you feel emotionally grounded and capable of returning to yourself afterward with loving-kindness.

Most of us have heard the voice of an inner critic. They show up like an overzealous guardian, intent on preventing harm. Their language may be harsh, yet underneath is often fear—of humiliation, dismissal, or irrelevance. In their way, our critic is trying to protect us, even when their strategy wounds. When we recognize their voice as one part[9] of us, we can begin to relate with care.

It can help to give your inner critic a name. Mine is Becky. When she interrupts—"You don't know what you're doing," "You're embarrassing yourself"—I say, "Becky, not now. Later." Naming her creates space. I remember she is a *part* of me, not the entirety of who I am. I speak to her the way I speak to my teenager—clear about boundaries and loving in tone. Sometimes she has a useful point. The task isn't to silence her forever but to keep her voice in proportion and the dialogue grounded.

I can create distance in the moment. Later, I hear her out. Here is one way to begin.

Step One: Let the Critic Speak

Start by inviting your inner critic to speak freely. Don't shut them down. Let them have their say.

You: Okay, you've been trying to get my attention. I'm listening; tell me everything.

Let them speak without interruption. They can rant, exaggerate, be cruel and unapologetic. Speak their words aloud with your voice. Record it if you want.

Here's one of mine:

> You're such a fraud. You act like a healer and use big words to sound intelligent, but you're just a self-important, undereducated fake who pretends to be intellectual. It won't be long before everyone realizes you're a liar, a fake, and someone gets hurt because you think you know so much.

I give her space to be truthful. It may feel like she's being unkind. I remember that I've stonewalled, rejected, and criticized her too. I've shouted, "Get the hell out of my head!" She has been trying to help, and I've often ignored or threatened her to defend myself. This time, I listen as the highest self

---

[9]Richard C. Schwartz, *Internal Family Systems Therapy* (Guilford Press, 1995). This therapeutic model describes how individuals can dialogue with "parts" of the personality—such as the inner critic—in order to foster understanding, compassion, and healing within the self.

I can muster—accepting and nonreactive. I remind myself: These *feelings* are real. The *stories* may not be.

After you've listened, **pause**. Let **silence** come back into the room.

Ask yourself:

- What did that feel like in my body?
- Where did I clench or go numb?
- What part of me believed it?
- What part of me didn't?

Even if it's just a flicker, notice your doubts about their rant: the sentence that almost made you laugh or roll your eyes. You might not hear the absurdity until you let the critic finish. Listen for the *feelings* beneath the *judgments*, and you may hear *fear*. It's like hearing your kid scream, "I hate you!" Instead of being reactive, we hopefully get curious. "You sound *really* angry. Can you share more?"

Sometimes they don't sound like *you* but like a teacher who belittled you or a parent who withheld approval. You may recognize the tone, the cadence, even specific words. **If the voice feels borrowed, trust that.**

** If you notice yourself getting tense, activated, or freezing, pause and skip to "Step Five: Reentry Practice" at the end of this section.*

Step Two: Begin the Conversation

Now that the critic has spoken, begin the dialogue with steadiness—calm, secure, nonreactive. You're not here to prove them wrong; you're here to get curious. Speak to them gently; they are scared and risking being truthful. Step into a steady, caring role.

Start with simple, open, curious questions.

- "What are you afraid will happen if I keep going?"
- "Who taught you to speak this way?"
- "What are you trying to protect me from?"
- "What would make you feel safer?"
- "Are you worried I'm trying to get rid of you?"

You want to know what they're scared of and how they're protecting you. Ask something you'd ask a child who's in distress. Ask something you wish they'd asked you when you were overwhelmed or flooded. Keep it simple, honest, and kind. Stay present long enough for vulnerability to arise. Keep asking open, nonjudgmental questions until you have a nuanced picture.

Step Three: Contextualize

Once you've listened and asked questions, begin to place what you've heard in context. This isn't about debating or disproving them. It's about seeing the whole picture: their fears, history, and present needs.

Gently test their claims against what you know:

- "Is this fear about the present or the past?"
- "Does this voice belong to me or did I absorb it?"
- "What evidence do I have that refutes this story?"
- "Can I accept *some* of it without buying it *wholesale*?"
- "What *else* is true at the same time?"

Look for patterns: Does this critic show up at beginnings? Endings? When you're alone? In front of others? Noticing these cycles helps you respond with regulation.

Bring in compassion and proportion. **You might say:**

- "I see you are trying to protect me, but I don't need that right now."
- "I know you want to keep me safe from pain. The way it's coming through is painful."
- "I understand you are worried. I can handle this."

Contextualizing doesn't *exile* them; it reframes your relationship, allowing you to hold their fear and your truth together. From this steadier place, you choose what to carry forward and what to set down.

Here's an example with me and Becky:

A Conversation with Becky (a Short Scene)
(A quiet studio. The Artist sits cross-legged on the floor.)
Artist *(quiet, steady)*: Okay, Becky. You've been trying to speak. I'm ready to listen.
Becky *(tight, clipped, fast)*: Finally. This new work is a disaster. You're not ready. You look like a mess. It's embarrassing.
Artist *(long breath in, slow exhale)*: You sound really anxious. What are you afraid will happen?

Becky *(sharp, rising)*: That you'll screw it up. That they'll see right through you.

Artist *(gently)*: So… you're scared I won't be taken seriously. That I'll be dismissed.

Becky *(bursting)*: Yes! You used to be someone. If you mess this up, they'll forget you. You'll be irrelevant.

Artist *(softening)*: That sounds really painful. Did that happen to you?

Becky *(a beat, smaller)*: When I was a kid, I got attention when I was brilliant. Otherwise, nothing.

Artist: You're trying to protect us, huh?

Becky *(defensive, faltering)*: Yes. I keep you sharp. On edge. That's how you stay ahead.

Artist *(calm)*: I appreciate you looking out for me. That edge got me through a lot. Now it keeps me from doing what I love. I have strength and skills I didn't have back then.

Becky *(snaps)*: So I'm supposed to just back off?

Artist *(steady)*: Not back off—shift roles. I can take over protecting us. Maybe you can be my friend and we can make this together. It's actually fun to make art…

(A pause.)

Becky *(sounding young, unsure)*: I don't know how to do that.

Artist *(warm)*: That's okay. I do. We can have conversations about what we're making and what you're feeling. You don't have to disappear. But you can't be in the driver's seat.

Becky *(half sincere, half playful)*: Can I ride shotgun?

Artist *(smiling)*: You're in the backseat. You can yell directions if you want. I'll choose which ones to follow.

(Silence.)

Becky *(after a beat, softer)*: Okay. I'll try.

Try This

Set a timer for ten minutes. Write or speak your own scene with your critic. Give them a name. Let them talk. Then respond—not to silence them but to understand. If they won't soften, stop. Move. Breathe. Remind yourself: *That is one part of me. I am more than that voice.*

Step Four: Return to Yourself

After the conversation—however it unfolded—pause.

Not to analyze or fix. Just to acknowledge that something opened. That you stayed with a part of yourself you usually try to shut down. That matters.

Sometimes the inner critic, like a distressed toddler, just needs to be heard—allowed to express what they're holding so they can loosen their grip. When we listen without flinching, we sometimes reach the honest root beneath all that control: *I feel scared. I feel ashamed. I want to be seen.*

And sometimes, as with any toddler, space isn't enough. What's needed is a clear, nonviolent boundary—something you do for yourself. You might speak a steadying phrase: *That's enough. Not now. This isn't helping.* The act itself is care. It protects you, and it keeps them from doing harm they doesn't intend. Naming the behavior reminds you: *I'm still here. I'm in charge now.*

To help the critic release their grip, you may also need a gesture. A stomp. A stretch. A shake. A physical completion of the conversation, so your body can shift gears. This isn't performative. It's physiological. If the voice lives in your nervous system, it needs an embodied way out—not just a thought.

You don't need to forgive the critic or agree with them. You do need to recognize them as *part of you.*

Step Five: Reentry Practice

After working with your inner critic, your system may feel stirred—open, raw, tender, or alert. Before you return to your day, take a few minutes to reground.

- Place one hand on your chest, belly, or any place that feels comforting.
- Take a full, slow breath in through your nose, and exhale gently through your mouth, letting your exhale be longer than your inhale.
- Name five things you can see, four things you can touch, three things you can hear, two things you can smell or imagine smelling, and one thing you know to be true right now.
- Let your shoulders soften.
- Shake out your hands or tap your chest.
- Roll your spine slowly or walk around your space. Let your head release, eyes wander, tongue float.
- Make sound if it helps—hum, sigh, yawn, sing. Unhinge your jaw.

You showed up. You stayed. You met something hard with attention. **Offer yourself a small gesture of thanks.**

And when you're ready, **begin again**.

Tuning In: Trusting What's Already There

This practice starts with what's already in the room, what your body already knows. Let it be enough.

1. **Awaken your instincts.**
   Try an Authentic Movement practice: Follow your inner impulses without judgment. The goal isn't to *invent* movement but to listen to the body's urges attentively. There is no "right" size, action, or quality. Movement may be large or small, still or repetitive, precise or formless. The only requirement is **honest attention**. Move in silence or with ambient sound. Every few minutes, **pause** and ask:
   - What clues am I seeing?
   - What is surprising me?
   - What keeps repeating?
2. **Practice beginning with faith.**
   Stand in your space. Out loud, say, "This piece begins with…" Immediately let your body dance the end of the sentence. Move before thinking interferes. Repeat several times, using new language each round. When one of your beginnings feels resonant, repeat it a few times until it has found itself (but no need to set it as choreography).
3. **Allow your movement to develop.**
   Add another sentence in text and finish it with movement. Try one of these, or your own text:
   - "This piece refuses to…"
   - "In this piece, my ribs…"
   - "In this piece, when I leave this spot, I…"
4. **Mark the moment.**
   Continue to create from these half sentences, spoken aloud, letting each phrase become a cliff's edge, falling off speech into movement. Use each sentence as many times as you like until you find a movement ending that resonates. Write your own sentences, or try some of these:
   - "This is where I started to…"
   - "This is where I almost stopped…"
   - "This is where I said yes to…"
   - "This is the story where I…"

- "This is where I leave my..."
- "This is where I return to..."
- "This is where I begin to..."

Move as soon as the text drops out, no overthinking! Let the words trigger action, gesture, stillness, or even sound. When one has a physical or emotional charge, follow it; see what unfolds. You are not trying to build choreography, but to notice the moment when your impulse lands as authentic and meaningful.

Studio Lab: The Leap Before the Landing

This practice invites you to act on instinct, letting bold declarations and impulsive choices lead before meaning is fully formed, and before you're ready.

1. **Declare a truth (even if you don't believe it yet).**
   Write a bold, declarative sentence about your current project or process. Don't analyze or deliberate; go with your first impulse. Even if it feels "dramatic" or "irrational."
   - This piece is about *longing.*
   - This work requires *three dancers, one chair,* and *absolute silence.*
   - The entire performance will be performed forward and then in reverse.
   - **Optional addition:** Write three in a row. The third is often the most surprising!
2. **Take the first action.**
   Choose **one** of your statements and choreograph it.
   - If it was about longing, create a phrase that holds or resists longing.
   - If your piece requires a chair, interact with one—sit, climb, drag, avoid.
   - If your performance is in reverse, choreograph a section, then rewind as precisely as you can.
3. **Keep moving forward.**
   Once you've made the first move, commit by making three rapid decisions. Think of these not as improvements but as *continuations.*
   - **Expand** or **repeat** your original action in a new way.
   - Change one element: **space, time,** or **weight.**
   - Add a **counterpoint**—something that interrupts, contradicts, or complicates the first action.
4. **Step back without undoing.**
   Observe what you've made. Do not erase. **Ask:**
   - What ideas does this stimulate?
   - What is surprising me?
   - What does it want next?

Instead of fixing it, continue. **Add a next layer—a sound, a rule, a shift in direction,** or **an object** that recontextualizes what's there.

Pagework: Writing into Faith

Freewrite on some or all of these questions.

1. **When did you last feel deeply lost in your process?**
   What carried you forward—instinct, support, time, structure, surrender?

2. **Think about a moment when doubt stopped you mid-process.**
   What did your doubt need from you, the room, or someone else to be able to keep going?

3. **Recall a time when you trusted an intuitive choice without knowing why.**
   What happened? Did analysis arrive later, and if so, how did it shift the outcome?

4. **Write a review from the point of view of someone who adores you.**
   It can reflect on your art, your teaching, or your being. Format it as a glowing review, letter of recommendation, five-star Yelp post. Go big; be hyperbolic. No censoring!

   Option: Write the harshest review you can imagine, then read it back with compassion or humor.

5. **Recall a moment when you relinquished control of your creative process.**
   What conditions allowed that surrender? How might you create more of them?

Movements + Maps: Faith in Letting It Happen

This score invites you to engage actively with surrender, allowing your instincts to guide you before stepping back with clear, critical eyes.

1. **Create without a plan.**
   Let go of expectations. Choose the most immediate medium—movement, voice, objects, text, sound, or an unexpected form. Work in a stream-of-consciousness style: Let your first impulse lead to the next without stopping to evaluate. If something feels "wrong," exaggerate rather than censor. If it feels too *serious*, make it *ridiculous*. If too *chaotic*, *lean in further*. If it feels too *repetitive*, shift one thing and *keep going*.

2. **Capture and preserve your work.**
   Record or document what you've created. Resist the urge to shape it into meaning.

3. **Leave the material alone.**
   Step away for at least twenty-four hours.

4. **Observe without judgment.**
   Return to the material as if encountering a stranger's work. Describe what you see:
   - "A body searching for balance"
   - "A person arguing with an invisible presence"
   - "An apology disguised as a dance"
   - "A slow collapse that never completes"

5. **Generate three new snippets.**
   Use three of your descriptions as titles or prompts for three pieces of new material. For each title, create a small product—a movement phrase, bit of dialogue, or scenic design inspired by the title alone.

6. **Weave the unknown together.**
   Place your original material and the new responses in conversation. Build a short piece using this vocabulary. Let them interrupt, contradict, or echo one another. Experiment with sequencing. What happens when they are layered, juxtaposed, or repeated?

   Observe relationships forming between them. DJ them: **edit, delete, repeat, cut,** and **paste.**

Contributor's Note: On Faith

by Okwui Okpokwasili

When I was seven years old, my mother went into labor at the end of her second trimester, prematurely giving birth to one of my younger sisters six months into her pregnancy. My sister weighed 2 pounds, 13 ounces and could fit into the palm of my father's hand. My sister was in an incubator for seventy-seven days. During this time, my mother slept at the hospital, dutifully pumping breast milk, touching and talking to my sister, telling her about the siblings waiting for her to come home. My mother was practicing (and in the throes of) a profound faith that my sister would survive and thrive. And this faith demanded an unceasing labor.

There was the bestowing of my sister's name, which translates into "the gift and mercy of God," so that at its every utterance was an expression of gratitude and acknowledgment of inevitable relief.

This was foundational to my understanding of faith. It was to make a plea and to believe that plea would be heard. There was no guarantee of redress, no certainty that you would receive a desired outcome. It was simply to make the utterance and to labor in service of that utterance.

I admit, faith is not the word that immediately comes to mind when I think about an art practice. I think of an affinity for the elliptical. A lust for attuning to the quiet revelation in a moment. Of being kind of nosey. Of having a lack of concern for outcome but an unshakeable impulse to try things and to test things out, to wonder and to wander. But, of course, it is faith that has led me to believe that I can shape these particular instincts into a guide for my artistic practice. A practice that does not compel me to find answers but to be led to the next question, to be open to possibilities I may not have foreseen. The heart of my art practice is in service of making the utterance and shimmering in its resonance.

Some essential labors in sustaining my faith:

The practice of listening. To hear songs in the whirring of the fan on a hot summer night and to hum with it or in counterpoint. To sing with others where you cannot tell where your voice ends and theirs begins. To eavesdrop on conversations on a subway train or in the grocery store and record those fragments in a journal, to begin to get to know a character who might make their way into a piece.

The practice of seeing. Initiating a movement score that can begin with the questions: What is your last memory of being physically touched? Was it a brush across your back? Was it a hand on your face? Were there arms around your waist? And from the memory of that last imprint of touch, close your eyes, slowly begin to retrace it, so slowly that you branch out into a new thread that has no end. And then sit and watch what emerges with wonder.

Studio Provocations: Questioning Faith

I said to my soul, be still, and wait without hope… there is yet faith.
(T. S. Eliot, *Four Quartets*)[10]

Faith in the Product

What part of this piece do you trust most?

- Is it an image, rhythm, relationship, moment of stillness, a performer?

What's one moment you don't fully believe in yet, and what would it take to believe it?

Name one gesture or image to bet the whole piece on.

Try: Let that choice lead the next rehearsal.

Faith in Process

Where are you hesitating because you want *proof*?

Try: Press forward with this section without defending, explaining, or answering it.

What can you learn from your first impulses?

Try: Spend an hour making four fifteen-minute sketches. Begin with a first impulse, keep adding choice after choice, without changing or second-guessing. End with four mini-sections.

Faith in Collaborators

Where in this piece do you need to trust someone *else's* body, timing, or instinct?

Try: Hand over the reins to someone else: a performer, a friend, a designer. Have them create a gesture, idea, or motif and build on that.

What's one action that would signal more trust in your collaborators (eye contact, gesture, breath, direct conversation)?

Do your collaborators have more or less faith in this project than you?

[10] T. S. Eliot, *Four Quartets* (Harcourt, 1943).

Faith in Material

Which doubt about this work could launch a new choice?

- Could doubt show up in rhythm, weight, or voice?

Where does doubt live in your body right now; can you dance it?

Try: Find doubt in your body and follow it for three minutes without correcting it. Resist the urge to resolve it. Let the dance remain uncertain.

How does faith look different from doubt in this piece's vocabulary?

Try: Watch your work live or recorded. List the moments where you feel faith and where you feel doubt. Is there any difference in their form or function? Can you borrow from the faith section?

Testing and Stretching Faith

What happens if you raise the stakes?

Try: Perform the next run-through as if it's the only chance you'll ever have to show this piece. What emerges under that pressure?

Where can faith let you simplify something?

Try: Say aloud, "We can let go of…" Attempt to finish the sentence without thinking, saying the first thing that comes up. Run it without that element. What opens up?

What's one wild choice you've thought of but not dared to try?

Try: Make that risk the center of the next draft or section.

Where might the *audience* need more faith to meet this work?

- Is there a place to invite them into uncertainty rather than resolve it?
- Is there one practical action you can take that would ask *more* from them?

Faith in Meaning

What do you want this piece to make possible?

- How does that longing show up in the process or material?

Which moment, if it landed, would make you believe in this piece?

- Is that moment already present or still to be found?

Are you waiting to *understand* this in order to *trust* it?

What future does this piece believe in?

9

Communication

Before You Begin: Priming Curiosity About Communication

Take a breath. Consider these questions. Let them settle in your body before moving forward. They are not for solving, but for sensing.

Who really hears me, and how do I know?

Why does it sometimes feel risky to say what I mean?

When do I say what I mean—and when do I hide, veil, or lie?

What might someone assume about me just by watching me move?

How do I decide what needs to be said and what can stay unspoken?

Where in my life am I clearest—and where am I most misunderstood?

Groundwork: Communication as Desire

Don't tell me the moon is shining; show me the glint of light on broken glass.
(Anton Chekhov, *Letters of Anton Chekhov*)[1]

Knowing Me, Knowing You

Stepping onto a crowded bus with my two kids in tow, I hear the "failure" beep pierce the air. My Metrocard is empty and cannot be refilled on the bus. The driver and I share a charged moment, silently negotiating. He doesn't want to set a precedent by letting me ride without paying, and he doesn't want to kick us off the bus, delaying everyone behind me. I don't want to be scolded or cause trouble. If I say explicitly, "I don't have enough money; can I ride anyway?" he will likely say, "No." Pretending I didn't hear the beep feels entitled and inconsiderate. **Direct communication won't get either of us what we want.**

I ease onto the bus, mumbling, "I didn't realize it was low.... I don't have any... " He mumbles back—neither saying, "It's okay, go ahead," nor indicating I should leave. He shifts his gaze to the person behind me, indicating that we are done with our exchange. The outcome is fragile; I see the potential for both humiliation and relief.

That moment on the bus—improvised, ambiguous, but deeply felt—reveals something essential about communication. What mattered was how we read each other, and how we made ourselves readable. The exchange was *indirect* but not *unclear*. It was negotiated through **tone**, **timing**, **posture**, and **gesture**. This kind of communication lives at the heart of art-making. What we call "style," "tone," or "presence" often hinges on how much we say without saying, how much we direct the audience's attention or let them find their own way in.

Communication is the bridge between intention and impact, shaping what others feel, sense, intuit, or wrestle with. It holds the tension between power and care, audience and artist, clarity and mystery. How we communicate—directly, indirectly, or somewhere in between—shapes how our work is felt, understood, remembered, or dismissed. Here I use *direct* and *indirect* in their everyday sense, not as Laban's categories of Space Effort.

[1]Anton Chekhov, *Letters of Anton Chekhov*, ed. and trans. Michael Henry Heim and Simon Karlinsky (Harper & Row, 1973).

The Myth of the Indirect Body

Movement is often treated as background and words as foreground. In many rehearsal rooms and critical conversations, verbal statements are assumed to be deliberate, while gestures are thought of as offhanded or decorative. This hierarchy shapes how work is made, how it is received, and even how it is funded. In many theater processes, directors coach the text line by line but leave movement to instinct or improvisation, even when the staging carries equal weight. Full choreographic passages may be built collaboratively in the room, yet the production budgets for a vocal coach and not a movement director. The message is subtle but clear: Words are crafted; bodies will sort themselves out.

Yet the body carries its own exacting vocabulary. A posture can reveal commitment or retreat; a shift in weight can announce decision or doubt. The clarity of movement isn't *lesser* than language—it's a *different* language. As trauma researcher Bessel van der Kolk writes, "the body keeps the score: it stores the imprints of traumatic experience in heart, gut, and postures, long after the mind believes the danger has passed."[2]

This echoes what performers know instinctively: Gesture, breath, and tone carry traces of lived history, often more vividly than words. Neuroscientist Vittorio Gallese, writing on embodied simulation, describes how seeing another's movement activates the observer's own motor system, an exchange that allows audiences to *feel into* a performance before analyzing it.[3] Performance scholar Erika Fischer-Lichte expands this further, noting that spectators are not passive recipients of words but participants in "a feedback loop of embodiment" where movement, affect, and energy co-create meaning.[4]

When we learn to read movement on its own terms, we discover that the body and speech are in constant negotiation. A hand may reach with tenderness or accusation. A stillness can hold focus as sharply as any line of text. A performer can scan the entire room with a wide awareness and still communicate precision or attend to a single point and communicate fullness.

What often reads as "vague" is not the expansiveness of attention but the absence of choice. Movement feels unmoored when the performer hasn't located what they are attending to—or when they are

---

[2]Bessel van der Kolk, *The Body Keeps the Score: Brain, Mind, and Body in the Healing of Trauma* (Viking, 2014), 27.

[3]Vittorio Gallese, "Embodied Simulation: From Neurons to Phenomenal Experience," *Phenomenology and the Cognitive Sciences* 4, no. 1 (2005): 23–48, https://doi.org/10.1007/s11097-005-4737-z. Gallese introduces the concept of "embodied simulation," describing how witnessing another's movement activates the observer's motor system and enables kinesthetic empathy.

[4]Erika Fischer-Lichte, *The Transformative Power of Performance: A New Aesthetics* (Routledge, 2008), 38–54. Fischer-Lichte analyzes the dynamic, participatory relationship between performers and spectators, describing a "feedback loop of embodiment" integral to meaning-making in live performance.

hiding rather than choosing. The audience senses this, even if they can't name it. Vagueness often reads as detachment; a clear choice may read as presence, whether the communication is direct or diffuse.

In the studio, one of the core questions becomes: Is this moment asking for singular focus, or multidirectional awareness? Is the performer moving from a chosen relationship, or drifting through an unchosen one?

When the answer is unclear, it's usually because the performer's relationship to the action hasn't yet been found.

Understanding that movement and speech are always in negotiation, we can start to notice *how* artists choose to communicate. Some work announces its message plainly; some lets meaning unfold through suggestion and delay. Each can be deliberate, precise, and capable of failure. What matters is the relationship between choice and impact: Is the mode of communication alive, chosen, and aligned with the work's priorities?

Direct Communication: Clarity as Invitation

Direct communication in art does not mean *literalism*. It means *clarity of desire*: the artist knows what they want to say, and they say it overtly.

Directness is a risk. It removes the veil of plausible deniability. It says, "This is what I'm asking of you. This is what I'm telling you. This is what I need you to see." It does so without apology.

Honesty and confrontation are not the same. Direct communication can be *definite* without being *aggressive*. It might be a monologue delivered with unwavering eye contact. It might be a dance that holds one shape for seven minutes, insisting, "This is not decoration."

Direct communication says, "If I want you to understand grief, I won't gesture toward it abstractly. I'll risk exposing it." It exposes the creator's beliefs, feelings, and priorities.

Works like Anna Deavere Smith's *Fires in the Mirror*,[5] a documentary theater piece built from verbatim interviews connected to the 1991 Crown Heights conflict, or Jerome Bel's *Disabled Theater*,[6] in which the actors describe their disabilities and perform their own dances, make bold, exacting choices. The audience knows what they are witnessing. Even when the artist uses symbolism and metaphor, the invitation is unmistakable, "Meet me here. I'll show you where I am."

Here's the paradox: The more precise we are, the more room we sometimes give the audience to feel. **Clarity is not control; it's trust.** It's giving the audience solid ground, leaving them free to *feel*.

---

[5]Anna Deavere Smith, *Fires in the Mirror: Crown Heights, Brooklyn and Other Identities* (Anchor Books, 1993).
[6]Jérôme Bel, *Disabled Theater*, performance with Theater HORA, Zürich, 2012.

Of course, not every artist wants to speak plainly. Some use indirectness to build ambiguity, asking the audience to do more interpretive work. This carries its own risk and requires equal intention.

Layering Meaning, Leaving Room

Indirect communication is a purposeful choice to veil, suggest, or evoke. It says, "There is meaning here; you must seek it." It makes the audience complicit. Indirect work uses metaphor, dream logic, juxtaposition, and delay. A motif may happen early and repeat frequently, only to be understood retroactively. Sound might come from different locations, establishing a mystery. Meaning is built through *attention*, not *explanation*.

There's power in ambiguity when it is earned. Not every question needs an answer. Works like Pina Bausch's *Café Müller*,[7] where blind, sleepwalking figures collide, embrace, and repeat gestures of longing and dependence, or John Jasperse's *Giant Empty*,[8] where minimalism and contradiction evoke the tension between presence and absence, leave room for interpretation and contradiction. They don't hand the audience a thesis—they offer them a mirror and ask, "What do you see here? What does it ask of you?"

Indirectness works best when the artist holds the reins firmly, creating a world built on clear, internal rules. Without that structure, the work often tips into obfuscation or avoidance, and the audience feels abandoned. When resisting literality, inner logic can fall away; that is where coherence dissolves.

At its weakest, *detachment* masquerades as *ambiguity*; indecision is labeled "nuance" and the artist has ceded meaning. At its best, indirect communication invites the viewer to step into the piece as a co-creator. The gap between *what is said* and *what is meant* becomes a generative space.

Avoiding Drift

Sometimes communication lands in a middle space: communication without a chosen purpose. The danger here is drift. When a choice hasn't been made, the work can feel vague and the audience senses it. This middle ground often masquerades as "subtlety" or "sophistication", but more often it signals that an intention hasn't been clarified. It shows up when we want intimacy and fear exposure, or crave complexity and neglect to layer meaning. Performers use generalized intensity or a detached demeanor, hoping the audience won't notice the missing *why*. But when our inner purpose is foggy, the audience knows.

---

[7]Pina Bausch, *Café Müller*, Tanztheater Wuppertal Pina Bausch, premiered 1978, Wuppertal, Germany.

[8]John Jasperse, *Giant Empty*, John Jasperse Company, premiered 2001, New York.

I felt this middle ground in rehearsal recently. We were close to performance, and the director was tying loose ends and solving production needs. She asked me to move a sculpture during a high-stakes audience interaction.

"Why?" I asked.

"It needs to move for the next section," she told me. She was focused on timing, transitions, and the arc of the work; I was tracking the embodied logic of my character. That made sense; we were racing the clock. But the action felt unmoored; the sculpture was meaningful, and I wanted to remain loyal to that relationship.

Together, we found a reason—not literal, but relational—that let me fold the action into the character's arc. That alignment mattered. Without it, I would have been faking it, and the audience would have felt the disconnect.

This is what an ambiguous middle ground looks like: tasks without threads, actions without inner logic. Not every action needs to be justified in words, but every action needs a reason that lives in the body. "Why am I touching this? Why am I looking here? What is this moment responding to, resisting, or remembering?" Without that, ambiguity slides into ambivalence and loses its mystery.

Reading and Being Read

The body is always speaking.

It reveals what we want, what we fear, where we're holding tension, what we haven't processed. The shoulders tighten, "I'm not ready." The breath quickens, "I want this." The gaze darts away, "Please don't look at me"—even as the voice says, "I'm fine." Our words, even our thoughts, might distort. Our bodies signal more directly, often without our awareness.

A brash, overconfident posture may register as insecurity. A performative calm may betray hypervigilance. Small children and animals offer clear body language; they haven't yet learned to mask. Adults, especially in leadership or performance roles, often have. This isn't intentional dishonesty; it reflects protective, cultural, and neurological survival.

Masking helps us navigate social expectations and norms, but also shuts down our internal signals. When we default to it, *impulse* and *intuition* are squashed. It is risky and personal to choose when, where, and with whom you feel safe enough to simply *be*.

Masking often reveals what we want to protect. Reading a mask offers a new layer of truth.

Somatic and trauma-informed frameworks remind us that *lack of clarity* is not the same as *lack of meaning*. Hesitation, stillness, bracing, and tension are all loud signals. *How* we are doing something is often more telling than *what* we are doing. A tight body might be protecting, surviving, or feeling overwhelmed. It might be about to implode or explode. If we don't learn to read these signals—or attend to how we are being read—we risk missing opportunities for authenticity and connection. We can practice identifying the *need* behind the *strategy*. Intuition gathers the senses into meaning.

Intuition as Integrative Sense

Intuition is often treated as poetic or mystical, but it functions like any other sense. It integrates physical *signals*—breath, muscle tone, heart rate, gut sensation—into *perception*. When we value these inner cues alongside external ones, intuition shifts from *guesswork* to *guidance*. It tells us when a gesture resonates, when a choice feels congruent, when something in the room changes.

We've been conditioned to trust what can be *measured*—pitch, diction, staging—and doubt what is *felt*. That dichotomy breeds self-doubt, which undermines play, curiosity, and risk. **Reclaiming intuition is not indulgent; it is essential.** It is the clearest barometer we have for truth telling. Though often mythologized as unknowable, it can be strengthened like any other muscle.

One rehearsal tool I use to strengthen somatic awareness is a deceptively simple partner exercise.

Students pair up, facing one another. One is the *requester*, the other the *receiver*. The requester asks for permission to initiate contact: "May I place my right hand on your left shoulder?" For the first five rounds, the receiver *must* say no, building tolerance for rejection and reinforcing no as a welcome response.

Next, responses can include no, yes, or yes *with conditions*:

"Yes, *if* you do it lightly."

"Yes, *but* only for five seconds."

Then, the verbal script is removed.

One person still requests physical contact, and the other consents, refuses, or modifies—but all communication is **nonverbal**.

Insight often emerges here.

I'll notice a student using ambiguous movement—a hand floating hesitantly toward their partner's shoulder. The receiver will tense, uncertain of what is being asked. Where is their partner asking to touch, and when will they land? The vagueness denies the receiver enough information to make an informed choice. When the initiating movement is clear, the response is immediate. When we signal clearly through the body, we invite genuine consent, not coerced participation.

This principle applies to our creative process. If we say, "I want collaboration," while directing rigidly, or we ask performers for vulnerability while staying emotionally inscrutable, our work may absorb the confusion. **Communication is not just something we say; it's something we *are*.**

Intimacy and the Audience

Choreographers often try to tell me about their work before showing it; I inevitably tell them I want to experience it before hearing about it. An audience can only respond to what exists, not what we'd *hoped* to make. Trust arises when *what we state* and *what we embody* align.

This dynamic holds in art and in life. Intimacy doesn't come from sharing space alone; two people can sit across from each other at dinner, one feeling nourished, the other unseen. Proximity alone does not create intimacy; it requires a shared reality.

After attending my partner's work event, a painful evening of meandering small talk, I might say, "Wow, your boss can really go on!" On the surface, it's commentary; underneath, I'm asking for recognition: "See what I endured for you." Because I've buried the real need, the ask comes out sideways; it's disingenuous. When I name the truth—"That was a lot for me; I think I'm craving a little appreciation"—the communication opens, and intimacy becomes available.

Art can misalign similarly. A piece might claim to be about "human rights" but actually is seeking admiration or validation. The *declared story* and the *embodied story* diverge, and the audience senses the gap. This is why I frequently bristle at *So You Think You Can Dance*. The show frames itself as a celebration of artistry and expression, but the story beneath is about perfection, admiration, and compliance. It's not virtuosity itself. I don't feel this dissonance in classical Chinese dance, breakdancing, Elizabeth Streb, or Cunningham—all of which prize virtuosity. But they do so honestly, without disguising what they want from me.

I often see contemporary dances described as exploring "the patriarchy," "mental illness," "climate change," or "racism." These labels prepare me for depth and intellectual risk. Yet, watching the work, I feel I'm meant to admire their beauty, sexiness, and technical prowess. The self-description points one way while the body demands something else. This sideways communication manipulates the audience.

Honesty is not about moral purity; it is about trust. I have long hoped for an artist to arrive at mentorship, saying, "I feel *not enough* in my life. But when I dance, people admire my physique and technique, and I feel like I *belong*." "I feel small; I want you to see me" is a powerful impetus for a solo. Saying, "This work is about the mass incarceration of Black men," while actually craving personal validation, lacks that same courage and vulnerability.

During that moment with the bus driver, we both knew what we wanted. Our exchange was indirect, but it wasn't *disguised*. We could be elliptical and still be clear because the *real ask* was on the table. In art, as in that bus ride, the question is less about directness or metaphor than about honesty: Are we letting our true needs be legible to those we are in relation with?

So, with every gesture, word, or image, ask: **What am I saying here, and how am I asking the audience to listen?**

Communication always reveals relationship—to the audience, the work, and ourselves. Are we hiding, performing, asking, demanding, or offering? This is how we invite others into our world without coercion, distortion, or disguise. **It is how meaning becomes shared.**

Takeaway: What matters is not whether communication is direct or layered, but whether it is chosen and aligned. When we are honest, meaning can be shared.

In Practice: Tips About Communication

1. **Make yourself *readable*.**
   Ask: How am I making my intention legible—through tone, timing, posture, structure?
2. **Know the inner logic.**
   Ask: What are the internal rules? Am I staying committed to them or breaking them intentionally?
3. **Track the desire beneath the theme.**
   Ask: What do I actually want from the audience—recognition, admiration, discomfort, agreement, care?
4. **Avoid the drifting middle.**
   Ask: Is this ambiguity intentional, or have I avoided committing?
5. **Name the relationship.**
   Ask: What relationship am I creating with the audience right now—confessional, confrontational, collaborative, observational?
6. **Respect the audience's sovereignty.**
   Ask: Am I inviting a response, or trying to control one?
7. **Track the hidden motivations.**
   Ask: Does what I *say* this work is about match what my choices are asking for?
8. **Give the body equal craft.**
   Ask: Have I shaped the physical language with the same precision as the text?
9. **Let intuition inform your choices.**
   Ask: What is my body signaling about this moment—congruence or incoherence?
10. **Commit fully to each choice.**
    Ask: Can I clearly name why this choice exists?

Frameworks: Practicing Inner Consent

This solo exploration adapts a partner-based exercise into a practice of listening, negotiating, and honoring your body's internal yes and no. Cultivating this sensitivity sharpens our creative clarity and supports honest collaboration—with ourselves and others.

1. **Create a neutral state.**
   Stand or sit comfortably with no agenda. Let your breath settle. Feel your contact with the ground. **Ask:** "Am I willing to *listen* before I act?"

2. **Make a request.**
   Ask:
   "Do I want to raise my left arm?"
   "Do I want to place my hand over my heart?"
   "Do I want to take a step forward?"
   Wait. Sense the body's answer.

   - "Yes" may feel easeful, open, aligned.
   - "No" may feel tight, uneasy, or inert.
   - "Maybe" like hesitancy or doubt.

3. **Try a *conditional* yes.**
   Ask a new question. When you sense a yes, *clarify the conditions*:

   - "Yes, *if* it's slow."
   - "Yes, *but* with eyes closed."
   - "Yes, for a *few* seconds."

   Do the action. Stay alert to feelings.

4. **Drop the words.**
   Without making verbal requests, begin to initiate small movements. Pause before each one; wait for enthusiastic consent. Let the movement complete or abort based on the body's readiness.

5. **Move from inner permission.**
   Ask your body what it wants you to know. Let the gestures grow or halt based on continued consent. If you notice a change midmovement, adjust or stop.

6. **Reflect.**
    - When was it easy to hear your own signals?
    - Did you override or doubt your internal voice?
    - How would your creative practice change if this kind of clarity guided your choices?
    - Where else in life do you say *yes* without checking in with yourself?

From the Field: *Make Thick My Blood*

Figure 9.1 Dawn Stern and Stephan Wolfert in *Make Thick My Blood*. Reproduced with permission of Ashley Garrett.

My career has branched from dancer to choreographer, professor to mentor, movement director to theater director. Directing a trauma-informed *Macbeth* for the veteran-centered theater company DeCruit was my first solo directing gig, and I was terrified. Imposter syndrome kept asking, What am I doing at the helm of this ship?

I had planned a five-week rehearsal process, but when COVID hit, it collapsed into once-a-week Zoom sessions—double-masked, filmed through a phone. The collapse of resources stripped away pressure. I dropped into something elemental: tracking breath, weight, space, and energy. With voices muffled and a 2D view, the body became the only metric. And it was enough.

Even when I couldn't hear the words, the posture, tone, and pacing carried meaning. A clenched jaw or hesitant breath conveyed more than Shakespeare's text. This wasn't a workaround; it was a revelation. The squares of the Zoom screen became strange little sanctuaries. I tracked their spines and shoulders and saw fear, conviction, tenderness, resistance. I could sense when an actor was struggling, excited, distracted, or in flow. The body told me, again and again.

One moment crystallized this. We were working on the "If it were done when 'tis done" soliloquy. The actor's body was saturated with internal conflict. The text began to feel ornamental. I asked him to murmur the speech, nearly inaudibly, and let his body be louder. It was private and yet more visible.

When masks came off and voices returned, our foundation held. We had trained ourselves to hear the body, to prioritize its intelligence. We discovered that clarity doesn't always come through articulation. It can arrive through presence.

Guidance: Art and Expression

I work at the intersection of art and healing, and I have long been unsettled by the way those two words sit next to each other. When someone says, "art and healing," there is often an implied diminishment. I hear, "Oh. So not *real* art. *Therapy* art. Self-indulgent art."

I reject that assumption.

Some of the greatest art in the world is profoundly healing. It locates us. It confronts us. It allows us to metabolize grief, rage, longing, terror, and joy. It changes us, connects us, and repairs the divides of fractured realities.

And yet I understand how the suspicion arose.

We use the word *art* to describe almost *any* act of personal expression. I believe *everyone* should dance, sing, draw, and write. I believe expression is a human necessity: vital, healthy, and often therapeutic.

But *expression* is not *art*.

This is not a hierarchy of value but a distinction of function. Expression can be private or shared. It may ask for validation, or nothing at all.

Art asks for something more demanding. It is not only the release of interior life, but the shaping of that experience *with another in mind*. It does not simply say, "Here I am." It asks, "Can we *meet* here?" It is constructed with *relationship* at its *core*. When I use the word *art*, I mean a particular kind of communication—one that rigorously constructs an experience where empathy travels in *both* directions.

This is where healing reenters the conversation. Healing, in art, is not *self-soothing*. It is not the unfiltered discharge of emotion. In art, healing occurs in the *meeting*, when something in my world and something in yours overlap, even briefly, and we recognize each other. Art offers an opportunity to experience true belonging.

The root of art, for me, is to *know* and *be known*. The formations are radically unique; art may manifest as play, resistance, fantasy, or disruption. It may use vocabularies, rhythms, and structures as varied as the makers, but it always crafts a world in order for the audience to recognize it.

No one can fully inhabit our interior world. This aloneness, for some, breeds loneliness. Expression allows us to feel and know *ourselves*, and sometimes to allow others to understand us better. Art does something more complex. It attempts to *bridge* that aloneness.

When I seek an audience, I have to ask *why*. Do I want to be *seen* or do I want to *meet*? There is nothing wrong with wanting to be watched. Having witnesses is a sounding board for self-awareness and can be incredibly validating. But when the primary aim is validation without reciprocity, I experience that as *expression*, not *art*. Art considers *the other*. It anticipates their presence. It shapes itself *in relation*. It does not ask merely to be *observed*; it asks to be *engaged*. When the audience gasps, melts, or sits in rapt attention, our separate realities briefly overlap. These moments aren't just entertainment. They heal, locate, repair, and ground us.

I wonder if we have diluted the power of healing in art because we have blurred this distinction. When self-expression is messy, uneven, or self-focused—as it often and rightly is—the word *art* absorbs those qualities. Healing becomes suspect, and depth sentimentalized. I don't want to diminish expression. I want to free it.

If we allowed expression to *be* expression—necessary, therapeutic, communal, private—without the burden of being called art, perhaps more people would feel invited to participate. And then we could reclaim art as a rigorous, relational act—one that includes healing as a consequence of meeting. For me, this distinction matters. Not to exclude, but to clarify responsibility.

Expression says, "This is inside *me*."

Art says, "Can we hold this *together*?"

Expression helps us endure our aloneness.

Art tests whether that aloneness is absolute.

And when—even for a moment—it is not, something in us is found.

Tuning In: Tuning the Body to Communication

This solo practice builds your ability to read, interpret, and align with embodied cues.

1. **Establish neutrality.**
   Stand, sit, or lie in a neutral position. Let your breath settle into a rhythm that feels accurate for this moment. Without correcting anything, simply observe:
   - Where is there tension?
   - Is your breath full, shallow, or paused?
   - What emotion is suggested by your posture?
2. **Make micro-shifts.**
   Soften your jaw, drop your shoulders, shift your weight subtly. After each adjustment, pause and feel:
   - Has anything changed?
3. **Choose a message.**
   Select a simple phrase to communicate nonverbally:
   - "I am here."
   - "I need something."
   - "I have something to say."
4. **Ask for internal consent.**
   Ask your body, "Are you ready to share?" Wait for a yes, no, or maybe. This might show up as ease, tension, hesitation, or clarity. **If the answer is no, respect it.** Wait. Shift the message. Or just listen.
5. **Express with breath alone.**
   Use breath to express the message without movement or voice. Slow inhale versus fast exhale, held breath versus audible release. What can breath alone communicate?

6. **Express with posture and gaze.**
   Allow your posture (spine, shoulders, gaze) to speak. Is the feeling any clearer? What would someone make up about a photograph of you right now?

7. **Let the movement emerge.**
   Begin to express with more movement, following the impulses. Stay inside the feeling, not the form. Try to release an imaginary audience. This is for you.

8. **Reflect and reset.**
   - What was most communicative? Where did clarity emerge?
   - When were you aligned, and when did you feel performative?
   - Did you override yourself at any point?
   - What would it feel like to create from this place more often?

Studio Lab: Let the Body Speak

This practice invites you to explore how the body communicates with nuance and clarity, letting movement reveal what the voice might censor: intention, contradiction, urgency, care.

1. **Choose your audience.**
   Imagine an audience—a specific person or group, or a metaphorical one: your future self, an unborn generation, your future spouse. Allow the relationship to have stakes, but not so intense that it overwhelms you.
   If the content is emotionally charged, plan a moment of grounding or care afterward.

2. **Speak freely.**
   Find a private space where you can move and speak without interruption. Set up a video or audio recording. Speak directly to your chosen audience. Be messy, unscripted, and honest. Try not to stop speaking, except for breathing.
   Notice where tension gathers, what *opens*, what *resists*.

3. **Let movement join the conversation.**
   Continue speaking, allowing the body to harmonize. Let your gestures, posture, or weight shifts either support or contradict your text. You can be literal, abstract, or metaphorical.

4. **Drop the words.**
   Stop talking, but keep the conversation going. Your audience is still watching, listening. Let your body continue the story. Is the message more urgent? More tender? More or less vulnerable?

5. **Watch and reflect.**
   Play back your video on mute.
   - What was clear in the body when you were only speaking?
   - What became obvious when you were only moving?
   - Were there moments when your text and movement contradicted one another?

6. **Shift the context.**
   Choose a short movement section. Describe the ethos ("wild," "somber," "hesitant."). Pair it with three soundscapes:
   - **Silence:** What story do you see?
   - **Contradictory ethos:** What subtext or new meaning emerges?

- **Aligned sound:** Does it reinforce the message or flatten it?

Notice how each version changes the story.

Optional prompt: **Reverse the process.** Try the whole exercise again, but in reverse. Start with movement only. Let your body initiate. Then add words.

What does your voice say when it follows the body's lead?

Pagework: Writing into Communication

Freewrite on some or all of these questions.

1. **Write about two different experiences of making: one when you created mostly for yourself, and another when you created for an audience.**
    - What choices shifted because someone else would encounter it?
2. **When you share work, what are you hoping for?**
    - To be seen? To be understood? To build shared meaning?
    - How can you tell the difference in your process?
3. **When you feel misunderstood, how does it shape your creative process?**
    - Does it change how you choose your next communication?
4. **Examine one piece of your work.**
    - Where is your communication direct?
    - Where is it layered or indirect?
    - Are those choices deliberate and aligned with what you want the audience to experience?
5. **Consider how healing shows up in your work.**
    - Does it arise through personal release, through careful structure, or through meeting?
    - What conditions make that possible?

Movements + Maps: Speaking to the Void, Speaking to the Room

This score invites you to explore the impact of intent and audience awareness, revealing how relationships shape the meaning of your work.

1. **Create a piece no one sees.**
   Craft a solo artistic event using any medium. Perform it for yourself without documentation. It could be a short song, dance, text, or sculpture from household objects.

2. **Create for an audience.**
   Identify an audience: a trusted friend, pet, stranger, or social media post.
   Consider them:
   - What do you want them to know?
   - How do you think it might affect them?

   Create directly for their gaze. Share it somewhere and ask for their response (not critique).

3. **Compare and reflect.**
   - How did their absence shape my choices?
   - What changed when I imagined an audience?
   - Did any additional feelings arise through sharing it?

4. **Distill a phrase.**
   From all your material, craft a very short phrase. This is a single "sentence" in words, movement, or collage, a concentrated gesture.

5. **Translate or transform.**
   Change the medium:
   - Turn the **movement** phrase into a **sketch.**
   - Turn the **visual** piece into a **short poem** or **movement score.**
   - Turn the **sound** into a **drawn** or **choreographed** gesture.

6. **Make something from it.**
   Create a new, small piece of art from your various sketches. This could be a short dance, a thirty-second film, a micro-poem, a sound score, a solo, a photograph, or a composition in any form. Be concise, deliberate, and grounded. Don't overthink! Title it. Giving it a name clarifies the offering. Decide whether or not to share it with an audience.

Contributor's Note: The Artifice Is the Vehicle

by David Dorfman

> There are only two worthwhile things to leave behind when you depart this world of ours: children and art.
>
> (Stephen Sondheim, *Sunday in the Park with George*)[9]

Communication is endless, ethereal, needed, joyous, mysterious—and it can be abusive, abused, infrequent, lonely, hopeful—

and yes, endless again.

Not endless like "forever." Endless like weather, waves, thoughts.

It loops, slips, knocks, and returns. It disappears and reappears.

Communication lives in the body—

electrical impulses firing from the brain, keeping us alive, even when we're not aware of what is going where.

Although I love to emphasize communication in choreographic classes as an intent-full action, it is always occurring, whether we are moving or still, searching for meaning or assembling randomly.

Communication does not require our intention, but it thrives on it. This is both liberating and confounding.

How do we harness our communication skills as kinetic, poetic/prosaic embodied creators so we share a unique experience that is at once vivid, engrossing, compelling, or repulsive, wild, memorable… or… ?

Communication onstage is saturated to the point of fullness. We don't often communicate with each other like this in "real life." The artifice is the vehicle.

I try to make dances that people will take home with them—that are moving, funny, unbearably sad.

Let's make dances that are experienced so deeply

they stay in a viewer's body forever.

Or at least enter us fully for a moment?

---

[9]Stephen Sondheim and James Lapine, *Sunday in the Park with George*, premiered 1983.

We communicate by finding routes that draw viewers in electrically, like those impulses that keep us alive. Sometimes this is invisible, scientific, or magical, unspeakable. Sometimes it's transparent and literal.

To communicate, our work needs to be more than witnessed.

It needs to be transmitted and accepted.

Offered and digested.

Not always understood, but metabolized—enough to spark more inquiry, more inspiration, more dancing.

field notes from the studio

Movement is Necessary.

Move like you're not you.

Nurture the literary power of movement and the kinetic pleasure of (spoken) text.

What is radical or conceptual for you?

Look for happy accidents.

Dance the most beautiful thing you've never seen.

Be human and humane.

Everything I've learned, I've learned from Art.

Invite and Indict.

Subtext equals Context and Content.

Studio Provocations: Questioning Communication

We need radical honesty—learning to speak from our root systems about how we feel and what we want. Speak our needs and listen to others' needs.... The result of this kind of speech is that our lives begin to align with our longings, and our lives become a building block for authentic community and ultimately a society that is built around true need and real people, not fake news and bullshit norms.

(Adrienne Maree Brown, *Pleasure Activism*)[10]

Strategic Modes of Communication

How are you communicating (speaking, moving, projection, sound, program notes)?

- What forms are you *not* using?
- What is each element responsible for?
- Are any repeating the same message?
- Have you tried inviting contradiction between them, like slow movement with chaotic text?
- Do these modes reinforce one another, contradict one another, or dilute one another?
- What happens if you remove one element—text, music, movement—and let the others carry the meaning?

Are you shaping the audience toward a shared understanding, or intentionally leaving room for multiple interpretations?

The Role of the Audience

Do you *need* an audience for this?

- Why?

What are you asking of them?

- To witness? To agree? To question? To participate?

Do they know you see them?

[10]Adrienne Maree Brown, *Pleasure Activism: The Politics of Feeling Good* (AK Press, 2019), 10.

Legibility and Empathy

When something feels obscured, what exactly is unclear—the content, the structure, or your intention?

Is there a shared language between you and the audience?

- If not, have you taught them how to read this work?

Do you want your audience to receive more through feeling, intellect, emotion, senses, or intuition?

- What concrete choices are shaping that experience?

Direct Versus Indirect Communication

Is abstraction inviting interpretation or avoiding being seen?

What must the audience clearly understand for this piece to work?

Where is meaning explicit and where is it implicit?

- Is that shift intentional?

Modes of Communication

Move through each channel in your work. For each one, answer the same questions.

Text (spoken or written)

- What information is the text delivering that nothing else is?
- If you removed it, what would be lost?
- Is it clarifying, complicating, or repeating?

Sound (music, silence, rhythm, breath)

- What is the sound telling the audience?
- Is it shaping emotion, pace, tension?
- If the sound disappeared, would the meaning shift?

Movement (choreography, pacing, stillness)

- Where in the choreography does the audience lean in?
- Where do they relax?
- Where do they drift?

Lighting and Design (costume, projection, objects)

- What does the design tell the audience about tone, stakes, or genre?
- If the performers disappeared, what would the room still be saying?
- Is the design shaping meaning or decorating it?

Honesty, Vulnerability, and Artistic Integrity

What does this work want—recognition, admiration, confrontation, communion?

- Is that *want* shaping the piece?

If the audience did not respond as you hoped, would the work still feel complete?

Where do you feel most vulnerable in this expression?

- Is there anywhere that would benefit from *more* vulnerability?

10

Material

Before You Begin: Priming Curiosity About Material

Take a breath. Consider these questions. Let them settle in your body before moving forward. They are not for solving, but for sensing.

Why do I feel drawn to certain materials again and again?

Who feels like a source of insight, texture, or disruption in my work?

When does something shift from just *material* to something that *moves* me?

Where do I most often find my material, and where might I be overlooking it?

How do I know when my discomfort with a material means I should let it go or learn from it?

What materials feel safe, and what habits or unexamined patterns have grown from that safety?

Groundwork: Listening Through Material

> Two questions form the foundation of all novels: "What if?" and "What next?" (A third question, "What now?" is one the author asks himself every 10 minutes or so, but it's more a cry than a question.) Every novel begins with the speculative question, What if "X" happened? That's how you start.
>
> (Tom Clancy)[1]

Matter, Motion, and Meaning: The Sacredness of Material

This chapter is a little different.

Like the others, it's anchored by a central premise. But this chapter unfolds, in part, as an inventory of the materials that shape creative practice. What holds these sections together is the belief that material is never arbitrary, yet we often take it for granted. Materials resist, collaborate, and carry meaning. Each type of material offers a unique note. Tuning them, individually and in relation to one another, invites the complexity of your harmonic voice.

We often forget how many decisions we are making in our "material." We reach for what's familiar or available without noticing the meaning, association, and power they carry. Once we awaken material, we can collaborate with it.

This chapter explores nine categories of material: **human**, **kinesthetic**, **intellectual**, **dynamic**, **tangible**, **historical/cultura**l, **emotional**, **environmental**, and **technological/digital**. I ask you to consider the following: What is the **role** of material in your process? What are your **responsibilities** toward it? How might your relationship to it **grow**?

The Nature of Material

Materials are the atoms of our art. Objects, bodies, light, sound, ideas, spaces, voices—anything we consider an ingredient is material. Some of it we consider deeply. The lighting designer may obsess over the angle or timing of a cue; you may write and rewrite a line of text. But, because material is everywhere, we always forget to consider some of it. If we were cooking with these ingredients, measuring some and adding others mindlessly, our food would have a dubious outcome.

---

[1]Tom Clancy, quoted on Goodreads, accessed September 18, 2025, https://www.goodreads.com/quotes/673018-two-questions-form-the-foundation-of-all-novels-what-if.

Collaborating consciously with our materials is both expanding and humbling. It amplifies possibilities and invites our material to offer us new ideas. Material can be intellectual—ideas, colors, references. It can be kinesthetic, emotional, historical, or technological. Each type offers a different kind of friction, possibility, and responsibility. My intention is to pause our artistic assumptions, defaults, and expectations to see our material as unique collaborators, able to breathe fresh ideas into our work.

These sections are meant to help you notice what you prioritize, overlook, and never question. This chapter is a thesaurus: a tool for expanding language and discovering nuance. A thesaurus reminds you of everything you might say, often inspiring sentences you'd never have written. I hope that this chapter does the same for the materials you work with.

Human

Human material encompasses not only what people *do* but what they *know*, how they *feel*, and what they *create*. We could discuss "human" material in limitless ways, but I'll focus on *collaboration*. **How** do you choose collaborators? **Where** do you find them? **Why** are they right for *this* project? **What** mediums do they practice? **When** do they enter the process?

How do you choose them?

Do you hold an open audition, inviting anyone who wants to show up? This might reflect a value of expansiveness, believing inspiration can arrive from unexpected places. Do you gather people through personal recommendations—friends of friends, colleagues of colleagues? This choice can reveal a desire for continuity, a sense of community already woven into the work. Do you invite those who have already chosen you—students, workshop attendees, or others drawn to your research? This suggests a value in shared language and mutual curiosity, where collaborators meet you midstream in your inquiry.

Reflect: What does your method of choosing collaborators reveal about how you relate to risk, control, and surprise?

Where do you find them?

Are they emerging from your local community, building a dialogue with the place you live and work? Do you travel to find them, entering new cultural ecosystems and learning their rhythms? Are they primarily people you meet in professional settings—festivals, residencies, universities—or people you encounter outside of art entirely: activists, family, strangers? Each source reshapes the work's texture: the city that hums beneath it, the social fabric it echoes.

Reflect: What ecosystems does your work repeatedly draw from—and which remain unexplored?

Why Are They Right for This Project?

Is it about skill—virtuosity in a particular form, craft, or technique? Chemistry—how you sense their imagination meeting yours? Shared stakes—a personal resonance with the subject matter, an alignment of values, or a hunger to disrupt what either of you already knows? Each reason shifts how power, care, and accountability show up in rehearsal.

Reflect: Are you choosing for comfort, challenge, alignment, contrast—or something you haven't named yet?

What Mediums Do They Practice?

Are you calling dancers for a movement-based work or sculptors for a performance installation? A poet into choreography, a videographer into live theater? Each medium carries its own training, assumptions, tempo, and hierarchy of values. If you go on a hike with a geologist, a painter, and a biomechanics expert, different experiences will awaken. The same is true in our artistic process.

Reflect: If you invited someone from a medium you rarely work with, what would you choose?

When Do They Enter the Process?

Do you bring them in from the very first question so their fingerprints are on every layer of research? Do you wait until the structure is mostly built, inviting them to inhabit something already shaped? Do you stagger the timing—sound designer in week one, costume artist in week four—so the work evolves as a conversation across time? Timing reveals how you hold authorship and co-authorship, when you want solitude and when you crave chorus.

Reflect: What pattern do you repeat about when collaborators enter, and what would happen if you disrupted that sequence?

Kinesthetic

I often hear, "There's no new movement," as if originality means inventing gestures the world has never seen. This assumes movement lives in its **shape** rather than in its **context**, **timing**, and **lived presence**. Books are written with the same words; what makes them distinct is precision, point of view, and the way those words combine. Movement asks the same of us: not to create unheard-of shapes but to choose and compose in ways that feel alive.

If movement is a language, what counts as a "word"? Is it a gesture, a direction, a weight shift, a way of looking? Then phrases—like sentences—are where authorship emerges, in how gestures combine, interrupt, repeat, dissolve, or linger. Familiar components can still disclose something startling. "New" rarely means unprecedented; it means truthful, particular, or unmistakably yours.

Many of us inherit vocabularies—ballet, Graham, breakdance, Practical Aesthetics, Bharatanatyam, Viewpoints, Suzuki. These forms offer more than steps: they carry tone, gaze, dynamics, spatial logic, and ideas about power and audience. Inheriting a form means inheriting both its beauty and its biases: what it elevates, ignores, or assumes about bodies. Authorship comes from locating where you align and diverge from the form, and how you recombine: shifting rhythm, muting virtuosity, bending spatial habits, changing how presence is held.

Outside a named lineage, this can be even harder to see. Working in open forms like devised performance can feel boundless: no fixed aesthetic to honor or defy, no canonized rules to follow. The freedom is exhilarating, and slippery. It's easy to see that alienation is central to Brecht, or psychological realism to Stanislavski. It's harder to see the inherited patterns in devised forms: the field's taste for irony, hybridity, or fracture over coherence.

When anything is possible, what defaults quietly reappear? Perhaps you always drift toward floorwork, disjointed phrasing, or "rawness" as authenticity. Perhaps you avoid unison because it feels too formal or eschew overt narratives because they're "unsophisticated." These are givens, too—subtle pressures from training, peers, critics, even the lineage of *antilineage*.

Inviting yourself to see these invisible containers can be as clarifying as naming a codified one. **Ask:**

- What choices do I repeat without questioning?
- What do I avoid because I think "we don't do that here"?
- Who told me—explicitly or implicitly—what counts as serious, radical, or cliché?
- If I try the "forbidden" thing—symmetry, melodrama, stillness, virtuosity—what will I find?

Field Note: Shifting Authorship

For a long time, choreographing the movement was the heart of my practice. I was shedding years of inherited aesthetic after dancing with Bill T. Jones and was seeking my kinesthetic voice. I was driven by questions of form, effort, physics, and anatomy.

Phrasework was a way to learn and communicate who I was. But eventually, I became more interested in being surprised, changed, having other bodies and intelligences shape the vocabulary. I began building prompts and frameworks instead of phrases. I stopped listing myself as "Choreographer," and became "Director."

The shift from generating kinesthetic material to stimulating, curating, organizing, and editing the contributions of others was a radical change in my artistic life. It changed my aesthetic, but more importantly it changed my ecosystem, transforming the tone of the room, the balance of power, and the hegemony. It allowed me to recalibrate my strategies with my values as they evolved.

Intellectual

Intellectual material is your **thought architecture**: the image that wakes you at 3 a.m., the line of dialogue scribbled in your notebook, the color palette you build from a childhood memory.

It's the decision to set *Twelfth Night* on a spaceship or to let water slowly pool onstage until the actors are knee deep. Honoring your frameworks, associations, visual imagination, and staging philosophies is how your work begins to sound, look, and feel like *you*.

But in a world saturated with imagery, it's challenging to separate imagination from memories. **What is inspiration, and what is imitation?** What is *honoring* an influence, and what is *appropriation*? Learning to zoom in and out on the *context* of what you love, its lineage, intent, and formal strategy, catalyzes your admiration into your vision.

Those images that haunt us, that live in our bodies after a performance, aren't there to be borrowed. They're there to illuminate. Like the contrast dye in an MRI, they don't become part of you; they help you see what's already there. They clarify your obsessions, hungers, and questions. To let *other* art serve *yours*, you must look beyond the surface details. Instead of asking, "What did they do?" or "How did they do that?," ask, "*Why* did that image resonate?"

Here's an example: You're in a dark theater. An image, sound, or choice enthralls you. You can't stop thinking about it. The image from that show feels like the perfect solution to a place you're stuck in your own work… if only it were *yours*.

Many artists freeze here, stuck between stealing (don't) and banishing the image. The original image becomes an intrusive thought; shutting it down shuts down your imagination.

But what if you zoom out?

Ask: What was that artist's intent? What tactics did they use? Why was it so powerful? Perhaps they used a duet to distill something universal. Or layered sound in a way that created both fear and confidence.

Now zoom in.

What part of *your* scene could use those tactics? What if you adopt the *strategy*, not the *image*? Can you borrow the scale, tone, juxtaposition, or rhythm? Studying the DNA of what you love, rather than copying its expression, allows you to tap into artistic inspiration scientifically.

Creating intellectual material with integrity doesn't mean ignoring your influences, but engaging them critically, consciously, and ethically.

Dynamic

If vocabulary names *what* we do, dynamics name *how* we do it. "A man walking to a bed" is *staging*; whether he shuffles, marches, or lunges tells a *story*. Dynamics create tension, contrast, and resolution, shaping how material is *felt*. Even the smallest shifts hold weight. A twitching hand. Darting eyes. A hesitation before speaking. A gaze that slices across the room. These micro-moments accumulate, layering narrative into gesture.

Three questions can unpack our dynamics: ***Who* is shaping them? Why *these* dynamics? Which *habits* are steering them?**

Who decides? Are dynamics meticulously directed, or do they emerge from performers' choices? Does the piece need uniformity, or space for personal expression? Neither is better. But noticing the origin of your dynamics clarifies your values, making them shareable with the people in the room. When we skip this step, we invite confusion. A director may quietly expect precision while espousing freedom. This mismatch can strain trust. Choreographers may keep dynamics they dislike because they are reticent to correct a dancer's style. Directors may micromanage every glance while also insisting the room is horizontal, collaborative, and egalitarian. These tensions surface when we fail to articulate how decisions get made.

Why these dynamics? Every shift in weight, volume, or tempo carries intent. Do you want the audience to see the character's anxiety, or see them hide it? Both express anxiety; one adds the subtext of shame. **Alignment** between *what* and *how* creates one kind of meaning; **dissonance** creates another. Contradictions—a loud laugh over a breaking heart, a still body holding frantic breath—often pull the audience closer.

Which habits steer them? Habits come from training, culture, personality, and lived experience. They express our uniqueness, but they can become a mask. Maybe you use forceful energy when you're unsure or avoid stillness because it's vulnerable. Naming these patterns allows us to stretch. Try the opposite. Slow what you always rush. Hold the silence you often fill. Let unfamiliar dynamics invite you to unknown feelings. Learn to tolerate the empty space in the wake of a paused habit.

Tangible

Performers are not objects, but objects *perform* with you. Objects signal potential: A phone suggests connection to the outside world, a ladder promises a vantage point, a rope implies tension. The audience will wonder what they're for, consciously or not. Objects hold memories and associations, and every detail—the curve of a leg, the scrape of metal, the exact shade of green—has the potential to affect the viewer. Throwing "any chair" onstage without inquiry dulls that potential; *specificity* is what gives an object resonance.

At the same time, treating objects as if they are fragile relics can distort the relationship we are trying to build. Consider how we handle even the most sacred things in real life—a newborn, a wedding ring, a beloved book. We hold them with care, yes, but also familiarity. We look away, carry them around, forget about them sometimes. Exaggerating reverence onstage to infer an object's importance can backfire because it fails to activate our mirror neurons. When we watch humans behave as *we* do, it awakens our embodied memory.

Every object also builds *rules*. The *way* it is touched, ignored, moved, or revered becomes the construction of your devised world. A performer who cradles a cup like treasure and tosses it aside seconds later breaks a contract with the audience. That fracture can be thrilling when intentional, but confusing when accidental. Clarity about the object's role—and when that role shifts—keeps the audience tethered to the story you're building.

It's like the contract of a fourth wall. Imagine a play that spends two acts establishing the audience as invisible, quiet witnesses. In act three, without provocation, a character suddenly looks out and speaks to us. It never happens again. The rule is broken without context, breaking the agreement we established about reality and power. But if that same character has just survived something life altering—their partner leaves, their belief system collapses, their child dies—and in the silence after, they peel off part of a costume, raise their gaze, and speak directly to us, we understand *why* the rule changed. The break lands because the rule was **seen, acknowledged, and purposefully broken**.

If we understand the rules, we can subvert them with *meaning*. Your care in choosing and handling objects creates solidarity with the audience and performers about realism, relationships, and rules, all at the service of consent and cohesion.

Field Note: The Waterfall Problem

Sometimes we imagine unattainable material. We obsessively picture a waterfall, campfire, or elaborate set. We lament our budget, schedule, and resources. Instead of giving up the dream, consider:

- What compels you about that imagined material?
- How can you create the outcome without the material? Could light, sound, projection, or movement be your waterfall? Would rushing vocal dynamics fill that gap?

This digs into the *meaning* behind the fantasy. My Princeton students encounter this in their midterm. First, they must imagine a scene from a high-budget dance theater work. Then I slash their resources, and they distill the essence. Finally, they create a live event that meets their fantasy using only basic resources.

> **For example:**
> *Image:* "The back wall opens, and a 1920s tenement sits behind it. In it are the characters' parents, 50 years ago, discussing having a baby."
> *Distillation:* "I want to pack the backstory with feeling, not exposition. I want to care about this character's awful parents. I also like the spatial framing of the reveal."
> *Solution:* The character finds her mother's journal. As she reads aloud, a recorded voice takes over and she lip-syncs her mother's words discussing the baby with her husband, allowing the character to feel her mother's wants and needs in real time.

Historical/Cultural

Every creative choice is marinated in culture and history. The words "strong monologue" or "beautiful movement" were built on someone's *opinion* and *aesthetic*, and someone shaped *theirs*. But history and culture are subjective.

History

When "ballet" becomes shorthand for "technique," and "realism" for "good acting," other traditions are sidelined. In nonballet forms, "ballet technique" often refers to vertical alignment, cross-lateral connectivity, and muscular control. These qualities are not more valuable than rhythmic complexity, breath support, or successive patterning, but they've been granted greater institutional legitimacy. Meanwhile, Irish step dancing prizes verticality, hip-hop thrives on cross-lateralism, and Horton technique is built on muscular integrity. Yet ballet remains the foundation of most university dance curricula, solidifying its position as the default.

In theater, realism is similarly privileged. Emotional authenticity, psychological motivation, and causal narrative logic overshadow rhythmic timing, heightened language, or stylized presentation. But these qualities are alive in many global traditions. *Noh theater* cultivates internal transformation through precision; *West African griot* performance carries emotional truth through rhythm and voice; *Brechtian acting* embraces estrangement to spark critical engagement. Using these biases to define excellence shapes how we train, curate, critique, and fund art.

Even if you've trained across multiple forms, notice which ones you treat as "baseline." Which aesthetics feel like "home," and which feel like "styles" you visit? When you call someone "technical" or "rigorous," whose histories are you centering?

Ask:

- Which forms were foundational, and which were electives or "add-ons"?
- Where do you unconsciously reproduce the hierarchies you were taught?
- Which inheritances do you want to keep?

Knowing the currents you're swimming in lets you follow, resist, or redirect them with intention.

Culture

Many artists say they don't have a *culture*. I used to feel that way too. I grew up in a fourth-generation, politically liberal Ukrainian Jewish family. We didn't practice Judaism, eat Ukrainian food, or observe any cultural rituals. But, watching *Political Mother* by Hofesh Shechter, my muscle memory started humming. The deconstructed folk dances resonated in my bones. I suddenly remembered my grandparents' Christmas parties, where the adults would dance traditional Jewish dances like the *bulgar*[2] and *patsh tants* in the basement. As a child, I wasn't allowed in the circle. I watched from the edges, mimicking steps and learning the rhythm. Joining that circle when I was twelve felt like being knighted. The sense of inclusion and belonging was profound. That rhythm was still alive, waiting to be activated through art.

Even if your culture feels distant or diluted, it's worth digging into. What gets cooked at your family's table? What songs were played while people cleaned up? What body patterns or relational habits repeat through generations? Your body may hold memories your mind has forgotten.

Ask:

- What dances, stories, rituals, or sounds do I remember from childhood?
- What did my family do at holidays or rites of passage?
- What body languages, rhythms, or relating styles feel like home, even if I've never called them "culture"?

Interculturalism

There are moments when another culture's material will crack you open. When I encountered *Pantsula*, a South African street dance born within Apartheid, its rhythm, explosiveness, and political edge floored me. But quoting *Pantsula* without context would flatten it. Its brilliance doesn't live in

[2]YIVO Institute for Jewish Research, "Dance," *YIVO Encyclopedia of Jews in Eastern Europe*, accessed June 17, 2025, https://yivoencyclopedia.org/article.aspx/Dance.

the steps but in its stakes. It's a code of resistance born under surveillance. Moreover, it is not my story to tell.

So what do I do when another culture moves me deeply, but I don't want to co-opt it?

I analyze. I research. I try to understand how it works and what it's doing. Maybe it's the authenticity of the movement vocabulary, the way lived experience is etched into the phrasing. Maybe it's the 1:1 relationship between music and movement. Maybe it's the density of communal interaction—partnerships shifting, bodies witnessing each other, call-and-response embedded in the structure.

Ask:

- What in my culture reaches toward similar effects?
- How can I evoke such urgency, rhythmic clarity, or communal energy?

This isn't just about avoiding appropriation but about finding deeper artistic curiosity. Unearthing *why* something feels alive is where rigor lives. **Let interculturalism *stir* your process, not decorate it.**

Every influence or encounter can clarify what we're carrying and what we're reaching toward; knowing that lineage lets us create with more honesty, complexity, and care.

Emotional

Emotions shape how we breathe, move, and speak. They're visible in our gestures and audible in our cadence. They change us physically, slowing our limbs, cracking our voice, raising or lowering our gaze. They are nuanced compositional forces that offer unique artistic challenges. Here are some reminders about emotional material.

1. **Emotions rarely arrive alone.**
   Feelings overlap, contradict, and shift. Joy carries grief. Anger hides disappointment. A gesture may look defiant while its timing betrays hesitation. Complexity feels real because it activates the nervous system; simplicity flattens it.

2. **Emotional material needs shape.**
   Raw vulnerability isn't automatically compelling. Personal catharsis does not guarantee audience connection. The work must invite others into feeling, not ask them to witness yours.

3. **Balance control and surrender.**
   Exposing emotion requires surrender; shaping it into art requires control. Performance lives in the tension between the two.

4. **Beware emotional shorthand.**
   Shouting doesn't equal anger; trembling lips don't equal sadness. Audiences don't need a label; they need the felt truth. Paradoxically, we often feel *more* when less is *shown*.

5. **Harness the power of withholding.**
   A child trying not to cry often moves us more than one wailing. The pause before confession, the breath before breaking—these liminal moments invite the audience's own emotions to rise.

6. **Craft the frame.**
   Real feelings onstage can be vital—they shift breath, timing, weight, and bring the work alive. But art needs *shape*. Even when you let yourself fall apart, there's still a frame: knowing when the collapse begins, what supports you in it, and how you return. This is one of the ways we navigate *expression* into *art*. **Ask:**
   - Where does this emotional arc begin and end?
   - What does the audience need to track it?
   - What structures allow me to repeat this without harm or inconsistency?

7. **Emotional history lives in the body.**
   Our nervous systems, postures, and muscular habits hold traces of past feelings. Fear tightens the jaw, grief softens the pelvis, joy lifts the sternum. These patterns are *readable*. They can be amplified, interrupted, or transformed—not only somatically but compositionally. Catalyze the audience's meaning-making habits to tell the story *you* want to tell.

8. **Emotional contagion is real.**
   Your state affects the room. Our calm can soothe; our panic can unnerve. Use this awareness: What do you want to seed in your collaborators, your audience, yourself?

9. **Rehearsal and performance require different emotional guardrails.**
   Raw feeling may be useful in process but is unsustainable and dangerous onstage. Craft emotion to create safety and consistency without self-harm or dissociation.

Environmental

Environment provokes and inspires in ways we often overlook. The uneven texture of a floor might dictate the quality of a step, changing choreography forever. A flickering lightbulb can spark a duet of hesitation. A beam of sunlight through a window becomes a score for chance. These aren't distractions; they're contributions.

Every space carries agency and stories. A performance in a factory-turned-theater holds echoes of labor and transformation. A dance in a public park must contend with wind, leaves, and strangers passing through. Even a generic black box has limits and gifts: acoustics, angles, sight lines, shadows. The space you rehearse in is already shaping what you make, whether you name it or not.

And environment extends beyond walls—it's season, weather, political climate. A rehearsal the day after an election lands differently. A winter morning feels different from a summer night. A room shifts when one performer is missing, when tension hums between collaborators. Context is meaning.

When we stop treating the environment as neutral, we gain another collaborator—one with its own memories, moods, and momentum. Sometimes the best way to hear it is to **step outside your default**.

Try a few short experiments:

- Rehearse a section in a stairwell, hallway, or parking lot; feel how the echo or slope changes timing.
- Take a passage outdoors and notice how wind or traffic alters attention.
- Swap scale—crowd a group into a small room or place a solo in a cavernous space—and watch what emerges.
- Work only along the edges of the room, or only in its center, to see what focus shifts.
- Change the time of day: Rehearse at dawn or late at night and sense what new rhythms appear.

When you return to the studio, the work will carry the residue of its journey through environments.

Technological/Digital

Technology in the arts has always sparked tension. We depend on digital tools daily yet fear they might dilute the humanity and depth we value in live performance. During COVID-19 lockdowns, many mourned the loss of touch, shared breath, and co-present energy; screens felt flat, empathy lagged, and connection frayed. Others found provocation in the shift—new spatial logics, unexpected collaborations, ways to make work across geography and time zones.

This ambivalence isn't new. Mathematicians once feared calculators. Painters resisted the camera. Every generation faces the same anxiety: Will this tool replace me? Will it flatten what I love? But innovation rarely erases artistry; it transforms it. Calculators freed mathematicians to explore higher-order math. Cameras liberated painters from photorealism, allowing them to invent

Impressionism, Post-Impressionism, abstraction, and Surrealism. Fear of technology often hides a deeper truth: Transformation is unsettling, yet history shows tools *expand* expression, not *erase* it.

Still, technology has no *inherent* wisdom. It's a material, like light or fabric, and its value depends on how you use it. A sound score isn't good because it's made with expensive software. Projection isn't relevant because it's trending. You're not obligated to adopt AI or even a laptop to be legitimate. *New* doesn't mean *better*.

I use AI for grammar checks, research, and to put pressure on my logic, freeing me to focus on my very human gifts of embodiment, intuition, and empathy. If a tool opens space for your artistry, use it. If it distracts or diminishes your humanity, set it aside. You owe no allegiance to novelty or speed, and allowing technology to make things easier does not make you lazy.

Technology is not a *threat* to imagination; it's an *invitation*. It can't replace soul, but it can extend reach. It can scaffold form, magnify detail, and open possibilities you didn't know were there. Screendance can travel where bodies can't. Motion capture can translate gestures into visual symphonies. Robotics can introduce nonhuman presence into choreography. Sound looping can build live scores from a single voice or step. Virtual and augmented reality can bend scale—shrinking the audience inside a fingertip or expanding them across a landscape. Sensors can turn breath, heat, or heartbeat into light and sound. None of these tools is necessary, but each offers a doorway: a chance to make work that couldn't have existed before.

Material never stops arriving. It comes through bodies, histories, accidents, weather, tools, moods, memory. You don't have to master every kind of material, but you do have to recognize it—to know when it's rendering the work without your consent, and when it's a white rabbit you should follow to Wonderland.

This thesaurus is a way to enliven every rehearsal, every object you touch, every room you enter. Each time you notice a new layer—an overlooked sound, an inherited habit, a shift in weather, an uninvited collaborator—you expand the vocabulary of your art. The work of attending to material is endless, and that's what keeps it alive.

Agreements as Community Organizers

Each of these descriptions of material is a place we can converge or diverge, telling a story about coherence or contradiction. **Unison** tells a story about shared meaning; the *type* of unison (space, timing, dynamics, body part, text, agenda) offers breadcrumbs about their connection. If the performers all move in the same direction, we may see **environment**. Speaking or moving together may imply **shared history** (How do they all know the same thing?). Dynamics can suggest **emotional**

context, such as a community in grief or protest. Uniform costumes tell a story about **function**. Shared colors tell a subtler story about **harmony**. Tempo, duration, phrasing, body parts, and kinesphere each shed light on the relationships in their own ways. The aggregate of our materials allows for a complex, nuanced story to be told.

Material keeps arriving—through bodies, objects, weather, memory, lineage, accidents, tools. Attending to it widens your vocabulary. Arranging it gives the work its rhythm. This work of attending and arranging is ongoing, and by the book's end we'll return to it under the name of priorities—the lens that gathers all material into coherence.

Takeaway: Attend to what is here. Collaborate with what arrives. Every body, object, and condition carries weight and possibility. The work deepens when awareness guides not only what you make but how you arrange it.

In Practice: Tips About Material

1. **Start with what's in front of you.**
   Before you invent, notice what's already here—people, sounds, air, light, habits. Begin with what *is*.

2. **Let collaboration change the plan.**
   When others enter the work, let their instincts shift your structure. Treat difference as possibility, not interference.

3. ***Feel* before you *frame*.**
   Let tension, viscerality, and breath guide your first decisions. Create from sensation before you edit for design.

4. **Test material with your body.**
   Move it, touch it, speak it aloud. Materials gain meaning when they pass through sensation.

5. **Let energy carry the story.**
   Dynamics—pacing, volume, stillness—generate meaning more than vocabulary. Shift one and watch the whole tone change.

6. **Work *with* the object, not *against* it.**
   Learn your material's behavior. Follow its responses and physics before imposing your intention.

7. **Honor what a form remembers.**
   Every technique, style, or gesture has a past. Learn its roots, name its influence, and decide what you want to carry forward.

8. **Craft emotion into form.**
   Feelings aren't the destination; they're raw material. Give them contour, timing, and frame so they can find the audience with mutuality.

9. **Let the room teach you.**
   Light, sound, temperature, and space already choreograph the scene. Change one and study what shifts.

10. **Let technology extend, not dictate.**
    Let technology expand the work when it opens capacities you cannot access otherwise. Feel no obligation to include it when it does not serve the inquiry.

11. **Watch what happens *between* things.**
    Meaning gathers at the edges of people, objects, timing, and tone. Nuanced composition stays attuned to those intersections.

Frameworks: Is This the Right Material?

Choose a material you're currently working with—an object, body, idea, or image. Use the chart below to clarify how it functions in your process and whether any adjustments are needed.

Category	Prompt	Rating (1–5)
Relevance	Is this the *right* material for the work you're making?	☐ 1 ☐ 2 ☐ 3 ☐ 4 ☐ 5
Surprise	Does this material challenge or disrupt your expectations?	☐ 1 ☐ 2 ☐ 3 ☐ 4 ☐ 5
Agency	Are you letting the material influence the process?	☐ 1 ☐ 2 ☐ 3 ☐ 4 ☐ 5
Ethical Fit	Does your use of this material honor its source/context?	☐ 1 ☐ 2 ☐ 3 ☐ 4 ☐ 5
Energetic Charge	Does it still feel alive or has it gone flat?	☐ 1 ☐ 2 ☐ 3 ☐ 4 ☐ 5
Resonance	Does the material reflect or deepen your core inquiry?	☐ 1 ☐ 2 ☐ 3 ☐ 4 ☐ 5
Relationship	Are you in a dynamic exchange with the material, not domination or avoidance?	☐ 1 ☐ 2 ☐ 3 ☐ 4 ☐ 5

From the Field: *us*

Figure 10.1 Alexandra Beller in *us* at HERE Arts Center. Reproduced with permission of Carl Skutch.

In 2007, I choreographed a one-woman show that never felt like a solo. I was the only human onstage, but my partners—a flag, a raghead mop, a garbage can, and a series of sex dolls—designed the piece as much as I did. These objects were characters, collaborators, and provocations.

The work, *us*,[3] explored my tumultuous relationship with the United States, imagined as a romantic partnership unraveling. Could any last therapy session, conversation, or desperate gesture persuade me to stay? What betrayals or silences made leaving inevitable? These weren't abstract questions. They rose from my own frustration with a country unwilling to embrace diversity or renounce violence. Dancing with objects allowed those tensions to manifest in ways my body alone could not.

Each object carried a distinct charge. The flag—worn as a dress, snapped as a rifle, spun like a lasso—embodied patriotism: It asked me to envelop myself in it and prop it up reverently. The mop became

[3]Alexandra Beller/Dances, *us*, dance performance, premiere at HERE Arts Center, New York, June 19–24, 2007.

a female ally in our fight for autonomy. The garbage can, looping a baby's cries and an antichoice presidential address, hovered as a suffocating presence. The sex dolls, filled and emptied, embodied women's objectification, disposability, and silencing.

These weren't props *standing in* for ideas. Their weight, texture, and resistance provoked visceral responses from me. Treating them as sentient partners required me, as in all consensual relationships, to partner with the unknown. They yielded and resisted, demanding my adaptation. Each asked for its own dynamic, its own way of moving. This wasn't choreography imposed on material; it was choreography spawned by it.

I began by listening. I played with the objects and let them lead. The sex dolls, when unplugged, wilted with quiet, devastating pathos; their slow deflation became the final image of the piece. The flag choreographed itself, improvising and transforming as I twisted and unfurled it. The mop surprised me most: dancing with it made me wash the flag, an unplanned gesture of cleansing I never could have scripted.

The process mirrored internal family systems therapy, where parts of the self are externalized into distinct personas to be witnessed and understood. In *us*, the objects were horcruxes—fragments of my fractured relationship with the country. Externalizing those tensions allowed me, and the audience, to see and contend with them.

The audience, too, was material. Seated on all four sides of a boxing ring, their presence was not passive. Their gaze became a partner, mirroring the vulnerability, rage, and longing coursing through the work. Together, our bodies—mine, the objects', and theirs—formed a volatile ecosystem.

Looking back, the power of this process lay not just in animating objects but in discovering the life already inside them. They transcended symbol and became substance. Material wasn't a vessel for meaning. It *was* the meaning.

Guidance: When Your Material Fails You

When the materials of your creative life—your studio, collaborators, funding, or ideas—vanish or change, it can feel like the work is slipping away. Loss shakes us, but it also reveals what remains: **unexpected material waiting to be realized.**

Every artist will face a canceled venue, missing collaborator, rejected funding, or dried-up idea. Our instinct is to grip tightly to what should have been. But loosening our hold can open space for emergence. A dancer with a broken leg discovers a captivating arm dance. A canceled theater leads to an abandoned warehouse that frames the piece magically. Disrupted expectations spark invention.

But let's not romanticize it. The ache of disappointment is real—the fatigue, the scrambling, the heartbreak. False positivity only dissociates us from the truth. Let the spark of invention *and* the shadow it casts coexist. Hold resilience in honest conversation with grief.

Emotions that surface—rage, numbness, longing—aren't distractions; they are material. The old adage to "leave it at the door" is a relic. Treat feelings as collaborators: Listen, engage, let them lead. When creation feels overwhelming, stepping away isn't failure; it's part of the process.

Desire may feel dangerous after repeated loss. Yet longing itself is connective tissue, even longing for what we can't have. A single spark—a movement, a question, an image—can reignite the work.

When disappointment strikes, **pause**. Feel what's true, and check in:

Do I need to step back, or am I ready to engage?
Am I forcing silver linings, or am I genuinely curious about what's next?
Only then ask:
What is still available?
What questions haven't been asked?
What fragments remain, and what might they become?

The most compelling material often lives in what we nearly abandoned. The detour isn't the end of the road; it's another way home.

Tuning In: Nine Gateways into Material

This practice moves through these nine gateways of material to let new ideas enter.

1. **Human**
   Enter with your body as the primary material. Begin with **breath**, letting it guide the first shifts. Notice it travel through your chest, ribs, and belly. Let a small action arise—shift your gaze, stretch your fingers, tilt your spine—and allow it to unfold until it feels complete. Feel weight drop into your **bones**, spiral through your **fascia**, skim the boundary of your **skin**. Let your **organs** swell, settle, spiral. Notice how each layer changes your sense of self—and where "you" meets "not you."

2. **Kinesthetic**
   Let one movement begin without planning—a sway, a bend, a reach. Feel gravity thread through it, carrying you into falling, swinging, or rebounding. Stay with the texture: buoyant, sluggish, jagged, smooth. Let sensation guide you more than shape or appearance. Allow each action to ripple into the next, one gesture setting another in motion. Notice when the body surprises you, and follow those threads a little longer.

3. **Intellectual**
   Begin in stillness—seated or lying down. Let your mind wander freely. Don't fixate; let thoughts drift, link, and ricochet like a mind map. Notice which thoughts repel, hold, or return to you. When one takes root—because it compels, repeats, or resists—begin there. Let that thought sculpt your body into a shape. Then another. Let it form, reform, and reshape you. Track how the body digests the idea—not by illustrating it but by allowing it to move you.

4. **Dynamic**
   Choose a simple action—lifting an arm, shifting weight, walking a few steps. Change its tempo: **sudden, sustained, suspended**. Change its weight: **light, heavy, delicate, forceful**. Let your control over the movement vacillate. Widen and narrow your focus, responding to more, then less. Notice the feelings or associations that emerge.

5. **Tangible**
   Take an object near you into your hand. Hold it with indifference, then with care, then somewhere in between. Explore its weight, edges, and texture against your skin. Move with it slowly—balance it, set it down, let it rest on you. Notice when you adjust to the object and when the object seems to adjust to you. Attend to the behaviors or feelings this object awakens, and sense what it can do that you cannot.

6. **Historical/Cultural**

   Bring to mind a movement, rhythm, or gesture you have inherited or witnessed—from family, training, or community. Let your body echo it, even as a fragment. Repeat it until it feels full. Then allow it to unravel, transform, or dissolve into something less familiar, shaped by your body's present moment. **Ask:** What does this movement remember? What does it still ask of you?

7. **Emotional**

   Close your eyes. Imagine walking through a house you once knew—real or invented. Move through its rooms, touch its objects. Notice where tenderness, grief, and fear arise. Let that sensation fuel your movement. If nothing arises, explore the neutrality itself.

8. **Environmental**

   Let the room lead. Dance with its sound—hums, echoes, silence. Dance with its light—angles, shadows, warmth. Feel the air's temperature, the architecture's pull. Allow the environment to interrupt, redirect, or sustain your rhythm. Sense how your movement leaves an imprint on the space, even as the space leaves an imprint on you.

9. **Technological/Digital**

   Treat AI as a creative partner. **Use this prompt:** "I'm exploring movement based on this sensation: [describe sensory details]. Give me 7 images that are

   - Concrete and physical
   - Visually specific
   - Nonpsychological (no emotional labels)
   - No advice, no explanation
   - One short line each

   Avoid metaphors that name feelings. Stay embodied."

   Example: Input: *"My shoulders are heavy, my breath shallow, my legs floating."*

   AI output: "A balloon tied to a stone."

   Improvise based on each image AI offered, then begin to curate and create with them.

Studio Lab: Collaging Material into Meaning

This exercise invites you to work with everyday objects as compositional elements, allowing their relationships to reveal tone, tension, and narrative. By treating material as both literal and symbolic, you let form lead to meaning.

1. **Gather a collection of objects.**
   Collect five to ten objects from your space. Choose a mix of things that are personal, neutral or mundane, with varying textures, sizes, and functions.

2. **Arrange and reframe them.**
   Place them in a contained, clear area, a spatial frame. Arrange them with attention to shape, weight, and relation, without trying to tell a story. Consider:
   - **Proximity:** What's near, far, connected, or isolated?
   - **Orientation:** What leans, towers, or lies flat?
   - **Tension:** What feels grounded, precarious, in transition?

3. **Shift the narrative through small adjustments.**
   Swap, remove, or rotate an element. Watch meaning shift. Repeat multiple times.

4. **Deconstruct and abstract.**
   Choose the object that feels most charged and **remove** it. **Replace** it with something unexpected. **Shift** the purpose of an object so it no longer functions as intended. Play with **scale**: let something small dominate; hide something large.

5. **Engage the body in the installation.**
   Stand still inside the installation and let it orient you. Circle it slowly. Let your body mirror, resist, or echo one element. Improvise, noticing when you are drawn toward or away from something.

6. **Reflect.**
   - What object held the most weight for you and why?
   - What surprised you about how meaning shifted?
   - How did composition affect emotion or tone?

Pagework: Writing into Material

Freewrite on some or all of these questions.

Write about a time when…

1. **What you wanted wasn't there.**
   Something you needed vanished or was denied—funding, a collaborator, a space. How did you respond—replace, adapt, mourn, transform? What does your response show about the way you meet limits? Now ask: When something is missing in your current work, do you reach for substitution, reinvention, or delay? What choice feels available now?

2. **The material took over.**
   Recall a moment when a material behaved in a way you didn't plan—an object broke, the weather intruded, an emotion surged, technology failed or surprised you. How did the work change because of it? Do you tend to resist, absorb, or highlight these intrusions? In your present process, where is material already steering you? What would happen if you let it lead further?

3. **Your body remembered before you did.**
   Write about a time when a movement, rhythm, or ritual surfaced uninvited, as if your body carried memory you had forgotten. What did it feel like to follow that? How could attending to these embodied memories shift your creative lineage? What cues does your body give as you watch your own work—tightening jaw, leaning forward, holding breath, drifting focus, sudden alertness? Describe those reactions in concrete detail. In what ways do you follow them, amplify them, override them, or ignore them?

4. **You almost abandoned something.**
   Think of a material you nearly discarded—a gesture, draft, prop, image. Why were you ready to let it go? What changed your mind? Did saving it alter the piece or your sense of what is valuable in your process? Where in your current project are you hesitating—trimming something back, overexplaining it, or avoiding it altogether? If you stopped protecting the piece from that material, what section would have to grow, collapse, or shift to accommodate it?

5. **The smallest thing held the most weight.**
   Remember a moment when something overlooked—a silence, a pause, a glance, a shadow—carried unexpected meaning. How often do you give attention to what seems peripheral? What might happen if you treated the subtle or "minor" as central?

Movements + Maps: The Weight of What We Use

This score invites you to engage deeply with the dialogue between performer and object, space and substance, and between what is tangible and what lingers in absence.

1. **Create a short movement phrase.**
   Let each movement feel as defined and weighted as an object. Imagine each one has texture, density, color, and history, like a gallery installation. One movement might be a vintage sailboat, another a fossil, a 1940s offensive cartoon. Hold onto this phrase; you'll need it. This is your "original phrase."

2. **Arrange three to five objects.**
   Choose objects tied to memory, desire, tension, or your current emotional state. Touch, observe, listen to them. (*Optional:* Write a short sentence about what each object evokes.)

3. **Improvise with each object.**
   Notice your response: Are you pulled in, repelled, softened, sharpened? Create one movement in relation to each object and one of these spatial orientations each time:

   - **Above:** Loom, hover, suspend.
   - **Under:** Yield, fold, shelter.
   - **Around:** Circle, hesitate, orbit.
   - **Through or beneath:** Carve, disrupt, ghost.

4. **Create vignettes for each object.**
   Make a movement for each: a direct gesture, evasion, confrontation, tender repetition. Let each interaction be like a short sentence.

5. **Develop a walking phrase.**
   Create a walking phrase to get you from vignette to vignette. Your walking phrase must include **three shifts in tempo** and at least **one sudden change in direction**.

6. **Remove the objects.**
   Repeat as if the objects remain. Let absence become its own material. What does the movement ask to become now? Notice whether the memory of the object stays in your body or dissolves.

7. **Combine your original phrase with the object phrase.**
   Collage, edit, delete, and recombine parts of both. Let one interrupt, expand, or contradict the other. **Explore:** Does one dominate? Do they weave? Do they fracture or integrate? Refine your timing, rhythm, and sequence until the phrase feels layered and alive.

Contributor's Note: Remembering Remembering

by Bebe Miller

I am a choreographer because I watch. I watch the space between events and the timing between people. I watch the degree of energy in reconsidering a thought. I watch the laying of hands—on foreheads, furniture, puppies, space, the missing person described from memory. I watch carefully, carelessly, glancingly, stupidly. I watch based on how I've watched, what I've seen.

Humans are built on memory. We build our place in the world through what we remember, and we navigate the events we encounter according to our habits and perceptions. We ricochet onward and navigate by way of constant sensory information, through familiar as well as unfamiliar terrain. We organize our faces, postures, our relation to the weather, the landscape, and the paths we find ourselves on, aligning ourselves with the interior catalogue of events that collect and regenerate throughout the course of our lives.

Dances are built by humans. The layers of remembered events we pass through daily are the fascia of the body's reasoning, the matrix of the dance's form.

We remember remembering.

I think that part of the reason I choreograph dances has to do with revisiting memory in some weird, made-up way. I am taken away by the chance to crystallize fleeting encounters I may have seen or remembered, stopping time and action long enough to read them from the inside—from the flesh, from a distance. I fact-check my attention, choreographically: What's the rhythm? Where's the focus? What's the next dream move? I don't carry the catalogue of my life in my head; well, not all of it anyway. But I do collect kinds of time, kinds of impulses and resolutions that I see around me.

Memory is the container; remembering activates the practice. I abstract the nutrients, shift the emphasis and make something new. I rearrange sensation and image, according to the form that emerges. It is the thrust of intention that sends an arm into space just so, rather than its placement there. I follow the timing between gestures, the rise of attention between people, the toss of their weight, the offhand smirk or the tilt of a shoulder. Held in position a bit too long. My reasons for dancing do not need to be—nor are they—the reason for watching.

My reasons for dancing—for dance making—might sit alongside the reasons one watches these dances, but then how would I know that? We come together empty-handed, hearts and minds at the ready.

Studio Provocations: Questioning Material

What matters is not to ask what things mean, but rather how they work, how they matter, how they come to matter. The question is never merely about the material, but about how we question materiality itself.

(Trinh T. Minh-ha, *Woman, Native, Other*)[4]

Human Material

What if your performers had no shared vocabulary?

Try: Build a duet where each performer has distinct, secret rules. Notice the tensions that emerge.

Who is shaping the material?

Try: Let collaborators decide the order, tempo, or emphasis of your phrase. Step back and watch how authorship shifts.

How do the relationships generate material?

Try: Give two performers this alphabet: A, B, C, E, I, L, M, N, O, R, S, T, Y. Each creates a word bank, trades lists, writes ten sentences from the other's words, then trades again. Each chooses three sentences and creates a phrase for each. Layer the phrases—speaking, moving, fragmenting—and notice where overlap or misalignment creates meaning.

Kinesthetic Material

How are you using stillness?

Try: Extend its duration. Does pacing or emotional weight shift?

What is the topography?

Try: Draw one continuous doodle per performer without lifting your pen. Give each performer their doodle as a map for spatial pathways and intersections.

Intellectual Material

What questions are fueling your process that the audience cannot yet perceive?

---

[4]Trinh T. Minh-ha, *Woman Native, Other: Writing Postcoloniality and Feminism* (Indiana University Press, 1989), 28.

Try: Write those questions down as text and stage them physically—spoken, projected, or carried as objects. Let them inhabit the work rather than hover outside it.

What rules about composition are you following?

Try: Identify one rule you've been unconsciously following—symmetry, narrative logic, evenly spaced groupings—and break it. Invert the pattern, scramble the sequence, or remove the rule.

Dynamic Material

Where does tension accumulate?

Try: Build a section that sustains that tension without release. Track what changes in breath, timing, and audience focus when resolution is withheld.

How does the work's energy shift from beginning to end?

Try: Draw a single line across a card that tracks its intensity over time. If it crescendos, draw a rising diagonal. If it decrescendos, draw a falling one. If it stays steady, draw a straight horizontal line. If it surges and drops, draw a zigzag. Let the line represent how force, speed, volume, or emotional charge builds or recedes. Lay the cards out in order. What patterns do you notice? Then rearrange them. Watch the dance in that order. What emerges?

Choose one dynamic (e.g., weightlessness, chaos, precision).

Try: Find one section where that dominant dynamic feels habitual. Adjust only the dynamics—keep the choreography or text intact. What new tone emerges?

Are your sections a similar pace or duration?

Try: Radically alter one section—double its length or compress it to half. Observe how pacing shifts tone, urgency, or meaning.

Tangible Material

What objects appear and what do they mean?

Try: Reassign their meaning—a rope as weapon, lullaby, lifeline.

Where does light come from?

Try: Rehearse with light from an unconventional source—phone screens, under costumes, through a cracked door.

If your piece had a primary texture, what would it be?

Try: Layer in a conflicting texture. What new information emerges?

What if an object became the protagonist?

Try: Rework a section, letting the object drive the action.

Historical/Cultural Material

What cultural lineages appear in your movement, sound, or design?

How would the piece land in a radically different cultural context?

Try: Stage a short section, imagining that audience.

What styles have you inherited?

Try: Exaggerate or subvert one intentionally.

If you could borrow from another tradition, what would you quote?

Try: Evoke its energy or architecture without appropriating material.

Emotional Material

Where does emotion feel performed, and where does it feel lived?

Try: Keep the choreography or text intact. Adjust only breath, focus, and timing. Notice what changes in credibility.

Where do multiple emotions already coexist?

Try: Locate a moment where tone is layered—tenderness with irritation, humor with grief, steadiness with panic. Adjust only the timing: extend a beat, compress another, delay a reaction. Notice how the balance between the emotions shifts.

How does the emotional temperature rise and fall?

Try: Identify one place where the temperature changes quickly. Slow that change down. Then try the opposite—make it abrupt. Compare the effect.

Environmental Material

How is your space generating the material?

Try: Rehearse in a hallway, stairwell, or bathroom. What becomes urgent or absurd? Can you bring that back to the studio?

How does time itself craft the work?

Try: Rehearse a section at dawn, late at night, or in shifting light. Notice how fatigue, circadian rhythm, or atmosphere alters tone.

What environmental factors are you ignoring?

Try: Bring one to the forefront and let it drive the scene.

Technological/Digital Material

Are you using technology by choice or default?

Try: Add or erase technology for one section. What do you gain or lose?

What could you do if the work were a film?

Try: Re-create a cinematic effect live.

Could a simple tool (projector, AI, mic, phone) be used in a way that's never occurred to you?

Try: Use it for one surprising function.

What happens when technology leaves the room?

Try: Run one section without any tech—no sound system, no phones, no projections. Replace with bodies, voices, or simple physical tools. Notice what is revealed or lost.

11

Context and Culture

Before You Begin: Priming Curiosity About Context and Culture

Take a breath. Consider these questions. Let them settle in your body before moving forward. They are not for solving, but for sensing.

Who taught me what matters in art, and do I still agree?

Why do I feel visible in some spaces and invisible in others?

Where do I feel most at home, and where do I feel like a guest?

How do I recognize what I birthed and what was handed to me?

What parts of my culture show up in my work, whether I name them or not?

When do I feel most in sync with the culture around me, and when do I feel out of step?

Groundwork: Mapping Context, Meeting Culture

> Bodies are mirrors that absorb, remember, and reflect society's politics, art, religions, aesthetics, hopes, fears, strengths, failings—both the officially sanctioned versions and the sub-rosa closeted taboos. Bodies are barometers measuring the pulse of society.
>
> (Brenda Dixon Gottschild, "The Black Dancing Body as a Measure of Culture")[1]

A Note on Reading This Chapter and a Disclosure

This chapter attends to how power, access, and history shape artistic choices. I write as a white artist who has benefited from visibility I did not always recognize and who has also met exclusion in other parts of identity. Power does not sit on a single axis; resources, recognition, and the "benefit of the doubt" move through race, class, gender, ability, geography—and also through the systems that tell us what counts as "legitimate" art, what tempo of productivity is expected, what forms are deemed worthy. Read yourself in relation to power, not only identity. If you have had access, notice what has been treated as "neutral" or "universal." If you have met erasure or gatekeeping, may this language affirm what you already know and invite new forms of agency. This chapter is not only about race or justice but about the invisible systems—of art, productivity, and expectation—that shape how we create and how we are seen. The aim here is clarity, curiosity, and responsibility.

Art as Context, Art as Culture

It would be comforting to have a fixed, shared reality, a world where facts are unchanging and right and wrong are clearly defined. But human experience is messier than that. We build our realities from facts, feelings, perspectives, and beliefs that are colored by our context.

My sons are both colorblind. Their sunsets are not my sunsets. Are their facts *wrong*? Calling this "missing" information centers one reality as the norm. Science itself shifts beneath us. History reminds us that truth evolves. What we accept as a "fact" is conditioned by time, culture, and power.

This is even more true of art.

Every creative act is born with a cultural inheritance. Stuart Hall reminds us that cultural identity "is not a fixed essence but a positioning… subject to the continuous 'play' of history, culture, and power."[2] Assumptions, styles, structures, and default forms have been passed down to us. Every artistic choice

---

[1]Brenda Dixon Gottschild, "The Black Dancing Body as a Measure of Culture," *Choros International Dance Journal* 7, no. 1 (2018).

[2]Stuart Hall, "Cultural Identity and Diaspora," in *Identity: Community, Culture, Difference*, ed. Jonathan Rutherford (Lawrence & Wishart, 1990), 223.

reinforces or challenges our stories about value, legitimacy, and meaning. These legacies shape how we communicate, how we use time, space, and money, and even the theatrical "givens" we rarely question—the proscenium stage, the dark theater, the teacher-student relationship.

The question is, Are we *examining* or *reproducing* our artistic inheritance?

Artistic Colonization

Colonization concentrates power: A dominant group or idea overtakes the many. Beyond geography, this pattern repeats in aesthetics, privileging certain lineages, methods, and looks while diminishing others. In dance, we see colonization when "dance technique" is automatically equated with ballet or prioritizes Western alignment, phrasing, and dynamics.

In many institutions, "strong technique" implicitly means ballet—an inheritance that positions other lineages as stylistic or secondary, no matter their rigor. As Brenda Dixon Gottschild has argued, ballet is treated as the neutral yardstick, while Africanist aesthetics and other lineages are framed as deviations or add-ons.[3] Technique is simply the strategy for consistently and repeatably practicing skills toward foundational efficiency. Empathy, interoception, spatial awareness, and dynamic clarity all have techniques. When only one lineage is granted the title "technique," other lineages are pushed to the margins as "styles" or "electives," and erasure takes root inside the very language we use.

The same colonizing logic shapes how we classify art into genres, binaries, and categories. Anyone who has applied for funding knows the early demand to define: before describing the work, you must choose a label. Genres carry assumptions that preshape interpretation, signal allegiance, build invisible walls, and often invite judgments about what counts as *better* or more *legitimate*. Art becomes the ultimate clique.

What happens if we dissolve these containers and approach *all* art as a continuum of ideas about time, space, meaning, relationship, material, shape, and environment? What if we interrogate work through the lenses of politics, identity, process, mathematics, physics, mythology, and history? Where do we align, and what stories do we *share*? Let's loosen the borders and play. What unexpected connections might we discover if we resist the urge to categorize?

---

[3]Brenda Dixon Gottschild, *Digging the Africanist Presence in American Performance: Dance and Other Contexts* (Greenwood Press, 1996), 16–18.

Dismantling Binaries in Art

Cultural narratives often flatten complexity into binaries—man/woman, black/white, rich/poor—shrinking our ability to perceive the full spectrum of lived experience. Creative practice inherits similar simplifications. These are often taught as "opposites."

- **Process/product:** as though the journey and the outcome live apart.
- **Technique/somatics:** as though virtuosic movement resists mindfulness, or intuitive movement lacks rigor.
- **Entertainment/high art:** as though accessibility and depth cannot share space.
- **Abstract/narrative:** as though meaning must be either explicit or absent.
- **Individual/collective creation:** as though genius occurs alone and collaboration dissolves authorship.

Between these imagined poles stretches an entire spectrum—an ecology of options rather than a single crossroads. Continuums hold adaptability, contradiction, and specificity. Most of our colors live between the extremes of primary hues; humidity and temperature blend into endless variations of weather. Not only are there infinite *shades*, but we live in a world humming with contradiction. We experience this in sun showers, the taste of salty and sweet, and feeling the wave and the undertow simultaneously.

Human experience carries similar multiplicities. We can grieve and laugh in the same moment. We love and harm, falter and blame, forgive and feel wounded. Authentic work often emerges from what resists neat classification: grief underscored by "happy" music, joy edged by rage. These intersections can hold some of our richest material. Working beyond binaries expands perception, allowing art to meet life in its wholeness.

Breaking the Frame

Art lives in these layered states. We inherit rules, habits, and frameworks that compress our instincts and vision. These rules live in the architecture of stages, in who speaks and who listens, in what we praise and what we overlook. Over time, they become absorbed by our unconscious, constricting our intuition. Once visible, we can choose what to keep, stretch, or release.

Some common inheritances include the following:

- **Fixed structures:** Proscenium stages, "clear beginnings and endings," narrative arcs.
- **Aesthetic hierarchies:** What counts as "sophisticated" or "beautiful" often echoing Eurocentric, patriarchal, or class-based values.
- **Human centrality:** Human bodies, voices, and emotions are at the center of much performance. What changes when objects, landscapes, or environmental forces become equal agents in the work?
- **The "universal":** The concept of a universal experience invariably reflects *dominant* cultural norms rather than shared human truth.

History is full of artists whose work arose from reimagining these defaults: **Beckett** let *stillness* carry *force.* **Bartók** wove *folk lineages* into *concert form.* **Pina Bausch** dissolved borders between *dance* and *theater.*

Interrogating these inheritances begins with noticing them. Where did they originate? Which ones serve us, and which restrict our vision? Which have I actively chosen, and which are unconscious biases unaligned with my values? What repositions when the question changes from, "What category does this fit into?" to, "Where do these things already meet each other?"

What do **Basquiat** and **Björk** share?

How do **Cunningham** and **Wes Anderson** overlap?

Where does **Bharatanatyam** echo **Irish step dance**, or **hip-hop**?

These connections may feel improbable, even dissonant, at first. Sit with them longer and deeper patterns appear—commitments to rhythm, time, and audience; idiosyncratic craft; devotion to both history and invention. **Basquiat** and **Björk** both rework public perception as material, layering irony, myth, and vulnerability into their compositions. **Cunningham** and **Wes Anderson** sculpt affect through precision, spatial architecture, and deliberate timing; emotional undercurrents arise from formal clarity. **Bharatanatyam**, **Irish step**, and **hip-hop** arise from distinct lineages yet share percussive footwork, communal storytelling, and a demand for exactitude that transcends genre.

Beneath every tradition lives a shared palette: time, space, weight, relationship, flow, physics, control. Each culture fashions these forces through its own histories, intentions, and values. Gravity pulls on every body. The planet's axis and rotation create the same constructs of time. Tension and release, proximity and distance, stillness and motion—these conditions exist everywhere, even as each tradition interprets them in its own language.

Recognizing these commonalities does not *erase* the idiosyncrasies that make a culture unique and sacred. It lets us look past what at first feels foreign—the costumes, the syncopation, the vocabulary—and notice patterns that live underneath. Butoh may appear unlike our work: nearly naked bodies, stylized gesture, aching slowness. Yet in its use of gaze, light, and set design, we may find affinities closer to home than with colleagues working in our own genre.

This decoupling from invisible rules asks for more than curiosity. It requires humility, research, and accountability. Engaging with cultures beyond our own means decentering ourselves and staying answerable when we misstep. We cannot "know" another culture through brief exposure; we can only approach with care, listen for what is asked of us, and meet that with respect.

> Dominator culture has tried to keep us all afraid, to make us choose safety instead of risk, sameness instead of diversity. Moving through that fear, finding out what connects us, reveling in our differences; this is the process that brings us closer, that gives us a world of shared values, of meaningful community.
>
> (bell hooks, *Teaching Community: A Pedagogy of Hope*)[4]

Shifting Our Lens: Expanding and Contracting Perspective

The same awareness that helps us notice common forces across traditions can help us question the norms and conditions of our field. Dominant forms—beginnings, middles, ends; realism; virtuosity; familiar stage spaces—arrive preloaded, offering what looks like a complete palette while concealing potential material. We rearrange what's *inside* the structure without asking whether the structure *itself* is a choice. It's like inheriting a dollhouse and assuming your only choices are wallpaper and furniture, never imagining the walls could open, the roof invert, or gravity reverse.

We feel this in everyday life. An imposing salesperson asks, "Should I follow up by phone or email?" The question assumes we want a follow-up. They have condensed the frame only to include the options *they* desire. By restricting our choices, they erase the larger question ("Would you like a follow-up?") and, with it, our consent. We end up choosing between two options we never wanted.

This is where **Whole-Part-Whole** becomes useful. Developed in Laban/Bartenieff Movement Studies, it describes a rhythm of perception—zooming out, in, and back out. As Irmgard Bartenieff describes,[5]

---

[4]bell hooks, *Teaching Community: A Pedagogy of Hope* (Routledge, 2003), 197.

[5]Irmgard Bartenieff, *Body Movement: Coping with the Environment* (Gordon and Breach Science, 1980), 45.

this rhythm supports the dialogue between detail and context. Choreographer Liz Lerman often uses similar perceptual shifts in her community-based processes, where attending to a single gesture of an elder or nonprofessional mover transforms how the whole ensemble is perceived.[6]

- First, **zoom out**—take in the widest frame possible.
- Then, **zoom in**—study the details with care.
- Finally, **zoom back out**—let the details reshape your understanding of the whole.

This practice interrupts inherited defaults. In public discourse, it creates space to question the ground we're standing on before debating what color to paint it. In art-making, it prevents us from arguing about curtain speed when what we truly need to ask is whether we *want* a curtain at all. Without that wider frame, we rearrange details instead of generating a world. We shake the snow globe and expect a new landscape.

Whole-Part-Whole doesn't *discard* context or culture; it brings them into focus. It shows where *norms* masquerade as *aesthetics*, offering more colors than we were told *existed*. Every shift—out, in, out—exposes the structure and the space within it.

This is the work of the artist: to notice. To trace where defaults have compressed us, where they stabilize us, and where they invite reimagining.

Takeaway: Every work begins inside an inherited frame. The artist's task is to see it, question it, and choose what to carry forward, stretch, or let fall away.

[6]Liz Lerman, *Hanging by a Thread: Thoughts on Community and Connection* (Wesleyan University Press, 2012), 67.

In Practice: Tips About Context and Culture

1. **Notice your defaults.**
   Slow down to notice your automatic choices about structure, process, timing, bodies, or space—how long you hold a beat, when you default to unison, how touch is introduced.
   Ask: What standard do I follow even though it doesn't quite fit my process?

2. **Interrogate the frames you inherit.**
   Look closely at the systems, traditions, and aesthetics you've absorbed—costuming norms, body size on stage, how fictional gender aligns with performer gender, which language is spoken by default.
   Ask: What do I stand for in life that I abandon in the studio?

3. **Question artistic givens.**
   Challenge familiar templates—beginnings, middles, ends; realism; virtuosity; human centrality.
   Ask: What changes if I remove or invert one of these?

4. **Expand and contract your lens (Whole-Part-Whole).**
   Zoom out to see the cultural, political, and historical forces at play. Zoom in to study the details—when you resolve tension instead of sustaining it, what gets repeated, whose ideas are centered. Zoom back out to notice pattern they create together.
   Ask: What am I taking for granted as inevitable?

5. **Honor the context and your sources.**
   When engaging material beyond your lived experience, research deeply and listen actively. Learn who carries the form, how it has been used, and what histories travel with it. Approach with care, resisting surface-level borrowing. Approach with humility and care, resisting surface-level borrowing. Build sustained relationships with the work and its lineage.
   Ask: What responsibility comes with using this material?

6. **Attend to power dynamics.**
   Notice how agency is distributed between performers, collaborators, audience, and yourself—who makes final decisions, who improvises, who waits for permission, who is quoted in the program notes.
   Ask: Who can say no here without consequence?

7. **Stay curious, not certain.**
   Let questions guide your process. Make space for being surprised, challenged, and transformed by what emerges rather than clinging to fixed answers.
   Ask: Where am I defending an idea instead of investigating it?

8. **Reimagine tradition.**
   Traditions carry memory, identity, and resistance—and they can also uphold exclusion.
   Ask: Am I repeating this because I believe in it, or because I was trained to?

9. **Look for shared forces without collapsing difference.**
   Across every tradition, gravity pulls, time passes, bodies meet and part. Noticing these shared conditions can open connection and deepen respect for how each culture shapes them differently. Seek *resonance*, not *sameness*.
   Ask: What would happen if I stayed with this a little longer before deciding I understand it?

10. **Consider the room you invite.**
    Audiences, collaborators, and communities shape the chemistry of the work. Identity, history, and temperament enter with them.
    Ask: What would unsettle this piece in a useful way?

Frameworks: Three Cultural Forces × Three Artistic Responses

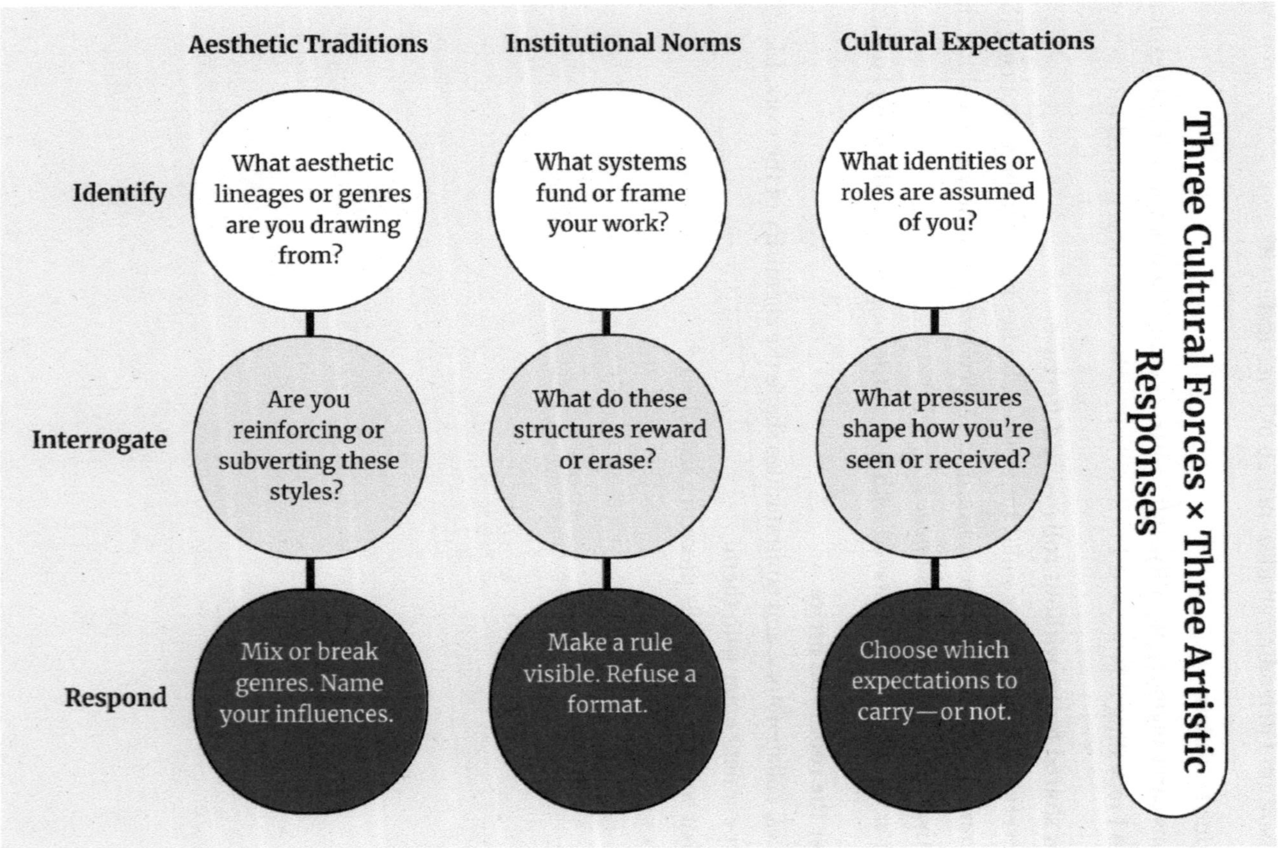

Figure 11.1 *Three Cultural Forces × Three Artistic Responses.* Chart connecting aesthetic traditions, institutional norms, and cultural expectations with creative strategies of identification, interrogation, and response.

From the Field: *Fandango for Butterflies (and Coyotes)*

Figure 11.2 The cast of *Fandango for Butterflies (and Coyotes)*. Reproduced with permission of Maria Baranova.

When I was asked to choreograph *Fandango for Butterflies (and Coyotes)*,[7] I felt honored—and terrified. This play was built from interviews with undocumented immigrants navigating daily uncertainty and the raw logistics of survival. The cast and creative team were all Spanish speaking, with first- or second-generation roots in the United States. Their connection to the material was visceral—rooted in family histories and lived experiences I could never embody.

The stakes felt impossibly high: to move carefully enough not to harm, yet boldly enough to serve the story. How could I, someone without this lived context, offer *guidance* without *presumption*? How could I ensure the movement didn't feel imposed or artificial? My body, training, and artistic instincts felt insufficient. Irrelevant even. I worried that my instincts, training, and even my body might fail this story. The desire to contribute without overstepping was a tension I carried throughout the process.

[7]Andrea Thome, *Fandango for Butterflies (and Coyotes)*, directed by José Zayas, produced by En Garde Arts, premiered at La MaMa Experimental Theatre Club, New York, February 6–15, 2020.

I decided my role was to **catalyze** and **curate**—to evoke material from the performers and craft it. My job was not to *impose* a movement vocabulary, which, in this context, risked feeling colonial. Instead, I assembled, collaged, and composed with the movement *they* devised.

My role was to illuminate and celebrate *their* experiences inside a stable, resilient structure. And to hold a frame that was sturdy enough for them to play, explore, and risk vulnerability. The work needed steadiness without apology, strength without force, control without coercion.

We followed the characters' memories of waiting, walking, and facing unknowable danger. I combed the text for words where physical and emotional forces collided, like "lost," "holding it together," and "unmoored." I linked staging choices to the verbs in their stories. No one could leave the stage; invisible tethers bound them together. There was never perfect unison; something always lagged, resisted, or pulled away. We built up scenes only to dismantle them immediately, creating a structure of disorientation and impermanence. The performers' movements created a fractured but fluid vocabulary that reflected the instability that underpinned the story.

My power as a choreographer wasn't about asserting expertise but amplifying the voices and bodies in the room. Collaging their gestures into metaphorical narratives was far richer than anything I could have invented. At the same time, honoring their stories required a structure that was specific, integral, and clear. The stories were often violent, and the choreographic foundation needed to be resilient. It was crucial that I also maintain a strong frame, make clear choices, and be a true leader without resorting to authoritarianism or manipulation.

Humility did not mean absence of strength. Presence, rigor, and challenge remained essential. Leadership in this show meant holding a strong frame that left space for others to step into it.

Guidance: Finding Joy

Burnout is heavy—often heavier for artists, whose work and passion are inseparable. It can feel like a hollowing out of purpose, a disconnection not just from energy but from meaning. In the wake of artistic fatigue, finding joy and inspiration is not a silver lining; it's mission-critical.

Our field doesn't always make that easy. We are taught to revere rigor, discipline, and sacrifice. We valorize the dancer performing with a broken foot, the writer who hasn't slept in days, the actor surviving a tyrannical director. I inherited this belief too. I built my early career on excellence and output, taking pride in how much I could bear. Joy appeared often, but never as a *priority*; it showed up as a side effect, a surprise, or a reward. Not the core method.

And so I had to ask, What if joy was the *method*?

I don't mean "earned" reward or pleasure as a distraction. Joy is not about escaping difficulty but about coexisting with it. Some of the most powerful, moving work I've made or witnessed has emerged not in the absence of pain but through the insistence of joy's presence within it (think of the film *Life Is Beautiful*). Joy is not the opposite of struggle; it's what gives struggle shape, texture, and humanity.

Crafting this requires repatterning. Our most influential systems reject joy as a value. We are taught that suffering legitimizes art. That pain is a sign of depth. That joy is naive, unserious, or indulgent. That "real" artists grind themselves down to the bone. This myth doesn't just harm artists; it impoverishes art.

For artists from historically marginalized communities, joy can be a radical act—defying the message that worth must be *earned* through hardship. Centering joy doesn't mean ignoring injustice. It means insisting on wholeness. On humanity. On presence.

Joy takes time, and time often feels scarce. We say, "I'll take a break after this show," or "I'll make space once I've caught up." But what if joy isn't something we earn *after* we work? What if it's what makes the work *possible*?

Joy doesn't follow a schedule. It doesn't arrive on demand, but we can create the conditions for it to find us. It can sneak in through silliness, through play, through quiet watching. It's an inside joke during tech, an anecdote in rehearsal, the conspiratorial look in a collaborator's eye. **They're not side quests; they're access points.**

When I allow for those moments—when I don't push them away in the name of productivity—something shifts. My process softens. My ideas open. My body breathes differently. I become more curious, more attentive, and more willing to take risks.

Centering joy means treating it as **a condition of practice**, not just a by-product, and building processes that allow it to emerge. That might look like starting rehearsals with laughter or scheduling rest into rehearsals.

It also means designing your artistic life to include pleasure—not just accomplishment, but felt, embodied pleasure. Noticing what feels generative and fills the well and what brings you back to yourself. (See "Groundwork: The Compass of Faith" in chapter 8 for tips on this.)

It means acknowledging when joy is absent and getting curious about *why*. **Ask:**

- What parts of your process feel dead or dutiful?
- What stories have you inherited about what "counts" as valuable or valid in art?
- What if pleasure is part of your integrity?

This doesn't mean that joy is always available or that art-making will always feel good. But we can remain attuned to what brings vitality, presence, or connection. That is still joy, still fuel.

Sometimes joy isn't something we add; it's the story we tell about what we're *already* doing. We can approach cleaning a house as drudgery and grind or we can put on an amazing playlist, enjoy the physicality, and delight in the vigor. The same is true in art-making. Drilling a difficult phrase, wrestling with a scene, repeating something until it lands—these can feel exhausting if framed as punishment, exhilarating if framed as devotion.

Challenge can be its own pleasure—the satisfaction of staying with something until it deepens, sharpens, transforms. The work is to shed the cycles of abuse and grind culture while keeping the aliveness that comes from caring deeply enough to work hard.

So, if you're stuck, lost, overworking, or burned out, pause and ask, "Where is the joy?"

Not the dopamine of applause or the relief of being finished. But the quiet aliveness that says, "I'm here. I care. I want to keep going."

Find those sparks and follow them. Let them recalibrate your process, shift your priorities. Let joy transform how you lead, collaborate, and make decisions.

Not earned. Deserved.

In Practice: Tips for Centering Joy in Your Creative Practice

1. **Redefine rigor.**
   Rigor isn't punishment; it's devotion. It needs joy as *fuel*, not *reward*.
   Try: Ask yourself, "How can I find pleasure in this work right now?"

2. **Build rituals that welcome joy.**
   Joy can be invited through repeatable practices that ground and open you.
   Try: Begin rehearsals with a *joy ritual*—music, a movement game, or shared laughter.

3. **Let play disrupt the script.**
   Silliness and absurdity are not distractions; they loosen rigidity and spark surprise.
   Try: Add one playful disruption to your next session and notice what shifts.

4. **Follow what feels alive.**
   Let your body guide you toward vitality, whether in daily practice or during tough choices.
   Try: Keep a joy journal for a week, and when making decisions, close your eyes and notice which option makes your breath or spine expand. What made you smile today?

5. **Resist the suffering artist myth.**
   Depth doesn't require depletion. Worth doesn't necessitate burnout.
   Try: When exhaustion feels like you've proven yourself, ask, "Whose voice is telling that story?"

6. **Learn joy's texture.**
   Joy can be loud, quiet, focused, or kinetic. Observe the variations to be able to discern it when it arrives.
   Try: Pause mid-process and scan your body: Where is there tension? Where is there warmth? Let sensation guide your next step.

7. **Rest as compost.**
   Rest isn't the *opposite* of work; it's the fertile ground that *sustains* it.
   Try: Build pause points into your schedule—not as rewards but as part of the cycle.

8. **Honor the small joys.**
   A funny rehearsal moment, a beautiful mistake, a tiny breakthrough. These are not *extra*; they are the *pulse*.
   Try: End each rehearsal by naming one unexpected joy that appeared.

Tuning In: Moving with Context

This practice explores how culture, family, and art live in your body as instinct, structure, and choice.

1. **Choose music.**
   Select a piece of music connected to your lineage—or the version of it you carry.
   - If you know your cultural background, choose music from that place, time, or community.
   - If your lineage carries trauma, disconnection, or erasure, choose with care.

   Pick music that feels grounding or sparks curiosity, not harm.

2. **Practice somatic listening.**
   Find a comfortable position—standing, sitting, or lying down. Close your eyes if that feels safe.
   - Notice your breath: its rhythm, depth, and sound.
   - Sense your weight settling into the surface beneath it.
   - Feel into your skeleton, muscles, skin, organs, and fluids.
   - Notice the temperature, sound, and light around you.

   Let your body arrive before you begin.

3. **Let the music enter.**
   Start the music, allowing it to move you:
   - Let your **feet** find the rhythm—stamping, tapping, swaying.
   - Let your **spine** respond—curling, arching, rippling with syncopation.
   - Let **gestures** emerge—hands clapping, arms lifting, hips shifting.

   If you know dances from your culture, invite them in improvisationally. If not, imagine what they might feel like—the pulse of a drum, the swing of a partner, the circle of a communal dance.

4. **Invite an ancestor.**
   Imagine an ancestor—known or unknown—stepping into the room.
   - Watch them dance. Are they grounded? Buoyant? Sharp? Fluid?
   - Join them: Copy, echo, or answer their rhythm. Let their movement mingle with yours, weaving inheritance and invention.

5. **Dance together.**
   Let the dance become a conversation.
   - Move side by side, trading gestures.
   - Allow rhythms to overlap—yours and theirs, imagined and remembered.
6. **Reflect.**
   Come to stillness. Notice your breath, weight, and heartbeat.
   - How did the dance feel in your body?
   - What, if anything, felt like home?

Studio Lab: Rule-Building for World-Making

This lab practices noticing rules and building new ones so our choices create the worlds we mean to make.

1. **Watch the first ten minutes of a (fiction) film.**
   Choose a film you've never seen.

   As you watch, **notice and name the rules** that emerge. Rules are the contract between the work and the audience that shape how *this* world operates. They may be **explicit** (characters use direct address for monologues) or **implicit** (the color scheme changes in memory sequences). **Look for the following:**

   - **Exposition:** How do we learn about the facts? (Dialogue? Voiceover? Visual cues?)
   - **Relationships:** How is intimacy or conflict shown? (Body language? Gaze? Text?)
   - **Realism versus stylization:** How do the stylistic choices feed meaning?
   - **Camera/editing:** Do you notice a logic to the camera and editing choices? (Moving main character while everyone is frozen when she is having a revelation?)
   - **Repetition and patterning:** What motifs in sound, duration, color offer clues?

   Write down every rule you can name, even the obvious ones.
   Example: "No one speaks above a whisper." "The camera never shows feet." "Music only appears in dream sequences."

2. **Choose a theme or question.**
   Select a focus for this creative experiment from the list below or create one:

   - A secret that changes everything.
   - Homecoming after exile.
   - Releasing an old identity.

3. **Build your rules.**
   Create **three to five rules** that define your world. They can be about:

   - **Movement**—only grounded movement, no eye contact, stillness after every action.
   - **Sound/voice**—no speaking until the end, music only between scenes.
   - **Time/structure**—time moves backward, each scene is shorter than the previous.
   - **Space/objects**—only travel along a grid, objects change meaning whenever touched.

   Make them purposeful: Each rule should reinforce your theme.

4. **Make something with the rules.**
   Step into your rules as if they are the gravity of your world—unbreakable laws.
   - **Let the rules choose *for* you.** Instead of deciding what comes next, **ask:** What does the *rule* demand? If all gestures must be circular, how does that shape walking? Falling? Stillness?
   - **Notice emerging tensions.** Which feels constricting? Which sparks surprising solutions?
   - **Accumulate meaning.** The repetition of a gesture or constraint may feel symbolic, ritualistic, oppressive, or tender; build story from that resonance.
   - **Explore transgression.** At some point, **break one rule**. Does it feel shocking, relieving, comedic, rebellious? Let your body respond rather than planning the outcome.

   When you finish, feel what remains of the world.
5. **Reflect.**
   - Which rules felt generative? Which felt restrictive?
   - Did any unintended patterns emerge?
   - How might you expand or tighten these rules for a longer work?

Pagework: Writing into Context and Culture

Freewrite on some or all of these questions.

1. **Trace an inheritance.**
   Write about a creative instinct, artistic value, or stylistic choice that's always been part of your work. Trace its origins through personal experience, cultural inheritance, or artistic training.
   - What systems or traditions does it reflect?
   - Does it feel like a choice or a habit?
   - How might you amplify, challenge, or reinvent it?
2. **Imagine a radical witness.**
   Imagine your work being viewed by someone with a radically different cultural background.
   - How might they interpret or feel about your work?
   - What parts might resonate, and what might feel unfamiliar, opaque, or harmful?
   - If your audience was entirely this demographic, what would you change?
   - Is any part of that change useful now?
3. **Follow the thread of joy.**
   Reflect on a moment in your creative life when you felt undeniable joy.
   - What **conditions** allowed that joy to arise?
   - How did it **affect** your process or outcomes?
4. **Sit inside a tension.**
   Write about a time when opposing forces (tradition vs. experimentation, precision vs. improvisation, product vs. process) recalibrated your process.
   - Where was the conflict?
   - How did you navigate contradiction?
   - How might they have supported each other more?
5. **Reclaim a story you've avoided.**
   Write about a story, subject, or theme you've felt reluctant to explore because of fear, stigma, or its emotional weight.
   - What feels risky or vulnerable?
   - Can you reframe it?
   - What creative tools, structures, or supports would help you explore it with care and integrity?

Movements + Maps: Shifting Frames—Expanding Context and Culture

This score invites you to interrogate, disrupt, and reshape your artistic lineage.

1. **Identify the "givens."**
   Below is a list of fifteen common "givens" we inherit from training or culture. Read through them and circle five that feel most present in your own work. Add others you notice in your practice or lineage.
   - The audience faces the performers.
   - There is a clear beginning, middle, and end.
   - Silence indicates "waiting." Action indicates "doing."
   - Speech carries information; movement carries emotion.
   - Gaze and eye contact follow social norms.
   - Space is divided into "performer" and "audience" zones.
   - Gravity is assumed—movement flows with natural weight and resistance.
   - Sound and movement align—gestures match rhythm, music, or text.
   - Movement builds toward a climax or peak moment.
   - Repetition signals importance or theme.
   - Big movement conveys big emotion; small movement conveys subtlety.
   - Time feels linear—actions follow cause and effect.
   - Transitions are marked by clear beginnings and endings of sections.
   - Breath is private—rarely shared, amplified, or audible.
   - Facial expressions mirror emotions.
2. **Exaggerate two. Oppose three. For example:**
   - Transitions at the beginning and end are marked *hyperbolically*.
   - Mark the passage of linear time *extravagantly*.
   - Movement must convey facts. Text creates a *poetic* context.
   - Let repetition be the norm. A *new* movement signals meaning.

3. **Build and perform it.**

   Use these new rules to create a short piece.

4. **Reflect.**

   - Which rules felt hardest to notice or to break?
   - Did new meaning emerge from exaggeration or opposition?
   - What might you put in your pocket for your next process?

Contributor's Note: Context, Culture, Continuity

by Brenda Dixon Gottschild

Life moves in circles, ellipses, spirals—forget about linearity!

My journey in dance/theater spins concentrically around actualizations as an artist-performer, writer-scholar, and practitioner-observer. These "me's" are equally driven by the same passion for the performing arts and my belief in performance as a highly charged, sociopolitical phenomenon. The odyssey began before I realized I was pursuing it. It was who I was: an African American girl who wanted to be a dancer (for as long as I can recall), loved books, loved sketching, loved school (where my shyness could be hidden by academic achievement), and, at some point, became aware that being Black was not the default setting for being American.

Recently, I came upon a paper I'd written for my high school English honors class in which I explained to my (white) teacher that what I saw as the problem in the United States is the way "the Negro" (the terminology of 1958, when I wrote this) is treated. In a social studies class, I wrote essays pleading the case for abolishing capital punishment and for statehood in Hawaii. My circumstances nurtured this McCarthy-era radical adolescent spirit: growing up in Harlem, an ethnically diverse community in the 1940s/1950s; going to integrated New York City schools in Washington Heights (the white neighborhood north of Harlem); and sharing honors classes with a handful of African Americans and a majority of Jewish kids, many of whom had lost relatives in the Holocaust. (Julius and Ethel Rosenberg's sons, Michael and Robert Meeropol, attended my junior high school. Their adopted father, Abel Meeropol, wrote the words to the song "Strange Fruit.") In other words, I grew up in a world of lower-middle-class urban otherness that felt natural. I wore the cloak of social/racial consciousness as closely as my love of dance, and from adolescence onward I continued to merge dance and social activism.

I am motivated to action as an antidote to—dare I repeat bell hooks's legendary phrase—the "imperialist white supremacist capitalist patriarchy." The sixteen-year-old me—the high school senior who explained racism to her teacher—has not yet rested her case. The beauty is that dance and social activism are symbiotic concentricities. Would that I might see, in my lifetime, the universal social justice that is the focus of my dancing mind, my thinking body.

Studio Provocations: Questioning Context and Culture

People generally see what they look for, and hear what they listen for.
(Harper Lee, *To Kill a Mockingbird*)[8]

Inheritance and Cultural Heritage

What in this work has a lineage you can name?

- Whose phrasing, spatial logic, or initiation pattern lives here?

If your ancestors were in the room, how would they respond?

- What might make them lean forward?
- What might make them uneasy?

Where does your work repeat cultural defaults without your realizing?

- Which of those repetitions feel alive?
- Which feel automatic?

Identity and Privilege

What part of yourself is visible in this work?

- What parts stay offstage?

What does this piece assume the audience agrees with?

Memory and Ancestry

What feels absent in this piece?

- Is that absence intentional?

If you stripped away your idea of technique, what would remain?

Who would recognize themselves in this work?

---

[8]Harper Lee, *To Kill a Mockingbird* (J. B. Lippincott & Co., 1960).

Politics and Power

Who makes the final decision—the performers, the audience, or the structure itself?

What are you asking your audience to consent to?

- Do they have a real choice?

Where are you applying control, and where are you riding this process?

Tension and Recontextualization

What rules are you consciously breaking?

- What is one more you could break?

Where are you using contradiction to create believability?

- Where does friction make the work more alive?

If someone walked in for one minute with no program notes, what would they assume this piece values?

12

Priorities

Before You Begin: Priming Curiosity About Priorities

Take a breath. Consider these questions. Let them settle in your body before moving forward. They are not for solving, but for sensing.

When do I feel like my day belongs to me?

Who benefits most from the way I spend my time?

What routines support my creativity and which ones stifle it?

Why do I keep showing up for what I love even when it's hard?

How do I sort what's important from what's merely demanding?

Where would I spend my time if no one needed anything from me (and I had what I needed)?

Groundwork: In Practice with Priorities

> In becoming forcibly and essentially aware of my mortality, and of what I wished and wanted for my life, however short it might be, priorities and omissions became strongly etched in a merciless light, and what I most regretted were my silences.
>
> (Audre Lorde, *Sister Outsider: Essays and Speeches*)[1]

Choosing What Matters

I lost this book once. Eighteen months into my writing process, I sat down, ready to write, and the entire file was missing. Not deleted, just gone. The draft, which started as a transcription for my intern, was attached to her university account. Postgraduation, all her files—and with them, my book—had been deleted. Her university told her there was nothing to be done. "The file is gone," she told me, "There's nothing left to try."

I refused to believe there were no options. I called her university and had the same conversations. But instead of simply asking what we should do, I explained what the book *meant* to me, how much I'd poured into it, how losing it was life altering. **Something shifted.** People who had dismissed her made calls, followed threads, and searched manually. Within days, the book was back in my hands.

What changed?

It wasn't just my words; it was the stakes. **Priorities, clearly named, compelled them to act.** Afterward, many friends said, "How lucky!" But luck was only one strand. You have my book in front of you today because I *prioritized* it enough to make *others* care. This raised a crucial question for artistic practice: How do we create art that conveys the urgency, importance, and humanity of our work to the audience?

The Architecture of Priorities

Making art involves sensing, clarifying, and advocating for your priorities. Each chapter has explored one of the fundamental forces that support this process—the bones, breath, and movement of your work. *Priorities* are the connective tissue holding them in relationship.

I teach actors about expression, embodiment, and function. They are often blown away by the myriad options Laban/Bartenieff offers them. New dynamics, postures, gestures, and spatial choices become

[1]Audre Lorde, "The Transformation of Silence into Language and Action," in *Sister Outsider: Essays and Speeches* (Crossing Press, 2007), 82.

available. Frequently, their first monologue in the workshop is *chaotic*. They try everything—very loud, very quiet, restrained, wild, furtive, and exposed. The piece lacks *priorities*. We don't learn **who they are** or **what they value. Refusing to decide hides you from the audience.** Endless possibilities are tantalizing, but *deciding* is a way to declare, "This is me! This is what I believe, feel, and desire."

The Courage to Choose

There's a kind of "being lost" in the rehearsal room that feels alive with possibility. It's intoxicating. Ideas bloom, connections emerge, and nothing is set in stone. When it feels like it could go *anywhere*, we imagine countless, often contradictory, winding paths. This fertility is sumptuous for a time, like a world-class buffet. But this state of openness can't last forever. Staring at the infinite choices whets the appetite but fails to nourish us.

It's easy to linger here, mistaking indecision for creative freedom. If we never decide, the work only exists in our mind—which is to say, it doesn't exist. What we think of as creative openness can sometimes be **avoidance**: fear of making the "wrong" choice keeps us from making *any* choice. Hypothetical art has no impact. Anne Bogart describes the pressure of decision-making.

> Art is violent. To be decisive is violent.... The moment of decision is a terrible one. It is the moment in which all other options die, and it is an act of violence to choose one thing over another.
>
> (Anne Bogart, *A Director Prepares*)[2]

Deciding means letting go of potential. In physics, potential energy is *stored energy*. Action begins when a force releases it into motion. Priorities *are* that force. They turn impulse into movement and direction, declaring what matters.

Prioritizing isn't just choosing *what* to do; it's deciding *when* to do it, *how long* to stay there, and when to *let go*. Tempo and duration determine which system leads—intuition or analysis.

- **Speedy decision-making** allows your **body** and **intuition** to take the lead.
- Taking **more time** allows your **analytical side** to be rigorous and thorough.

The Dance Between Part and Whole

Art-making is a constant negotiation between the whole and its parts. The big picture suggests, pressures, and sometimes dictates the details. In a work centered on climate collapse, I eliminated entrances and exits, and blackouts, denying the relief of a pause. There were no sections, costume

[2]Anne Bogart, *A Director Prepares: Seven Essays on Art and Theatre* (Routledge, 2001).

changes, or obvious musical variations, suggesting the continuous passage of time. These choices mirrored the crisis: no way in, no way out, no turning away, no stopping the next event. You saw the organic effect of every human action on the rest of the group.

I let the *whole* to determine the *details*. Sometimes a detail shines a light on the bigger picture. I once directed a piece with existential isolation as its central theme. Every structural choice reinforced that idea: solos, silence, stark lighting. But then something happened in rehearsal. Just as we were about to run a duet, one dancer grabbed her partner's hand. It was a small gesture but saturated with feeling. It taught me something about my theme. It wasn't simply about isolation; it was about *longing*.

That single touch rewrote everything. Suddenly, the solos weren't about accepting or lamenting their aloneness but *listening* for synchronicity. The silence became *expectation*; the stark lighting became something the dancers could rebel against. The material hadn't changed. Our priorities had. The details illuminated a hole in my foundation. Shoring it up made the work complex and evocative.

The way a single dissonant note resolves can reveal the harmonic logic of the whole symphony. It signals what tension means and how we define conclusion. In architecture, the placement of a doorway alters how an entire building is navigated. Across disciplines, details echo outward, and the whole reverberates inward. Part and whole exist as a spiral of influence, each revealing what the other could become.

The Risk of Being Seen

Clear choices don't just sharpen the work; they unmask *the artist*. The more *precise* we become, the more *visible* we are—our hopes, our wounds, our longings. Craft can feel like armor, but it also functions as magnification. Refinement makes the meaning *legible*, like bringing something into focus under a microscope. Saying what matters exposes us. What if no one *else* cares? This is the strange intimacy we enter with the audience when we attempt to build a shared reality.

Knowing what matters to *us* is one thing; getting *others* to care about it is another. The power of art lies in its ability to make the audience feel the urgency of our priorities as if they were their *own*. This is where **communication** comes into play. The *language* of our work—its movement, imagery, sound, and text—must resonate in the body as well as the mind. It must beckon the audience into our story, making them feel not like *spectators* but *participants*. This is the tension between expression and art.

Honoring the Process

Priorities change. They move with us. A shift in tone during rehearsal, a grant rejection, a conversation that lands wrong, a life change at home—each one alters the landscape. Our ecosystem adjusts to every internal and external shift, and with it, our priorities recalibrate. They are not fixed declarations we make once and defend forever. They require attention. They require attunement. The work asks us to notice when something has moved—when a value no longer aligns with our behavior, when the room feels different, when the stakes have quietly changed.

Prioritizing is not a one-time act of clarity. It is a continuous practice of alignment.

Inviting the Audience to Care

If priorities name what matters, the next task is transmitting that urgency to *others*. The audience will not feel what you feel unless they sense why it *matters*. This depends on honesty, clarity, and recognizability.

- **Honesty** begins with knowing what you truly want. The audience feels when your choices cost something, when you have risked being seen and let the work carry your real stakes. The way I had to explain why this book mattered to retrieve it, we must let the work explain what is nonnegotiable.
- **Clarity** emerges through craft. Articulation and precision sculpt expression, condensing lived experiences into saturated imagery. A gesture, line of text, silence—clear choices make vulnerability *legible*.
- **Recognizability** invites the audience into their own associations. They need to see themselves in the work. Contradiction, complexity, and unfinished edges give them space to enter. When we fail to build rules or things resolve too neatly, we fail to meet the audience.

The Anatomy of Art

I titled this book *The Anatomy of Art* because the vitality of our body and our artistic practice depends on what we nurture, what we neglect, and how closely we pay attention. This attention lets us sense when we need rest, pressure, stimulation, or action.

Our artistic practice, like our body, is sensitive and resilient. It is stabilized through structure and animated by impulse. It adapts to stress, compensates for imbalance, and strengthens the systems we attend to. It requires fuel and recovery. It responds to its environment and carries inheritance in its habits. It is catalyzed by *ideas*, but recognizes that only *actions* create change.

Anatomy names *systems* so we can study their individual functions, bringing them back into conversation with one another for integration. Circulation, respiration, digestion, sensation—these do not operate in isolation. They overlap constantly, influencing and informing one another. Separating them allows us to perceive patterns of coordination, strain, and support that would otherwise be overwhelming. We break the body down in order to understand how it works together. The anatomy of our art asks for the same attention.

Time is like our heart. It sets the pulse of the work, marks the span of a project, and alerts us to excitement and fatigue.

- Space is like proprioception and equilibrium, orienting inner impulse within outer architecture and allowing us to sense distance, proportion, and relationship.
- Meaning is like the brain, revealing patterns between sensation and perception, memory and desire.
- Environment is the climate surrounding the body, shaping how we breathe, move, and respond.
- Process is digestion and metabolism, breaking down experience, absorbing what nourishes, discarding what does not, converting material into movement.
- Facts are a skeleton, offering structure and resistance, something for meaning and desire to leverage so that action has consequence.
- Faith is our lungs, expanding and contracting, adjusting to exertion and rest, sustaining the body through repetition.
- Communication is the nervous system, listening to the inner and outer worlds simultaneously and calibrating threat, need, and relationship.
- Material is cells, the basic elements that combine and specialize to build structure, form, and progression.
- Context and culture are DNA and mitochondria, carrying inherited patterns and stored energy across generations.

And **priorities** are like hormones, altering the state of the whole body, accelerating some processes, quieting others, redistributing energy in response to what matters. When something matters deeply, the body changes. Heart rate shifts. Breath alters. Attention sharpens in response to danger, adaptation, or possibility. Audre Lorde writes of regret not for mistakes, but for silences, for the *not doing*. Priorities move through your creative practice in the same way, quickening the rehearsal that needs momentum, slowing the section that requires refinement, pulling you back to the central question when you drift, urging the conversation that has been avoided, concentrating your time and resources where the stakes are highest.

Takeaway: You have one body and one artistic life. The vitality and resilience of both depend on how closely you listen, how honestly you choose, and how consistently you align your actions with what matters.

In Practice: Tips About Priorities

1. **Name the big picture.**
   Define what this work is circling and what questions it keeps returning to. Update your strategies when your vision shifts rather than following an old script.

2. **Keep asking, "What else?"**
   Even after choosing, stay curious. This question refines choices and keeps them alive without losing focus.

3. **Move between the whole and the parts.**
   Check that details serve the larger vision, and notice when details reshape the vision itself.

4. **Align your choices with your values.**
   Before committing, ask if the action reflects your values and core themes. If not, recalibrate.

5. **Invite the audience in.**
   Consider how the work allows recognition and engagement rather than dictating meaning.

6. **Hold contradictions lovingly.**
   Let complexity live in the work. Humor and grief, structure and fluidity can coexist without resolution.

7. **Reassess as you go.**
   Creative work evolves. Pause to ask, "What am I prioritizing now?" Adjust focus as the work reveals itself.

8. **Share your priorities with your collaborators.**
   Clarify what matters most and invite others' insights to expand the vision. Listen slowly and nonjudgmentally to the priorities of those around you.

9. **Treat constraints as clarifiers.**
   Time, budget, and limits can sharpen focus. Ask what's **essential**, not what's **missing**.

10. **Balance your gut and your critique.**
    Trust instincts, then question them. Distinguish between what feels right and what feels familiar.

From the Field: *Antonio's Song: I Was Dreaming of a Son*

Figure 12.1 Antonio Suarez performing in *Antonio's Song: I Was Dreaming of a Son*. Photographer unknown.

One of my favorite projects was working as movement director on *Antonio's Song: I Was Dreaming of a Son*, written by Dael Orlandersmith and performed by Antonio Edwards Suarez.[3] The one-person autobiographical show demanded Antonio transform into fourteen essential characters—his wife, son, mother, father, and more—each with their own nonverbal language, rhythm, and presence.

The process posed a paradox: How could he embody these roles—channeling the pain, complexity, and emotional weight of his past—without inviting old wounds to reopen? How could we individuate each character in a way that felt effortless and organic?

Antonio's movement is generous and fluid, full of unexpected phrasing and openness, his "Antonio-ness." But this show demanded he dissolve those instincts and invent new expressive DNA

[3]Dael Orlandersmith and Antonio Edwards Suarez, *Antonio's Song: I Was Dreaming of a Son*, by directed by Mark Clements, performed at Goodman Theatre, Owen Theatre, Chicago, April 28–May 28, 2023.

for each character. How could we build a process that allowed him to *become* his dying father, bullying peer, or an abusive mother and that was sustainable through years of rehearsal and performance?

We had two priorities: Protect Antonio's emotional well-being, and create work so raw it shook audiences to their core. Could both coexist? These goals seemed counterintuitive, even contradictory. Yet, by constantly considering both priorities, we found a way to achieve both.

We began with free improvisation: Antonio chose a monologue, moved anywhere and everywhere, ignoring ideas of what was "too literal" or "too abstract." Then we stripped away the words—first spoken internally, then gone—until only the physical tone remained. In silence, his body revealed more than his text ever could. I noticed how his mother's presence filled the room, how his father's breath anchored him, how one character prowled, another fluttered, another seemed bound in plastic.

As we stripped away the text, each character surfaced through physical choices alone. I tracked shifts in body organization, weight, dynamics, spatial intent, gesture, and focus. His mother expanded through chest and arms; his father was rooted in breath and stance. Working systematically through these physical principles, each role developed its own expressive DNA. The turning point came when we realized Antonio could transform through physical patterning rather than reopening psychic wounds. The structure itself became both safeguard and risk.

I choreographed from his natural priorities. The result harnessed his inner wisdom but did not ask Antonio to relive each trauma. With this scaffold, each character awakened in his body as radically distinct but repeatable. The structure provided him with both freedom and safety, allowing him to access the work's emotional truth without being overwhelmed. The result was profound: Antonio could enter and exit each character without harm, and audiences felt each transformation viscerally—shaken, moved, and entirely inside his story.

By honoring both priorities equally—Antonio's safety and the audience's experience—we created something sustainable for him and unforgettable for them.

Guidance: On Choosing, Frameworks, and Making Work That's Yours

There's an enduring myth about creativity, that it is ephemeral, unpredictable, bestowed only on the lucky few by the whims of inspiration. But we are not passive vessels of divine creativity. We are observers, architects, navigators. The ability to create is a practiced, honed, profoundly personal skill.

Formulas are tempting. They promise certainty, efficiency, the comfort of never entering the studio or rehearsal without a plan. But because they repeat, they yield similar outcomes. A framework, on the other hand, is not a path to follow but a *field* to move in. It gives you coordinates, boundaries, rhythms, and questions. It lets you test, return, and expand. It is a device to help you locate yourself, not go where someone told you to.

That has been the spirit of this book: not to hand you a formula but to give you frameworks to test, return to, and reshape. How *you* use them is what matters.

The most crucial thing I can tell you is this: **Know what you care about.** No system or exercise can replace clear intention. We are all working with the same ingredients. These are the topics of each chapter. Your *priorities* are what separate your work from everyone else's, allowing your genius to become visible.

A framework might be a list of questions, a set of contrasts to play with, a chart, a score, even a single image that organizes your choices. What matters is that it holds **structure** without defining the **outcome**. That is something you can practice: building frameworks of your own.

Ask: What is the most specific container you can name that still leaves space for imagination?

When you feel uncertain, lost, or frozen by endless options, return to your framework. When you feel stuck, reshape it. Use your frameworks to cut away excess, strengthen what matters, and expand what's constricted. Use them to find clarity in the chaos. Use them, most of all, to make work that is *yours*.

Because no one else can.

Tuning In: Priorities—a Closing and Opening

This final embodiment exercise is an opportunity to reflect on everything you've explored in this book, making space for departure and reinvention.

1. **Ground in what has been.**
   Stand, sit, or lie down in stillness. Take five deep breaths, each one carrying a different intention.
   - **Breathe in gratitude:** Acknowledge the journey you've taken.
   - **Exhale:** Release any guilt about *how* you engaged.
   - **Breathe in recognition:** Notice what has changed.
   - **Exhale:** Release fantasies of what you thought would happen.
   - **Breathe in possibility:** Open to the unknown artist in your future.
   - **Exhale:** Let go of any pressure to "hold on" to past versions of yourself.
   - **Breathe in readiness:** Open to possibility.
   - **Exhale:** Release fatigue.
   - **Breathe in presence:** Honor the moment exactly as it is.
   - **Exhale:** Release the past and future.
2. **Shape your process.**
   Find one posture, shape, or tension that represents where you **started** at the beginning of this book. **Hold it.** Let your body shift until you find a shape that feels **now**. Let this be intuitive; no need to "show" progress. **Stay here and feel it.**

   Go back to the first shape and improvise to end at the second. Let the middle space change, grow, adopt, notice, and metabolize. Notice when you are ready for something new.
3. **Move toward the unknown.**
   Move with this invitation: **Follow what feels most alive.** If **stillness** feels alive, stay still. If a single repeated motion feels right, let it repeat. If **impulse and expansion** arise, trust where they take you. At some point, **pause and listen.**

4. **Carry it forward.**

   Walk slowly through your space, as if crossing from this process into whatever comes next. As you move, create a sentence that anchors you, like,

   - "I trust my body's information."
   - "I welcome uncertainty."
   - "I create with clarity and courage."

   When you feel complete, stop and take a final breath.

5. **Reflect.**

   - What discoveries do you want to carry forward?
   - What do you no longer need?
   - What artistic commitments feel most alive in your body?

Studio Lab: Goals and Values

This final exercise invites you to synthesize your instincts, values, vulnerabilities, and evolving artistic priorities.

1. **Define your "artistic compass."**
   In answering these prompts, respond quickly, instinctually, and honestly. The answers are your artistic compass.
   - A creative risk I took that felt **energizing** was…
   - A creative habit I've **relied** on that I now question is…
   - A moment in my practice when I felt **fully myself** was…
   - Something I used to **believe** about art but no longer do is…
   - A constraint that **unexpectedly freed me** was…
   - The part of my artistic process that brings me the most **joy** is…
   - When I get **lost** in my process, I need to remind myself that…
   - I know I am on the right path when I **feel**…
   - A word or concept I find myself **returning** to over and over is…
   - Something I am still **searching** for in my work is…
   - I know I am on the right path when I **feel**…

2. **Identify your priorities.**
   Pull out five to ten words or short phrases that stand out. These are creative priorities alive in this moment. They might include themes, artistic values, sensations, or questions.

   Some examples might be "Urgency," "Precision," "Letting go," "Surprise," "Imperfection," "Trust."

3. **Develop a process that aligns with one priority.**
   Choose **one** word or phrase from your list. Create a process that allows you to embody and investigate this priority. If your priority is
   - **Clarity**, create a process that strips away everything unnecessary. **Try:** Use a limited vocabulary, repeat movements until they feel distilled, or impose a strict structure.
   - **Discomfort**, work against your natural preferences. **Try:** Move in unfamiliar ways, use awkward timing, or change your usual rules.

- **Play**, set up a game or challenge. **Try:** Improvise with specific rules, create quickly, or invite randomness.
- **Depth**, practice patient inquiry. **Try:** Commit to staying with one idea, movement, or image far longer than usual.

Spend ten to fifteen minutes actively engaging with your chosen priority.

4. **Close and reopen.**

From your exploration, find one movement, phrase, or stillness that holds the essence of what you've learned. This could be a posture, repeated rhythm, or movement phrase.

- Do it once as the final moment of a performance.
- Do it again as the first sentence of a conversation.

Pagework: Writing into Priorities

Freewrite on some or all of these questions.

1. **Write about the driving force behind your current project.**
   - What question or theme feels urgent?
   - How does this priority align with your personal values?
2. **Reflect on a big artistic decision you've made recently.**
   - Why this choice?
   - How does it serve your larger vision?
   - What is one more decision that flows naturally from it?
3. **Your artistic compass is the way your values, dreams, community, resources, and daily realities align to point you toward one choice and away from another. In what direction does it point?**
   - What dream or long-term desire is quietly influencing your decisions right now?
   - Which of your current choices reflect your stated values, and which feel out of step with them?
   - How are your daily realities reinforcing or redirecting your artistic path?
   - How is your community shaping your direction—through support, expectation, collaboration, or absence?
4. **Write about a moment in your work where two priorities contradicted each other.**
   - How did you navigate that tension?
   - How might they coexist?
5. **Think of a time you advocated for your priorities in a collaboration or institution.**
   - How did you communicate?
   - What strategies helped?
6. **Imagine a future scenario where you must defend your priorities.**
   - How might you prepare?
   - What values would anchor you?

Movements + Maps: Creative Compass and the Art of Choosing

These two scores offer complementary approaches to creative decision-making.

Creative Compass names what matters and embodies it.

The Art of Choosing invites disruption, testing, and daring to change course.

Score One: Creative Compass

1. **Define what matters most.**
   Choose three central priorities for your current project. Write each on a separate paper or sticky note.

2. **Embody each priority.**
   Create a simple movement, gesture, or spatial relationship from each priority's essence. Transition between the movements. How do they relate or contrast?

3. **Layer and collide priorities.**
   Do two at once. Let them harmonize, contradict, or create tension. Adjust their relationship: Do they resist one another? Merge seamlessly? Require negotiation?

4. **Break a priority.**
   Take one and deliberately work against it. If your priority was "precision," introduce chaos. If it was "openness," explore restriction.

5. **Revisit and reassess.**
   Return to your three original priorities. Have they shifted? Do any ask to be replaced or redefined? Write or verbalize what you've learned about each and how they might evolve in your project.

Score Two: The Art of Choosing

1. **Name and destabilize.**

   Identify a core idea, theme, or emotion that holds urgency. **Name it** in one sentence. For the first half of rehearsal, deliberately **work against it**. At the halfway mark, **return to the theme**.

2. **Commit, then cut.**

   Create a sequence or phrase. **Cut half** of it. Then **cut one more** essential movement, gesture, spatial choice, or word. What do you fight to keep?

3. **Anchor one thing.**

   Make one foundational choice: an effort quality, a spatial limitation, a repeated gesture, a line of text. Let everything else *respond* to that anchor.

4. **Urgency without rush.**

   Create with urgency but without rushing. Let the movement feel inevitable but deliberate.

5. **Introduce irreversibility.**

   Build toward something irreversible: a decision, shift, destruction. Let it change the rest of the piece. Can you anticipate the shift without trying to control it?

6. **Create a residue.**

   Make an epilogue that continues from your "ending."

7. **Reenter with new eyes.**

   Revisit the beginning and **revise** it.

Contributor's Note: Making Work, Making Sense

by Kate Hamill

When I was a younger artist, I believed—however naively—that my priorities would always remain constant. But looking in the rearview mirror, my primary priority back then was to work, to work, simply to work... my hunger to get the jobs (and thus get approval) outranged my artistic sensibilities. Not surprisingly, I spent those first few years adrift—often in a state of desperation, tension, or panic. I only started to advance artistically when I began creating my own work, for and by myself, which necessitated pursuing what interested me, instead of some imagined external judge.

Since I started prioritizing my taste, many of my "musts" have become clearer: I only make feminist work; I enjoy making ensemble-based, irreverent work; I make highly theatrical work; and I appreciate heightened language. But even as I clarified artistic priorities, I found that I was not always focusing enough on the work environment—that it is as important to me to have respectful, fair, and collaborative workplaces as it is to pursue the art. I'm still, always, reexamining how to balance those priorities best.

How can I, as a freelance artist, rigorously pursue my individual artistic goals while ensuring the collectives I work with are equitable, kind, and generous? Every workplace and project is different, and I strive to learn lessons from each process. But the guiding principle that has helped the most is not only to pursue artistically what most sincerely activates *me*, not the tastemakers, not the gatekeepers, but also to follow the dictates of my conscience rigorously. Processes will differ. Priorities will shift. But you and your conscience are the constant.

Frameworks: Fifty Quick Actions for Discovering Your Priorities

This list is your artistic Magic 8 Ball. Pick one action randomly when you hit a wall.

Try: Cut these into cards and make your own deck. Shuffle, pull one, and let it guide your next rehearsal, journaling session, or creative decision.

1. **Write the problem in one sentence.** Fix it as if it's a *personal relationship* issue.
2. **Summarize the piece like a TV Guide logline.** Stage a thirty-second trailer.
3. **Describe your piece to a nonartist.** Adjust based on their questions.
4. **Cut one thing. Then cut one more.** What are you craving?
5. **Add a gratuitous layer (hat, chair, drum).** Keep it until it finds a reason to exist.
6. **Name one thing missing.** Use that to drive the next section.
7. **Choose a cliché.** Embrace it without irony, then distort it until it's new.
8. **Notice what scares you.** Amplify it.
9. **Pick a boring task.** Do it until an idea interrupts you.
10. **Choose one moment and zoom in.** Spend ten minutes refining its details.
11. **Name a mediocre part.** Repeat it with variations until it transforms.
12. **Write a to-do list.** Start with the last item.
13. **Repeat the most annoying moment ten times.** Then let it break open.
14. **Name one part of the piece that's brilliant.** Clone it. Then change it.
15. **Do one section with "just enough."** What changes?
16. **Pick two opposing options.** Make both.
17. **Translate into a new medium.** Then translate back based on what you liked.
18. **Change one big element (tempo, space, force).** Keep everything else constant.
19. **Name the part you've been avoiding.** Start there.
20. **Exaggerate one element to absurdity.** Then dial it back 80 percent.
21. **Watch your work like a stranger.** Write three observations.
22. **Impose a constraint** (e.g., one limb, one prop, one emotion). Explore fully.
23. **Take the most minor part.** Make it central.
24. **Find something accidental.** Make it intentional.
25. **Rehearse it like opening night.** Then mess it up completely.
26. **Let a mistake live.** Follow it.

27. **Keep only 10 percent.** Build something new from that fragment.
28. **Write every section on a card.** Shuffle them and do the new order.
29. **Watch each performer as a solo.** Overlap them randomly.
30. **Say something outrageous about your piece.** Play it out.[4]
31. **Open a book at random.** Use the first word to steer the next section.[5]
32. **Take a ten-second moment.** Stretch it to two minutes.[6]
33. **List every way to ruin the piece.** Reverse these.[7]
34. **Ask why five times in a row.** Follow where that leads.[8]
35. **Put an obstacle in the way.** Build the work around it.
36. **Overfill the stage.** Track what still matters.
37. **Implement an eject button.** Anyone can call "Stop!" when they lose interest.
38. **Take two unrelated elements from your piece.** Make them collide.[9]
39. **Write your problem in the center of a page.** Branch out only with questions.
40. **Pick an unrelated idea.** Force it into the work.

Inspired by *Oblique Strategies:*[10]

41. **Ask your body.** Move before thinking. Let it choose what's next.
42. **Use an old idea.** Insert it unchanged; watch it recontextualize the work.
43. **Emphasize a flaw.** Let it grow, repeat, or become focal.
44. **Strip down to one element.** Movement, sound, or image. Let it lead.
45. **Start at the end.** Work backward to discover what leads there.
46. **Do the opposite of what you'd typically do.** Especially if you dislike it.
47. **Transform, don't erase.** Every edit must evolve, not delete.
48. **Choose the easy solution.** Embellish it until it surprises you.
49. **Remove the most obvious moment.** Fill its absence deliberately.
50. **Repeat an accident.** Let it evolve into a central motif.

---

[4]Edward de Bono, *Lateral Thinking: Creativity Step by Step* (Harper & Row, 1970).
[5]De Bono, *Lateral Thinking.*
[6]Anne Bogart and Tina Landau, *The Viewpoints Book: A Practical Guide to Viewpoints and Composition* (Theatre Communications Group, 2005), 16.
[7]IDEO, *The Field Guide to Human-Centered Design* (IDEO, 2015).
[8]Toyota Motor Corporation, "The 5 Whys Method," in *Lean Manufacturing Toolbox*, accessed October 3, 2025.
[9]IDEO, *The Field Guide.*
[10]Brian Eno and Peter Schmidt, *Oblique Strategies: Over One Hundred Worthwhile Dilemmas* (Self-published, 1975).

Studio Provocations: Questioning Priorities

The purpose of art is not to provide answers but to ask better questions. When we think we understand, we stop looking. When we question, we begin to see.

(Twyla Tharp, *The Creative Habit*)[11]

Who

Who is shaping the priorities of the work most?

Try: Redistribute influence or amplify it.

Who is the piece speaking to?

Try: Make a section for someone you've left out.

Who are you willing to disappoint?

Try: Make something intended to disappoint them.

Who are you most nervous to show this to?

Try: Run the work as though they are sitting in the front row.

What

What choice in this work has the biggest effect? (Rhythm, relationship, a staging choice.)

Try: Let it affect something *else*. (Use the rhythm for text, repeat that staging elsewhere.)

What detail in your piece reveals the whole? (Bodies stay near each other throughout.)

Try: Strip a section down until only that detail remains. (A scene remains in touching distance throughout.)

What do you care about too much to let go of? (One monologue you love.)

Try: Build an improvisation built on only that. (Actor improvises from only that text.)

---

[11]Twyla Tharp, *The Creative Habit: Learn It and Use It for Life* (Simon & Schuster, 2003).

What's the riskiest thing you can safely ask for? (Do this scene in a headstand.)

Try: Let risk lead for the next five minutes.

When

When does your attention drop?

Try: Repeat that section or beat seven times, each with a different agenda.

When does *the piece* want to end, even if you've planned otherwise?

Try: Stop there.

When are you deciding from the body, not the mind?

Try: Set a timer for two minutes and make a series of fast-paced choices from gut instinct.

When does the piece demand urgency?

Try: Amplify the urgency of a single moment until it feels excessive. (Speed it up, make it bigger, add bodies, overlap text.)

Where

Where are your priorities most visible in the work? ("The performers' individuality, seen in their personal movement vocabulary.")

Try: Take an ambiguous moment and flood it with your priority. (Have them do authentic movement while doing the scene.)

Where are you physically placing yourself in rehearsal?

Try: Position yourself very differently next rehearsal.

Where might this work live beyond the studio?

Try: Rehearse this somewhere *very* unusual.

Why

Identify a section or beat that wants attention. What theatrical convention does it follow?

Try: Break the rule.

Ask, "Why is *this* work worth making now, in *this* moment?"

Try: Speak the answer before beginning rehearsal, see what follows.

Why is *this* the medium?

Try: Create a version as a sculpture, poem, or drawing.

How

What happens if you prioritize *process* over *product* or vice versa?

Try: Flip them for the next rehearsal.

How does the energy shift when you let someone else choose?

Try: Hand over authorship.

How does a single choice change the whole structure?

Try: Alter one variable—tempo, level, direction—and run the piece again.

Conclusion

The man who has many answers
is often found
in the theaters of information
where he offers, graciously,
his deep findings.

While the man who has only questions,
to comfort himself, makes music.
(Mary Oliver, *A Thousand Mornings*)[1]

Here's What I Know

A book of questions implies that there will be answers. But as we close this book, I'm reminded that the best art rarely provides answers; it moves us to *ask* more. Making is not tidying things up but unfolding them, diving into the mess of life, and creating something from it. Nonetheless, as we close this book, I will offer some of the answers I have culled through my art-making and vigorous living.

Say yes.

Say no.

Say maybe. Not right now. Give me a minute to think about it.

Give yourself a break.

Work harder.

---

[1]Mary Oliver, "The Man Who Has Many Answers," *A Thousand Mornings: Poems* (Penguin, 2012), 43.

Answer with your body.

Be critical and well-researched.

Ride your intuition.

Be strict and restrain yourself.

Let yourself ramble.

Interrupt yourself.

Make a safe space.

Let yourself be truly uncomfortable.

Forgive yourself.

Demand something of yourself.

See a ton of art.

Hibernate and get reclusive.

Make something fast.

Take your time.

Laugh at yourself.

Recognize the importance of what you are doing.

These statements contradict each other. That's the point. Art is not about absolutes but about balance, negotiation, and risk. It lives inside the tension between discipline and freedom, instinct and analysis, rigor and play.

Kindness

Kindness is an essential force in our creative lives. Kindness is not *coddling*; it's *attending*. It's the generosity of your focus on your work, your process, the people with you, and yourself.

Kindness asks:

What does this work need from me right now?

What does this collaborator need?

What does my creative spirit need?

Kindness refuses to bulldoze a rough draft, a risk, a tired body, or a doubt. It can be ruthless about the work's integrity but gentle toward the people making it, *including you*.

Kindness is not the absence of critique, but the presence of care.

As an exercise, I once wrote three letters of recommendation for myself through the eyes of three mentors. As a neurodiverse perfectionist with a vigorous inner critic, I was startled at how easily I could list my strengths. Intelligent. Charismatic. Intuitive. Creative. Generous. It didn't erase my fears, doubts, or critiques of myself. I could hold my limitations and my gifts without inflating or erasing either. Practice holding the contradiction of loving yourself while other thoughts, feelings, and stories move through you.

Art's Manifesto

Art asks for your attention, rigor, openness, and playfulness. To question your assumptions and push past your habits. To fail and keep going. It asks you to trust the road with no idea where you're headed. To risk failure, mediocrity, brilliance, and misunderstanding. To offer yourself without knowing how you will be received.

This is the paradox: Art asks us to be *vulnerable* and *resilient*. To allow ourselves to *be changed* by what we make. Looking into the mirror of our creations, we face the unknown in ourselves. We ask something bigger to pass through us without consuming us.

Art gives us the freedom to imagine new worlds, rewrite the rules, and inhabit the impossible. We can say what "can't" be said, make the hidden visible, and hold complexity without resolution.

Art connects us, reminds us that we're not alone, that every facet of our reality is shared with *someone*. It is an act of empathy flowing on a two-way road.

And art gives us *purpose*, finding patterns in the noise, and forging meaning from pain.

As you continue your journey, I hope you'll carry these ideas with you:

- **Trust your instincts**, and don't let them close you off to discovery.
- **Build a process that's authentic to you**, and don't be afraid to disrupt it.
- **Take risks**, and take care of yourself.
- **Honor your strengths**, and don't be afraid to stretch beyond them.
- **Embrace failure**, and don't let it define you.
- **Listen to your inner voice**, and don't forget to look around.
- **Make something that matters to you**, and trust that it will matter to someone else.

Art doesn't tie things up neatly; it expands the terrain of what's possible. It's a labyrinth, a storm, and a question that leads to more questions.

But this is the gift: Art changes us every time we make it.

Let this be your permission slip. Your lantern. Your dare.

This book will wait for you on the shelf. Come back when you're tangled, lost, empty, or overflowing.

But now go.

Break something. **Ask** again. **Begin** anyway.

Don't just make art. Be made *by* it.

And if your heart is pounding a little, good. That's your cue.

Appendix A: Laban, a Brief Explanation

In every act of creation, we negotiate between structure and freedom, finding the space where meaning and innovation emerge.

(Irmgard Bartenieff, *Body Movement*)[1]

How to Use This Appendix

This appendix offers context for a system that has deeply influenced my creative process: Laban/Bartenieff Movement Analysis (LBMA).[2] You do not need to master these terms to work with the ideas in this book. Instead, think of this appendix as a glossary. Some entries may answer questions that surfaced while reading this book; others may spark curiosity for further study.

Why LBMA Appears Here

My first encounter with this lineage arrived by surprise at a conference two decades ago. After taking my class, a somatics teacher said, "I didn't know you were a Bartenieff teacher!" I'd never even heard the name. The comment introduced me to a framework that married intuition with science, poetics with architecture. LBMA gave language to impulses I'd been following for years and organized my scattered ideas into a system I could sculpt and share.

What Is LBMA?

LBMA is a system for observing, describing, and understanding movement across bodies and contexts. Rudolf Laban (1879–1958) developed a system for analyzing the body in the service of meaning and notating it for posterity.[3] Irmgard Bartenieff extended this work through clinical practice and pedagogy, articulating principles that continue to shape training in dance, theater, therapy, athletics, and education.[4]

---

[1]Irmgard Bartenieff, *Body Movement: Coping with the Environment* (Gordon & Breach, 1980), 20.

[2]Rudolf Laban, *Choreographie. Erstes Heft: Grundbegriffe der Choreographie* [Choreography, Volume 1: Basic Concepts of Choreography] (Kurt Wolff, 1926).

[3]Valerie Preston-Dunlop, *Rudolf Laban: An Extraordinary Life* (Dance Books, 1998).

[4]Irmgard Bartenieff and Dori Lewis, *Body Movement: Coping with the Environment* (Gordon & Breach, 1981).

LBMA's framework rests on four interrelated pillars, often abbreviated as **BESS:**[5]

- **Body:** *What* is moving?
- **Effort:** *How* is it moving?
- **Shape:** *Why* is it moving (impulse and intention)?
- **Space:** *Where* is it moving (orientation and pathway)?

Whole-Part-Whole

Whole-Part-Whole names a practice of widening and narrowing attention. Each chapter in this book isolates a facet—Time, Space, Meaning, Relationship, and more—and then returns to the constellation they form. Focusing on a single element deepens understanding; recombining reveals patterns. The cycle repeats, echoing the rhythms in Process, Priorities, and Context and Culture where vision and action attune each other.

When we separate and illuminate the parts—whether Body, Effort, Shape, and Space in LBMA or the facets of creative life named in these chapters—we gain nuance and clarity. We see connections we might otherwise miss. We recognize habitual pairings ("I always move delicately and slowly") and open new combinations ("What happens if I move delicately and quickly?"). From there, we can reassemble the whole with more conscious choice.

The Four Themes

LBMA identifies four recurring themes—sometimes called **Lemniscates**—that shape all movement:[6]

- Inner/Outer
- Exertion/Recuperation
- Stability/Mobility
- Function/Expression

These themes operate like gravity; they are present whether or not we notice them. Paying attention to them can illuminate imbalances or open creative options.

Example: A piece drawn from an **Inner** impulse might gain depth when grounded in an **Outer** context (research, environment). A performance demanding a particular **Exertion** from the audience (complex text, intense duration) may also need moments of **Recuperation** (humor, music, short beats).

[5]Laban/Bartenieff Institute of Movement Studies (LIMS), "Certification Program in Laban Bartenieff Movement Studies," https://labaninstitute.org/certification-programs/.

[6]Peggy Hackney, *Making Connections: Total Body Integration Through Bartenieff Fundamentals* (Routledge, 2002), 42–6.

Body: The "What"

In LBMA, the **Body** category examines the "what" of movement: which body part is moving and what action it is performing. It maps the mechanics of movement without yet layering in qualities or intentions. Think action verbs: *flex, extend, rotate, balance, locomote, scatter, fold, still.* This level of noticing often reveals details that get lost when we only name large gestures: initiating from "back of the knee" rather than "leg," or sensing how "gather" shifts when led by elbow versus sternum.

Example: In rehearsal, a duet feels presentational. I ask one performer to initiate a reach from the sternum rather than the hand; the moment shifts from display to invitation.

Developmental Patterns

These six foundational patterns—**Breath, Core-Distal, Head-Tail, Upper-Lower, Body Half, Cross-Lateral**[7]—appear in fetal development, human evolution, and the milestones of motor development. Each reveals a way the body organizes itself and relates to its environment. While they serve functional roles (rolling, crawling, walking), they also map onto creative growth: curiosity expanding and returning, integration of opposites, complexity emerging from simplicity.

The Nine Principles

Bartenieff also identified the **Nine Principles:**[8] lenses for observing, creating, editing, and critiquing movement. While they describe physical phenomena, they extend far beyond anatomy. We can track weight shift in the pelvis or in a political movement; we can sense dynamic alignment in the spine or in how an ensemble attunes to one another in rehearsal.

These principles mirror the chapters of this book: recurring forces that shape both the smallest actions and the largest cultural shifts. Each principle can be approached as a question rather than a directive—an opening for curiosity.

For example:

- **Breath support**—How do things enter and exit?
- **Core support**—Where do we find our inner strength? What holds us together?
- **Weight shift**—What architecture grounds us, allowing us to take action?
- **Dynamic alignment**—How does one change affect everything else?

---

[7]Hackney, *Making Connections*, 21–40.

[8]Bartenieff and Lewis, *Body Movement*, 30–55.

- **Rotary factor**—What are we turning from? What are we shifting toward?
- **Initiation and sequencing**—Where do we begin, and what is inevitable from there?
- **Developmental movement patterns**—How did we become who we are?
- **Effort intent**—How does our inner world become visible and legible?
- **Spatial intent**—Where are we? Where have we been? Where do we want to go?

These principles name dynamics already present in all movement, whether personal, collective, or cultural. They invite noticing, not mastery. They belong to our art as much as to our bodies.

Why Body Matters

Attuning to the "what" of movement—the actions themselves and the body parts involved—grounds us in reality before layering intention or quality. Artists often discover **habitual initiations** (always leading with the head, rarely accessing the back body) or **unused possibilities** (a gesture beginning from the sternum instead of the hand). This clarity supports both **function** (efficiency, injury prevention) and **expression** (freshness, precision, presence). In creative process, noticing the "what" opens pathways for choice: What happens if the same phrase begins in a different body part, or unfolds with a new action? These shifts ripple through meaning and connection.

Effort: The "How"

Effort describes the **quality** of movement—the inner life made visible. It is where intention becomes legible: the difference between *striking* and *caressing*, between *drifting* and *plunging*. Effort is often the most recognizable facet of Laban's work, widely used in theater training, dance, therapy, even corporate leadership.

Effort maps four **Motion Factors**:[9]

- **Weight** (Strong/Light)
- **Space** (Direct/Indirect)
- **Time** (Quick/Sustained)
- **Flow** (Bound/Free)

These factors combine into countless textures—"Light and Quick," "Direct and Strong," "Free and Sustained"—each shaping sense and function.

---

[9]Rudolf Laban, *The Mastery of Movement* (Macdonald & Evans, 1960), 84–97.

Effort in Creative Practice

Effort is where craft and emotion intertwine. A single shift—choosing "Quick and Direct" over "Quick and Strong"—can alter not only what an *audience* sees but how *performers* experience the moment. Directors use it to sculpt dynamics between characters, choreographers to design phrasing and intensity, and teachers to guide presence and energy.

Effort qualities can reveal **subtext** (a hurt gesture *masked* as "efficient"), **heighten narrative** (a slow, ongoing, heavy walk signaling "inevitability"), or invite **play** (experimenting with disparate couplings like using Light and Bound to explore gentle control). They also support **ensemble cohesion**: naming a shared Effort can create immediate kinesthetic agreement, even across cultures or disciplines.

Example: In rehearsal, an actor's confession read as too forceful. We shifted the Effort from "Quick and Strong" to "Quick and Light"; the scene suddenly held urgency without threat, and their partner's response changed completely.

Effort as an Invitation

Exploring Effort rarely stays abstract for long. Once you name a quality, you begin to notice it everywhere—on the subway, in rehearsal, at the dinner table. This is part of why Effort study often becomes a doorway into deeper LBMA training: It bridges observation and embodiment, logic and intuition, description and transformation.

In my own teaching, Effort often catalyzes breakthroughs: Dancers who feel "stuck" in their vocabulary discover textures they never imagined; actors find precision in emotional beats without forcing them; directors locate the energetic arc of a scene through movement before a single line is spoken.

Space: The "Where"

Space in Laban's work is more than coordinates or stage geography; it is the field where meaning, relationship, and intention take form. How we orient, reach, and navigate through space reveals our values and needs; it codes intimacy or distance, authority or invitation, safety or exposure. In art-making, spatial choices shape everything from how a story lands to how a performer feels inside their body.

In LBMA, Space[10] includes both **external mapping** (*where* we move) and **internal orientation** (how we *sense* and relate to our surroundings). We study:

Dimensions, planes, diagonals: The geometric pathways the body uses.

---

[10]Preston-Dunlop, *Rudolf Laban*, 215–30; Hackney, *Making Connections*, 75–90.

Example: A solo kept feeling flat. It was mostly using the horizontal plane. We added a diagonal leap, and suddenly the phrase tilted toward quest and risk.

Kinesphere: The personal "bubble" around the body: **small** (gestural/focal), **medium** (using *some* of its range), **large** (as far as you can reach without traveling), or **global** (reaching energetically into space we can't touch).

Example: Two characters were arguing, both using a small kinesphere. It felt safe and strategic; I asked one performer to pace across the stage, using a large kinesphere. It immediately changed the power conversation.

Spatial pathways and tensions: Lines of action move through central, peripheral, or transverse pathways.

Example: A monologue delivered with peripheral gestures felt evasive. When the actor repeated it with a central pathway straight toward the audience, the text landed as a direct challenge.

Countertension: How reaching toward one point requires counterbalance elsewhere.

Example: A lift wasn't working. Once the supporting dancer reached back and down as the flyer reached up and forward, it flew effortlessly.

Keys and orientation systems: What we prioritize when locating what is "front," "up," or "right" (is it relative to the *room*, your *body*, or *gravity*?).

Example: A scene directed toward the audience felt stiff. When the performers oriented primarily to each other's fronts, the same dialogue read as intimate, even on the proscenium.

Why Space Matters in Creative Work

Space is often the first thing audiences read without knowing it: the widening of arms, the lean toward or away, the relationship between one performer's front body and another's. Spatial awareness deepens everything from blocking a scene to designing choreography, teaching presence, or understanding power dynamics.

Working consciously with Space can do the following:

- Shift **tone** (an open diagonal feels expansive; a horizontal plane can feel grounding or communal)
- Transform **relationships** (changing proximity can suggest intimacy, tension, or estrangement)
- Influence **audience perception** (central pathways invite focus; peripheral pathways can evoke play, reach, or avoidance)
- Offer **structural clarity** (geometric patterns create coherence, contrast, or surprise)

Space as an Invitation

Spatial principles are everywhere—in architecture, nature, staging, even conversation. Once you begin noticing your own spatial habits—do you favor horizontal gestures? Diagonals? Do you move centrally or skim the edges?—you uncover patterns that affect not only choreography but also how you inhabit rooms, relationships, and creative processes. Exploring Space opens unexpected pathways for both personal expression and collaborative storytelling.

Shape: The "Why"

Shape asks one of the most elemental questions in movement: **Why did you move?** Was the impulse rooted in *inner exploration*, *expression*, and *being*? Did it arise to define yourself *in relation to the environment*? Was it a *negotiation*—an adaptive search for resonance between inner and outer forces?

Shape bridges **function** and **expression**. It maps how we **change form** in response to ourselves, others, and the world. Shape highlights intention through the body's morphing shapes, drawing attention to how shifts in volume, direction, and flow reflect our inner and outer needs. While intention threads through every aspect of LBMA—Body, Effort, Space, and Shape—this pillar centers the evolving dialogue between inner impulse and outer environment.

Example: A performer was defaulting to a concave posture during transitions. Naming it as "Shape Flow" revealed a habit of *disappearing* between scenes; introducing brief directional reaches toward the audience grounded their entire character arc.

Modes of Shape Change

LBMA identifies three primary modes of Shape change,[11] each highlighting a different relationship between self and environment:

- **Shape Flow**—movement primarily centered on *personal sensation* and inner volume (curling inward on a breath, expanding simply because it feels good to stretch)
- **Directional**—movement *aimed* toward or away from a specific point in space (reaching for a hand, walking toward a spot, orienting to a fixed direction)
- **Carving/Shaping**—movement that *negotiates* volumes in space, adapting moment to moment (winding through a crowded rehearsal room, molding your body to hold a partner's weight)

[11] Hackney, *Making Connections*, 62–74.

Shape in Creative Practice

Shape surfaces constantly in art-making: a dancer's torso spiraling inward, an actor's hand extending toward a partner, a singer's body lifting into resonance. When artists explore Shape, they begin to clarify the *intention* behind their movement:

- Is this gesture *exploratory*, with no destination?
- Is it seeking to land in a *particular place* or make contact?
- Is it *adapting* moment by moment, negotiating its relationships?

Why Shape Matters

Working with Shape can transform communication. Artists begin to notice where their habitual "why" lives. This awareness invites *balance*: attuning more deeply to themselves, clarifying intention for others, or blending both when needed.

In rehearsal and performance, Shape can unlock emotional clarity without forcing it—inviting meaning to emerge through the body rather than being imposed by concept alone. It becomes a bridge between impulse and expression, between personal truth and shared experience.

LBMA as Lens, Not Doctrine

LBMA widens what we can notice and make together. If these concepts resonate with your current questions, my course "The Anatomy of Choice" offers guided practice in applying LBMA to composition, directing, and rehearsal design—building phrases from Shape motivation, crafting Effort scores that clarify beats without pushing emotion, and designing spatial architectures that shift relationship and power onstage.

See the companion website for details and texts for further study.

Tuning In: Switching Lenses with LBMA

This practice is a way to embody the ideas in this appendix—noticing how meaning changes when you attend to Body, Effort, Space, or Shape.

Body

*Lead with the **body's** experience and clarity of initiation.*

- Choose clear **body part initiations**: tailbone, right elbow, occiput, pelvic floor, third eye.
- Select **verbs** to clarify your actions: folding, gathering, locomoting, rotating, jumping.
- Focus on **connection pathways**: head-tail, elbow-knee, pubic bone–sternum, heel–sitz bones.
- Imagine a **marble of attention** traveling body part to body part, sparking impulses that become verbs.
- Stay in **sensing and deciding** with the body; let thought follow sensation.

Effort

*Let the **"how"** and quality lead.*

- Every verb should have an adjective or quality embedded: *slash*, *dip*, *perch*, *vibrate*, *dive*, *lilt*, *tumble*.
- Explore contrasting dynamics: a fast drop followed by a hesitant glance, or a commanding walk followed by a tentative reach.
- Notice how phrasing and rhythm tell a story.

Space

*Make **space** an active partner.*

- Imagine every action interacts with space: pushing, pulling, yielding, tracing.
- Visualize traces of light left behind your movements.
- Vary the scale and directionality: How much space do you claim? What parts are active or avoided?
- Try reversing your spatial habits.

Shape

Let desire sculpt the body. Find your ***why****.*

- Begin in **Shape Flow**: Allow breath, sensation, and inner climate to expand, condense, curl, or lengthen the body without aiming anywhere. Feel yourself grow and shrink, expand and condense, spiral, curl, and breathe.
- Shift into **Directional Shape**: Let a clear spatial intention organize you toward or away from something specific. Draw sweeping lines, straight and curved, in the air.
- Move into **Carving**: Adapt continuously to space, texture, or another body as if molding yourself to the environment. Let every movement you make affect the space. Negotiate your volume with the room's.

Integration

After cycling through the lenses individually, allow them to blur and inform each other. Notice which lens dominates and which recedes. How does toggling between them change *what* you do, as well as *how* and *why*?

Studio Lab: Shaping Meaning Through Body, Effort, and Space

This practice builds on the LBMA concepts introduced in this appendix. It's an invitation to craft movement by layering what, how, why, and where—Body, Effort, Shape, and Space.

1. **Start with motivation.**
   Stand, sit, or lie down. Close your eyes. What desire, question, or state feels alive? What kind of relationship with the environment are you craving? Choose a **Mode of Shape Change** that fits.
   - **Shape Flow**—movement primarily about *self* and inner experience (breath, growing/shrinking, internal sensation).
   - **Directional (Arcing or Spoking)**—movement focused on *getting somewhere* or connecting to a specific location.
   - **Shaping/Carving**—movement negotiating both *self* and *environment*, adapting inner and outer volumes, focusing on the *journey*.

   Improvise for a few minutes in one of these modes, noticing what kinds of movements naturally follow from this agenda.

2. **Generate movement (Body).**
   Using the observations from your improvisation, create **ten distinct movements/gestures** (reach, turn, level change, stillness, jump). Do not link them into a phrase yet. Keep them as a "vocabulary bank." What **body part** initiates and what **action** is it performing?

3. **Apply Effort.**
   Add **Effort**. Color your movements with qualitative adjectives. Allow the adjectives to change the dynamic or emotional tone. Notice how **meaning** shifts.

4. **Modify Space.**
   Decide how each movement interacts with space. Make intentional spatial choices. Consider:
   - **Level:** high, medium, low
   - **Direction:** forward, backward, sideways, diagonal
   - **Size:** large, medium, or small kinesphere

5. **Compose a phrase.**

   You now have six to ten movements that have dynamic and spatial choices embedded. Create a fifteen- to thirty-second phrase by reordering, repeating, or deleting. Hold onto your space and quality choices.

6. **Apply disruptions.**

   When your phrase feels embodied, apply these disruptions one at a time:

   - **Reverse the tempo.** (Change *fast* to *slow* and vice versa.)
   - **Reverse the force/impact.** (Change delicate to intense and vice versa.)
   - **Change the size/space you take up.**

Contributor's Note: Move, Fill Space, and Affect Others with Your Words Through Explorations of LBMA

by Barbara Adrian

All movement begins with the breath. Sound is initiated as the breath moves through the vocal folds, causing them to oscillate, producing vibrations that ignite the resonators, which produce sound. The articulators shape the sound into unstructured and structured sounds, giving birth to emotions, words, and phrases. The sounds/words/phrases vibrate into the environment, vibrating the environment. Words not only impart information that answers the question of "what?" Words are also containers for "why?" and "how?" *Why* this word now? *How* is the word filled? When the "why?" and "how?" are specific to the character and given circumstances, then the words move us as we move them.

What is the "means whereby" that we can explore and make specific vocal choices that move beyond the literal dictionary meaning of a word and embody the "how?" and "why?," thus filling the unique given circumstances of the story? LBMA is a tool for releasing vocal choices into the words without judgment or preconceived ideas. Words expand, shrink, bend, twist, reach, rise and fall, and explode beyond their dictionary meanings.

Words and phrases can move quickly or be sustained, strong, light, direct, indirect, free, bound. Their trajectory into space can be straight, arc-like, or winding. Exploring these prompts can help you discover the *filling* for the words. Playing with LBMA can surprise you with unexpected vocal discoveries. The flexibility of the LBMA vocabulary allows the coach/actor/instructor/student to explore myriad possible choices by improvising vocally and physically without fear of being "wrong." The story depends on the shape, effort, and relationship to space and others that fill and move the words. One explores with curiosity and joy, discovering and making choices that bring the many potential layers of the story to life.

Appendix B: The Art of Feedback

> To ask the "right" question is far more important than to receive the answer. The solution of a problem lies in the understanding of the problem; the answer is not outside the problem, it is in the problem.
>
> (Jiddu Krishnamurti, *The First and Last Freedom*)[1]

Feedback is an act of balance requiring rigor without violence, curiosity without assumption, and respect for the artist's autonomy. Feedback thrives on specificity, directness, and strength and loses clarity in hierarchy, manipulation, and opinion. Poorly delivered critique can scar an artist, particularly when power dynamics, cultural incompetence, or personal biases are unchecked. Great feedback, though, can deepen the work, strengthening an artist's agency, faith, and courage. Every feedback exchange begins inside roles and power dynamics; naming them changes the air.

Excellent feedback and mentorship are rare. Too often, they lean on advice giving or the deadly refrain of "What I'd like to see is…" Opinions can also arrive in disguise, cloaked as questions. A mentor might say, "That section was very aggressive. Did you want it to be so angry?" The words arrive as a question, but the body of the message is still opinion. This kind of stealth—like the wolf hidden in grandma's nightgown—slips past the artist's defenses and can seed doubt where curiosity could have grown. When feedback is built on hidden opinions, the artist may end up manipulated by their mentor's taste. This can fracture trust in their voice and, over time, deny them their own compass.[2]

Opinions and Manipulation

Over decades of giving artistic feedback, I've learned to resist the magnetism of my opinions. My opinions create *my* art. To help you with yours, I need *curiosity*. More useful are questions like these:

---

[1]Jiddu Krishnamurti, *The First and Last Freedom* (Harper & Row, 1954).

[2]James Elkins, *Why Art Cannot Be Taught* (University of Illinois Press, 2001), critiques the nature of studio critiques as often being subjective opinion disguised as authoritative evaluation, challenging traditional methods of artistic feedback and pedagogy.

- What is *this* trying to be?
- What are *you* trying to make?
- What is *your* voice?

But to release my opinions, I must recognize what they *feel* like in my body. For me, opinions arrive as urgency—heat, pressure, the thought, "I have something to say!" That cue reminds me to slow down, get grounded, and invest in inquiry.

Being truly curious can be uncomfortable. I may not share your values or aesthetic. Your interests might not excite me. What *then*? As a mentor, I must stay curious about *the artist*. Why does this interest *them*? What inner need does this fulfill?

And what to do with my noisy opinions? I have sat with an artist whose work bored, irritated, or offended me. What a moment! Their showing ends, and their eyes turn to me, glimmering with expectation. I feel opinions coursing through me, colliding with my desire to nurture their sensitive artistic spirits. It's a profound, freighted moment—one where I must search for balance between what I think/feel/want and what is *useful*. A question filled with genuine *not knowing* is my only hope.

"What is the duration of the final section trying to accomplish?" I might ask, with authentic wonder. The section's slowness and length had frustrated me; watching it, I'd felt claustrophobic and powerless. When the piece had ended, I'd noticed my body was tight and my mind racing—signs of anxiety, even annoyance. Was this how they wanted the audience to feel? That question is fascinating to me. Suddenly, I have a mystery far more compelling than my opinion. My opinions become quiet and curiosity drives.

"I want you to feel bored, lulled, unstable, maybe even frustrated," the artist responded. Even *more* of a riddle!

"Can you share why?" Now I can genuinely learn about them—their worldview, fears, hunger, and defenses. Sometimes, their answers reveal something I'd missed: a context, goal, belief, or preference. Other times, they have an "Ohhhhh" moment, recognizing they'd skipped a step, made an assumption, or taken the "easy" route.

Feedback Methodologies

Liz Lerman's Critical Response Process (CRP)[3] is one of the most trusted frameworks for artistic feedback. Its emphasis on consent, clarity, and curiosity has deeply influenced me. Most of the

[3]Liz Lerman and John Borstel, *Critical Response Process: A Method for Getting Useful Feedback on Anything You Make, from Dance to Dessert* (Liz Lerman Dance Exchange, 2003).

following material is built upon it. At the same time, no single structure can serve all bodies, identities, or cultural experiences. Additional approaches, drawing from embodied, decolonial, and community-rooted practices, are doors into the same room.

Somatic, Decolonial, and Emergent Models

While this appendix draws from Lerman's CRP, it's vital to acknowledge that it is a star in a constellation of feedback frameworks. These practices have emerged from community organizing, social justice movements, Indigenous cosmologies, healing justice, and disability arts—models not always credited in academic or institutional settings but which hold essential wisdom about how we speak, witness, and co-create. These practices emphasize feedback as a living relationship, a nonverbal exchange, or an act of mutual transformation rather than linear evaluation.

adrienne maree brown's work in *Emergent Strategy* and *Holding Change*[4]

Brown frames facilitation as "shaping change," rooting feedback in relationship, pattern recognition, adaptation, and trust. Her practices encourage us to listen to rhythm, to honor quiet, and to reject extractive urgency.

Try This: Build brief one-minute partner exchanges into the start of your feedback session. Invite pairs to share something personal about their relationship to the work, allowing people to arrive with their whole selves before analysis begins.

Prentis Hemphill's work on boundaries, trauma, and somatic integrity[5]

Hemphill reminds us that "the body is the site of transformation" and that feedback is a form of relational negotiation, not just verbal analysis. Their work invites us to feel safety and discomfort without collapse or dissociation.

Try This: Before feedback begins, ask the artist, "What feels resourcing and what feels like too much right now?" Ask responders, "Can you stay in connection while those limits are set?" During the session, anyone may say "pause," and the group stops for one shared breath before continuing or recalibrating together.

---

[4]Adrienne Maree Brown, *Holding Change: The Way of Emergent Strategy Facilitation and Mediation* (AK Press, 2021).

[5]Prentis Hemphill, "The Ritual of Repair," in *You Are Your Best Thing: Vulnerability, Shame Resilience, and the Black Experience*, ed. Tarana Burke and Brené Brown (Random House, 2021), 155–62.

Disability justice and crip-informed models

Artists and collectives like Sins Invalid[6] and Leah Lakshmi Piepzna-Samarasinha[7] foreground feedback as care, not consensus. These models value access, intimacy, sensory variance, slowness, and pacing over clarity or polish.

Try This: Close the feedback session by asking, "What do you need to stay resourced after this conversation?," and invite the group to name one way they can contribute to collective access or care moving forward. End by acknowledging that the work and the people are whole beyond this showing, and that sustaining each other matters as much as refining the piece.

Restorative and transformative justice models[8]

In these systems, listening and accountability are communal, not punitive. Feedback becomes a practice of truth telling with care, surfacing harm without shame, and imagining what's possible together.

Try This: If tension, confusion, or harm surfaces, pause and form a simple circle with agreed guidelines (listen with respect, speak only your truth, no cross-talk), and move a talking piece so each person answers: "What did you experience?" and "What impact did that have?" Conclude by asking, "What is needed now?," and invite the artist to reflect back what they heard before any next steps are named.

Indigenous knowledge systems (varies by community)[9]

In many Indigenous feedback traditions, story, land, and ritual hold authority. Evaluation may happen nonverbally, over time, in relationship, or through symbols rather than direct commentary. Time and value are relational, not standardized. These reflections draw broadly from Indigenous traditions, which vary widely and should not be generalized.

Try This: Instead of offering critique, invite responders to share a story about a strength they witnessed in the work and what it made possible for them. Let the artist listen without interruption, allowing meaning to emerge through lived connection rather than analysis.

These frameworks don't contradict CRP—they widen its application. They ask us to listen with our bodies, to question what is "neutral," and to attend to what power, safety, and lineage do inside every exchange. If CRP gives us a table, these traditions invite us to gather on the floor, in the circle, around the fire, or inside stillness. They remind us that feedback is not a fixed tool but a cultural practice—one we are always co-shaping.

---

[6]Sins Invalid, *Skin, Tooth, and Bone: The Basis of Movement Is Our People—a Disability Justice Primer* (Sins Invalid, 2016).
[7]Leah Lakshmi Piepzna-Samarasinha, *Care Work: Dreaming Disability Justice* (Arsenal Pulp Press, 2018).
[8]Howard Zehr, *The Little Book of Restorative Justice* (Good Books, 2002).
[9]Robin Wall Kimmerer, *Braiding Sweetgrass: Indigenous Wisdom, Scientific Knowledge, and the Teachings of Plants* (Milkweed Editions, 2013).

Being an artist often means creating spaces where feedback is empowering and illuminating, whether you establish this as the one giving feedback or as the recipient. This includes designing for different neurotypes and access needs—choosing modalities (verbal, written, gestural), pacing, and sensory environment. Being able to choreograph how you receive feedback can be one of the most empowering and self-loving structures you can devise as an artist. Here are some suggestions for developing your own strategies for facilitating feedback.

Whole-Part-Whole and Instinct and Analysis in the Feedback Process

The Whole-Part-Whole structure dynamically toggles between systemic impressions and granular viewing, inviting responders to engage in both instinct and analysis. **Begin by anchoring feedback in the "whole"** of the artist's intentions, thematic arcs, and emotional resonance. Let this framing include how the piece affects your body. Are you drawn forward in moments of tension? Do you feel your breath shift in moments of stillness?

Then zoom into the "part" by investigating specific moments, choices, or dynamics that stand out, using embodied tools like mapping energy, naming textures, or exploring shifts in physicality. Here, feedback can be intuitive or analytical. Using intuition, we can draw on sensory and somatic responses to uncover deeper layers. This helps us *own* our subjectivity, use instinct, and draw from the well of inner wisdom. We can also be analytical, illuminating specific choices that feed or leech from the artist's vision. By contextualizing the "whole" first, you can repeatedly refer to it as you are probing details. Does a choice, design element, section, or vocabulary diverge from what the artist stated? Is that departure intentional or unconscious?

Finally, return to the "whole" to synthesize these details into the broader narrative, ensuring the discussion remains cohesive and aligned with the artist's goals. This layered approach allows instinct and analysis to support one another, offering expansive and deeply rooted feedback in the artist's vision.

Whole-Part-Whole, practiced this way, dissolves the divide between intellect and sensation. It allows feedback to become not just a conversation *about* art but a continuation of it—a shared act of noticing, listening, and shaping meaning together.

Critical Response Process

CRP has four distinct steps. Groups can give a time limit for each step—three to five minutes works well for small showings.

1. **Statements of Meaning:** Responders reflect on aspects of the work that resonated with them or felt meaningful.
2. **Questions from the Artist:** The **artist** poses specific questions to guide the feedback, focusing the conversation on areas they wish to explore.
3. ***Neutral* Questions from Responders:** Responders ask open-ended questions to clarify or deepen their understanding of the work.
4. **Permissioned Opinions:** Responders may offer opinions *only* with the artist's explicit consent and within agreed-on boundaries.

Step 1: Statements of Meaning

This step sets the tone for the feedback session by focusing on the work's strengths and meaningful moments. Responders share what stood out to them, what they found compelling, or what lingered in their minds. This is not about praise, fake compliments, or vague affirmation but specific reflections illuminating the work's impact.

Lerman says, "Responders state what was meaningful, evocative, interesting, exciting, striking in the work they have just witnessed."

Examples:

- "The shift in lighting during the second section created a powerful sense of transformation."
- "I was drawn to the stillness in the duet; it felt charged and intentional."

Additions and Alternatives

These additional methods focus on building trust with the artist. You can shift the modality toward uniquely creative, embodied, or culturally responsive ways of reflecting on meaning to suit your priorities, audience, and relationship with the artist. Below are four embodied modes that can serve as alternatives or complements to CRP:

Energy Maps: Have responders map the energy they experienced over time using lines, shapes, or textures in a drawing. Energy maps provide an intuitive way to chart your experience of the work. You might draw jagged lines to represent rising tension or use bold, repetitive circles to reflect cyclical patterns. Comparing the maps can reveal patterns, cycles, and themes that can be difficult to put into words.

Metaphorical Reflections: Invite responders to describe the work using metaphors or imagery. Metaphor translates sensation into image. For example:

- "It felt like watching waves crash—relentless and cleansing."
- "The trio moved like a flock of birds, constantly shifting and reforming."

Physical Responses: Ask responders to embody a moment from the work that resonated with them. They can do a thirty-second improvisation, create a single gesture, or recall a moment of physicality that stuck with them. This can offer a rich, nonverbal dialogue about how the piece affected them physically and emotionally.

Word Associations: Have responders list words or phrases that came to mind during the work, creating a collage of impressions. Word associations, especially unfiltered, can reveal surprising insights about how the work resonates.

Step 2: Questions from the Artist

This step empowers the artist to direct the feedback process by identifying areas of curiosity, doubt, or focus. Artists ask targeted questions about their work.

Lerman says, "The more artists clarify what they are working on and where their own questions are, the more intense and deep the dialog becomes. These questions need to be quite specific. It doesn't work to say 'tell me what you think.'"

Examples:

- "Did the transition between sections feel clear?"
- "Did the lighting support a sense of isolation?"

Encouraging artists to articulate their questions fosters self-awareness and ensures feedback aligns with their priorities. Artists can also specify how they'd like responses delivered: verbally, written, or embodied.

Additions and Alternatives

Some artists struggle to formulate their questions, particularly if they are new to this process or unsure of their priorities. You can help them by prompting reflection or offering categories to consider:

- **Intention:** "What did you want this section to accomplish?"
- **Audience Impact:** "Are you devising a specific quality or relationship with the audience here?"
- **Embodiment:** "Is there a moment not sitting organically in your body?"
- **Craft and Technique:** "Is there a specific skill or element you'd like feedback on?"

- **Context/Lineage:** "What lineages, traditions, or practices does this piece stand inside or depart from? How do those influences shape what you're exploring?"

Encourage artists to keep their questions concise and avoid directing their responders with excessive context or leading questions that point to an answer they desire. If they can't identify specific questions, consider asking,

- "Is there a moment you're unsure about?"
- "What part of the work feels most alive to you right now?"
- "Where do you feel yourself taking the biggest risk?"
- "Where have you been hitting a wall?"

Step 3: Neutral Questions from Responders

Responders ask open-ended, neutral questions to gain insight into the artist's intentions and process. These questions should avoid embedding opinions or assumptions.

Lerman says, "Questions are neutral when they do not have an opinion couched in them. For example, if you are discussing the lighting of a scene, 'Why was it so dark?' is not a neutral question. 'What ideas guided your choices about lighting?' is."

Examples:

- "What inspired the choice to use repetition in the final section?"
- "How do you see the audience engaging with this moment?"
- "What arc do you want this duet to take?"
- "How literally do you want the audience to understand the narrative?"

Additions and Alternatives

Here you can adjust the focus of the questions based on your goals, where the artists are in their artistic journey, and how long you've been together as a group. Here are a few additional ways to frame this step:

Embodied Inquiry: Frame questions around physicality or dynamics.

- "Do you hope for any specific physical experience for the audience here?"
- "How are exertion and recuperation functioning energetically?"

Cultural Context: Acknowledge cultural influences or sensitivities.

- "What cultural stories or traditions inform this work?"
- "How do you see your identity reflected in this piece?"
- "Who might be left out of this moment and is that an intended boundary?"

Contradictions and Tensions: Explore complexity and layering.

- "This section felt both tender and unsettling. How do you want that tension to function?"
- "How do you hope the audience feels the weight of this idea?"
- "How do you see rhythm shaping the emotional impact?"

Step 4: Permissioned Opinions

Opinions are only offered if the artist explicitly consents. Responders must state the category of their opinion and respect the artist's boundaries. For trauma-aware feedback practices, see David Treleaven, *Trauma-Sensitive Mindfulness.*[10]

Lerman says, "Responders state opinions, subject to permission from the artist. The usual form is 'I have an opinion about ______, would you like to hear it?' The artist has the option to say no."

Examples:

- "Would you like to hear an opinion about your music?"
- "I had a thought about the pacing. Would you like to hear it?"

This ensures that opinions are contextually relevant and aligned with the artist's needs. It can be helpful to do a short consent practice before giving opinions. Here is one I use:

Finding Your No

Our *no* can be challenging, especially if we have moved through the world in a less-privileged body, environment, economy, or identity. Many of us are brought up to bias toward people pleasing and saying *yes*. Finding our no is essential to self-care, empowerment, sovereignty, and health. It can require repatterning. I often do this short exercise before allowing opinions into the feedback room. It is also a precursor to using touch if there is a gap in self-awareness or consensual exchange.

---

[10]David Treleaven, *Trauma-Sensitive Mindfulness: Practices for Safe and Transformative Healing* (W. W. Norton, 2018).

Exercise:

Have artists pair up.

Person A asks person B if they can do something pedestrian, like put a hand on B's shoulder, compliment their hair, or ask B to watch A improvise.

For the first five to eight rounds of asking, the person B *must* say no. Even if B would be happy to say yes, they say no, actively relating to any discomfort that arises.

Upon hearing no, A responds with a version of, "Thank you for telling me."

After five to eight rounds of mandatory no, B adds possible responses and is now authentic. They can still say no, and they can also say the following:

"Yes."

"Yes, and... / if... / but..."

This adds a request, like, "Yes, but only for three seconds," or "Yes, if it's only the back of your hand," or "Yes, and I may lean into you."

Take some time to discuss how that felt on both sides. What was it like to say no? To hear no? What feelings, associations, stories, or beliefs arose for both of you?

Switch roles and repeat.

Additions and Alternatives

Lerman's four-part structure emphasizes consent, power dynamics, and nonviolent language. Before sharing an opinion, do the following:

- Slow down and reflect. Is this opinion truly necessary or helpful?
- Use neutral language.
- Frame opinions as *possibilities* rather than *judgments*. For example: "I wonder how it might shift the intimacy if the duet were slower."

Additionally, consider nonverbal or asynchronous options for artists who need less immediacy and direct communication. This can support artists' diverse learning or processing styles. **For example:**

- Write opinions on note cards for the artist to review later.

- Offer digital feedback through shared documents or recordings. I often use a shared Google Sheet with a column for the artist and a row for each person giving feedback. The artist leaves with written feedback from each responder. This is also a good hack for short sessions that don't allow for free-flowing conversation.
- Have the artist ask for a show of hands, a chorus of snaps, or other communal agreement about a specific opinion. ("How many of you felt distracted by the music?")

Before offering opinions, it's essential to name the cultural perspective you're speaking from. For example, if your artistic references differ significantly from the artist's cultural framework, let your first move be curiosity about the cultural logic inside the piece. Cultures vary widely in how rhythm, proximity, force, and touch associations create meaning and relationship. When your cultural norms become the measure, the conversation narrows. Multiple realities intersect, merge, and depart from one another. Your story enters the circle; it does not define it.

Feedback as a Creative Exchange

Feedback is a dynamic, collaborative act that invites artists and responders to engage with curiosity, empathy, and intention. It is not about *fixing* the work but uncovering its possibilities *together*. Owning your preferred feedback methods is a profound gesture of self-care toward your sensitive, strong, hungry, curious, and tender inner artist.

Quick Tips

1. Slow down. Take time to connect with your body before speaking.
2. Own your opinions as being about *you*. Attempt to set them aside as you start offering feedback. There may be a place for them later, or you may notice them disappearing or becoming moot as feedback progresses. To this end, only use "I" statements and resist talking about "you."
3. Find the most neutral language possible. If there is a less historically loaded word, use it.
4. If the creator performed, consider creating some dispassionate distance by calling them the "performer" or "character" rather than saying "you." ("When the performer suddenly started speaking, I felt startled, then found myself very attentive.")

5. Reflect on what is working to offer areas of fruitful investment to the artist, not to reassure them. Do not lie or sugarcoat.
6. Resist making "I liked/loved…" or "I didn't like/hated…" statements.
7. Offer suggestions only when requested; before giving advice, ask what the artist is already considering. Even when asked, I often turn the question around to them before expressing my thoughts.
8. Do not make any assumptions about the artist's intentions. If you have not heard from them, ask.
9. Speak within the context of their genre, style, and intention, even if aspects of their work do not appeal to you. This still leaves room to encourage invention inside their genre or style.
10. Frame feedback primarily through questions from and for the artist.
11. If you offer an opinion at the end, ask permission to share it and let them know what it relates to.
12. Be sure you have framed questions so that the artist has access to their *no*, especially if there is an implied or explicit power differential (like student/teacher or artist/presenter or simply deep respect and admiration from the artist to the viewer).